THE COMPLETE IDIOT'S GUIDE® TO

Small-Space Gardening

by Chris McLaughlin

ALPHA

A member of Penguin Group (USA) Inc.

To my sugar babies and future gardeners, Jillian and Scarlett.

ALPHA BOOKS

Published by the Penguin Group

Penguin Group (USA) Inc., 375 Hudson Street, New York, New York 10014, USA

Penguin Group (Canada), 90 Eglinton Avenue East, Suite 700, Toronto, Ontario M4P 2Y3, Canada (a division of Pearson Penguin Canada Inc.)

Penguin Books Ltd., 80 Strand, London WC2R 0RL, England

Penguin Ireland, 25 St. Stephen's Green, Dublin 2, Ireland (a division of Penguin Books Ltd.)

Penguin Group (Australia), 250 Camberwell Road, Camberwell, Victoria 3124, Australia (a division of Pearson Australia Group Pty. Ltd.)

Penguin Books India Pvt. Ltd., 11 Community Centre, Panchsheel Park, New Delhi—110 017, India

Penguin Group (NZ), 67 Apollo Drive, Rosedale, North Shore, Auckland 1311, New Zealand (a division of Pearson New Zealand Ltd.)

Penguin Books (South Africa) (Pty.) Ltd., 24 Sturdee Avenue, Rosebank, Johannesburg 2196, South Africa

Penguin Books Ltd., Registered Offices: 80 Strand, London WC2R 0RL, England

International Standard Book Number: 978-1-61564-0-966
Library of Congress Catalog Card Number: 2011910187

14 13 12   8 7 6 5 4 3 2 1

Interpretation of the printing code: The rightmost number of the first series of numbers is the year of the book's printing; the rightmost number of the second series of numbers is the number of the book's printing. For example, a printing code of 12-1 shows that the first printing occurred in 2012.

Printed in the United States of America

Note: This publication contains the opinions and ideas of its author. It is intended to provide helpful and informative material on the subject matter covered. It is sold with the understanding that the author and publisher are not engaged in rendering professional services in the book. If the reader requires personal assistance or advice, a competent professional should be consulted.

The author and publisher specifically disclaim any responsibility for any liability, loss, or risk, personal or otherwise, which is incurred as a consequence, directly or indirectly, of the use and application of any of the contents of this book.

Most Alpha books are available at special quantity discounts for bulk purchases for sales promotions, premiums, fund-raising, or educational use. Special books, or book excerpts, can also be created to fit specific needs.

For details, write: Special Markets, Alpha Books, 375 Hudson Street, New York, NY 10014.

Publisher: *Marie Butler-Knight*

Associate Publisher: *Mike Sanders*

Executive Managing Editor: *Billy Fields*

Acquisitions Editor: *Paul Dinas, Brook Farling*

Senior Development Editor: *Phil Kitchel*

Senior Production Editor: *Janette Lynn*

Copy Editor: *Amy Borrelli*

Cover Designer: *Rebecca Batchelor*

Book Designers: *William Thomas, Rebecca Batchelor*

Illustrator: *Hollis McLaughlin*

Indexer: *Angie Bess Martin*

Layout: *Ayanna Lacey*

Proofreader: *John Etchison*

Contents

Introduction

What exactly *is* a small-space garden and how does it apply to you? Perhaps you live in a city with a postage-stamp-size plot of dirt. You might reside in an apartment with only a balcony or tiny front porch to work with. Or maybe you live in the suburbs, which can seem large in comparison to the other two, but you're still facing the same gardening problems as far as soil and light.

Small-space gardening describes the gardening issues that many of us face: places with very little earth in which to plant, buildings or structures around us that complicate things even when we do find some ground, and plants that seem to swallow up everything once they mature.

In *The Complete Idiot's Guide to Small-Space Gardening*, we'll show you tricks to fool the eye, plants that don't require much room, and techniques that allow you to have any garden style you want within the little space you have. Trying to picture a lovely garden with little square footage might be a stretch at the moment.

In more than 30 years of gardening, nearly all of my gardens have been in small spaces of one kind or another. I can offer you proof that petite gardens are some of the most fun to work with and take little time and expense to create. Cozy cottage gardens, tropical getaways, elegant rose gardens, and vegetable gardens can all be created in a garden space that feels small enough to fit in your pocket.

There are a few important things that I think are important to mention before you dive into *The Complete Idiot's Guide to Small-Space Gardening*. The first thing is that for some reason, botanists enjoy messing with gardener's heads and are known to change the names of plants as they see fit.

This drives gardeners crazy, as we've spent many years memorizing the proper, tongue-tying Latin names just to have to start over. In any case, the botanical names in this book may change depending on the day you read through the pages. If there's any doubt as to the plant you'd like to learn more about, please check the USDA Plant Database (http://plants.usda.gov) for the most current botanical plant names.

Second, please don't eat or serve any plants that aren't commonly known to be edible. Also, if you have small children, do some research and be certain that they aren't poisonous before you add plants to your yard.

Last, all regions are different as far as which plants are invasive and which aren't a problem. Contact your local Cooperative Extension Office and check the databases in the Resources for Small-Space Gardeners appendix for a list those that are best not planted in your area.

How This Book Is Organized

The Complete Idiot's Guide to Small-Space Gardening is divided into five parts:

Part 1, Living with a Little Landscape, explains the benefits of small-space gardening, as well as the various definitions. It goes over the options you have to borrow garden space if you'd like more room, including community gardens, yard sharing, and guerilla gardening. The second chapter explains USDA growing zones, the AHS heat map, and microclimates, so you can get to know your own little corner of the world in a more intimate way.

Chapter 3 has basic, practical tips on design and includes some ideas on garden themes. The last chapter in this part gets into planting your little space to include all of the senses, not just the eyes. It goes into color, fragrance, touch, and sound. This is the chapter that has tips on mastering illusion, one of the all-important techniques for small gardens. We also have good ideas on how to create walls and use them to the best advantage within a small space.

Part 2, Principles for Petite Plots, discusses one of the main strategies of small-space gardening: containers. It gets into the various types of containers you can use and why you might want to choose each one. It discusses potting soil and we get into portable raised garden beds as containers. There are also directions on how to create a tri-level container planter and plant it the same day.

Chapter 6 offers solutions to those tricky areas that are narrow, sloped, windy, sunny, shady, and soggy. Next is the blessing of raised garden beds. We have thoughts on bed-framing materials, making your bed on your lawn, and square-foot gardening. We even have directions on how to make a cinderblock raised bed in a hurry.

The last chapter in this part gets into the specifics of one of the other all-important small-space techniques: growing plants vertically. We've got information on how plants climb and what structures will support them. There's also discussion on alternate ways to garden vertically and why many vegetables are perfectly suited for this technique.

Part 3, Small-Space Garden Themes, is all about various garden styles and how to use them in a little garden setting. This part begins with growing your vegetables and how to get the most out of them. We have structure ideas and instructions that you can easily pull off yourself. We also name some names of vegetable dwarf varieties to get you going in the right direction.

The next chapter discusses how easy it is to introduce fruit into a little landscape and which varieties are your best bet. We also have a chapter devoted to flower gardens and borders, where we discuss how to "stack" a garden bed, roses, and plant ideas for creating a woodland, tropical, or wildlife garden.

There are also ideas in this part for herb and rock gardens, plus how to make a hypertufa (fake rock) container. Chapter 13 discusses swapping or simply borrowing some of your lawn for a garden area. And in the last chapter we have the goods on how you can include water features in your small-space garden.

Part 4, Good Gardening Practices, is all about basic and important gardening practices that'll help keep any garden healthy, gorgeous, and producing. We talk about the biggest key ingredient to great gardening: living soil. We'll tell you what soil testing is about, soil personality, pH—and why you don't have to freak out about it. We have compost, vermicompost, and organic fertilizer talk here.

Chapter 16 discusses why you might want to consider organic pest control and offers techniques to keep the bad guys at bay. We also have some great ideas for organic weed control that actually work.

Part 5, Plants for Small Spaces, is the part you're looking for if you want to look up a specific plant for your yard or garden. This section is loaded with details on everything from annuals (sunny and shady) perennials (sunny and shady), and flower bulbs.

Chapter 19 will give you examples of non-flowering perennials such as grasses and ferns. There are fragrant plants, vines and climbers, ground covers, evergreen shrubs, or those that flower. The last chapter of this part is all about trees, whether for structure, shade, or fruit. Instead of just lists, we have profiles of these plants so that you can get an idea of their individual personalities and habits.

Extras

Throughout the book, you'll find the following sidebars that highlight information I want to be sure you catch.

DEFINITION

These sidebars provide definitions and details about the gardening terms and techniques used throughout this book.

TIP THYME

These sidebars will have extra hints and tips for small-space gardening success.

PLANTING PITFALL

These sidebars will have warnings and things to consider as you garden.

GARDEN GOSPEL

Here I share miscellaneous facts about small-space gardening.

Acknowledgments

I'm never more aware of how many fabulous people are around me as when I come to the end of a book. I have to thank my awesome agent, Marilyn Allen, for being on my team. A huge thank-you to my editors, Paul Dinas, Brook Farling, Phil Kitchel, Janette Lynn, and Amy Borrelli for their patience and guidance on this book. A big shout out to Alpha Books for having the terrific *Complete Idiot's Guide* series in the first place, plus having faith in me as an author yet again.

My eternal gratitude to Jenny Peterson for being my second set of eyes (you're the best, Maven). Also Sandy Dittmar of Iseli Nursery for her guidance on dwarf conifers. A thank-you to those who graciously offered their images: Jenny Peterson, Bren Haas, Teresa Soule, Stark Bros, and Moss and Stone Gardens.

As always, I am indebted to my family and husband for their patience and kindness while I'm breathing life into a book and, therefore, ignoring them.

I'm grateful to you all beyond words.

Trademarks

All terms mentioned in this book that are known to be or are suspected of being trademarks or service marks have been appropriately capitalized. Alpha Books and Penguin Group (USA) Inc. cannot attest to the accuracy of this information. Use of a term in this book should not be regarded as affecting the validity of any trademark or service mark.

Living with a Little Landscape

Here's where we figure out just how much space you're talking about, and how you can get to know it better and take full advantage of what you have. We discuss zones, microclimates, and what full shade really means.

There are some general small-space designing tips, how to give your garden good "bones," and some garden theme ideas to get your creative juices flowing. We have information on ways to "borrow" garden space, too.

There are thoughts on color choices, using optical illusion, and how to plant for all of the senses. The end of this part gets into walls, boundary fences, and fences for fun. After reading this first part of the book, you'll see that small garden spaces can have advantages over the big, economy-sized ones, and why size really *doesn't* matter—much.

Size Does Matter— But Not Much

In This Chapter

- There are advantages to small-space gardening
- Defining your small space
- You can always "borrow" more gardening space
- What is "guerrilla gardening"?

First of all, let go of any garden envy that's floating around in your head. I don't care if you just came from your friend's 5-acre spread or a vast plant collection at a public gardens. Gardening in a small space doesn't mean you have to live with less.

In fact, it can be much easier to create "wow" in a small space; it just takes a bit of planning and a little creativity. But it's common for people who have very little gardening room to become stuck and throw in the towel almost before they ever get started.

We don't want you to do that! Small spaces have big potential, and we have some great ideas for your little landscape—some tips that will be a jumping-off point for you to use your own imagination to transform your small-garden space into a delightful reflection of your personality.

In the first part of this book, we're going to talk about what it means to work within a little landscape, and how the definition applies to you. We'll get into borrowing more space if you want to spread out beyond your small space, too. You'll find your garden zone and learn about the magic of microclimates. We'll go into a bit of basic design principles, the role of trees and shrubs, and hardscaping.

Small-Space Gardens Have Big-Time Advantages

Scaled-down gardens are a combination of plant choice, design, and special techniques. It's forgetting about what a traditional yard or garden should or shouldn't be. A little optical illusion doesn't hurt, either.

Your style may be cottage flowers, or perhaps a more sleek, modern design. Maybe you'd like a tropical paradise, or you're a cook and you'd like to grow your own vegetables and herbs. You might be cacti crazy or a rose lover. Whatever you've admired in large gardens, I promise can be created in your small-space garden.

 GARDEN GOSPEL

Creating focal points or playing up a great yard feature is much easier in a small-space garden.

"Size isn't everything," and this is very true when it comes to gardens. You may not ever get to plow the back 40, but then, think of the money you'll save by not having to purchase a tractor. Yes, small-space gardening has its advantages—and we can prove it:

- Year-round color and interest, themes, vegetables, and perennial beds can all be part of the small garden with much less up-front investment than broad expanses of landscape.

- Planted areas fill in faster than large gardens. So you get a mature yard and garden feel quickly.

- Small-space gardens require less maintenance (such as weeding or pruning) and use less water than their larger counterparts.

- They can be reworked practically in a weekend, if you want to change over your outdoor living space with an entirely different theme.

- Vegetable gardens in small spaces often require containers or raised beds. Vegetables grow extremely well in both cases and usually with less work because there are little (or no) weeds in raised beds, and their roots have wiggle room.

- It's just plain handy to step out back or onto the balcony to do your gardening.

Define Your Small-Space Garden

So what's the definition of a "small-space garden"? I think the answer depends on where you're standing. For some, it means the ultimate in small spaces—an apartment balcony. It might mean the enclosed cement patio of a condominium or town home, or a postage stamp of earth in the city. In fact, if you've seen the suburban lots that homes are being built on recently, even suburbia doesn't have much elbow room anymore.

Whether you're living three stories above your neighbors or within the confines of a suburban tract home, the restrictive planting space creates challenges for all of us. Even gardeners with true acreage can have small spaces within that grand area that's a challenge to plant. The truth is that size does matter—just not very much. Let me show you how you can grow almost anything in any small-space garden.

GARDEN GOSPEL

Your garden will be at its best if you work with its natural style as much as possible. If your garden space is in shade, learn to love ferns and woodland plants. If it's situated in the blazing sun, use drought-tolerant sun worshippers.

Urban and Apartment Gardens

If you have a small-space garden in the purest sense—in an apartment or small urban home—you may feel that you don't have choices. I beg to differ. You're going to be delighted at the many ideas, plants, and products available to gardeners in apartments or living a city lifestyle.

In these cozy, intimate settings, you'll be planting things in containers, hooked onto walls, and maybe on a roof. If you love flowers, trees, or perennials, you can grow them. Do you have a balcony that sees mostly shade during the day? Your little garden can house plants that are so beautiful, your neighbors will wish their balcony faced yours.

TIP THYME

It's a horticultural fact that because plants are living things, they also die. No, you do not have a black thumb on your gardening journey—something is going to die. It's a great opportunity to try something new!

If you're interested in growing fresh vegetables, you'll do them the same way—in pots, baskets, and vertically. You're not going to believe the products available that'll make gardening in small spaces easy.

Suburban "Land"

Suburban gardening spaces can actually be just as claustrophobic as any apartment. There are foundation beds with no more than 12" to work with. Entryways with 2' × 3' sections of soil that are set into deep shade are typical. Today's developers leave precious little yard space for the homeowner, and anything more than a tiny backyard is considered a bonus.

GARDEN GOSPEL

Small gardens have big impact when you link your indoor style to the outdoors. Stand inside your home and look out into the garden area. A garden created from this point of view will help you make your indoor and outdoor spaces into a nearly seamless whole.

Suburbanites should count yourselves lucky because you have the "biggest" garden space of all the small-space gardeners, but you'll be contending with very narrow pathways, homes in extremely close proximity to yours (casting lots of shade), and very often a large amount of concrete instead of earth. If you're a vegetable gardener, you may have only a sliver of area that receives the full sunlight that's vital to growing crops.

Not to worry. You can adopt the same gardening techniques used for those in closer quarters, plus we have a few more tricks that those with at least a little earth can utilize.

Borrowing Garden Space

The goal of this book is to allow anyone who wants to get their hands dirty to garden in their own space. But if you've done everything you can possibly do in your own small space, you can always borrow some. More and more cities offer community gardens for their residents. There's also a relatively new, creative gardening strategy called "yard sharing"—and, for the adventurous, there's always "guerrilla gardening," which we'll get to in a bit. Trust me: where there's a will, there's a way.

TIP THYME

Don't think you have to settle for one garden style or theme. Themes are just a place to start. Get the most out of your garden space by planting edibles among your ornamentals. Blueberries, kiwi, strawberries, rosemary, artichoke, leeks, and eggplant make wonderful ornamental edibles.

Gardening with your community offers you more than just more garden space, it also brings your neighbors and community together. Just as gardening by its very nature is a lesson on sustainability, gardening as a unit reinforces the community bonds among you and our neighbors. Gardening can also turn eyesore spaces into places of beauty, provide food for all who tend the grounds, and offer extra bounty for those in need.

Community Gardens

Becoming involved with a local community garden is one of the first ideas to consider if you'd like to get into a larger gardening situation. The land for a community gardens is often provided by the city, local business, or donated by a private party. Very often the people who "run" the gardens are an organized group.

Each garden plot will have a personality that reflects the gardener who's tending it. Some garden plots will be fenced, some won't. You may see whirligigs, small benches, painted signs, and original garden designs within the plots. It may look like the gardens are there only for growing vegetables, but, although veggies may dominate the scene, if you rent a garden plot you can plant and grow nearly anything you'd like such as flowers or herbs. In fact, the vegetable gardeners will welcome more flowers as they invite desirable pollinating insects to their vegetable plants.

The general concept is basically the same for most community gardens, but they'll all have some differences in what they have to offer as well as how they function. Our community gardens have measured-out garden plots that are roughly 12' × 20'. They each have a marker at one corner labeled with a number. The garden's office has a list of which plots are available to rent, and keeps a log of which gardener is renting which space for the year. Those gardeners get first dibs on that same space the following year. Rental fees fluctuate across the country; ours is on the high side, at $100 a year.

One of the best things about the gardens is that they have nearly everything you need to garden successfully. Ours has a large compost pile as well as mulch for spreading in the pathways. They have wheelbarrows, rakes, shovels, and water hoses. Our garden even has beehives on the property to help ensure vegetable production. A few ladies leave a box out every other week for excess produce from the gardeners, which they take to the local food bank. Classes offered by the city are held at our community gardens, too, on topics ranging from gardening practices such as composting to learning basic watercolor painting of the flowers and environment.

Another reason people enjoy community gardens is to hang around like-minded people. Gardeners throughout the city garden on common ground sharing tips, successes, and failures—thus, everyone benefits. The gardens are also a great way to share your bounty and try new things that are offered to you.

Community gardens are an excellent choice for those who need more vegetable space, as well as those whose yard is in full shade.
(Courtesy of Brenda Haas)

The Benefits of Community Gardens

There's much more to community gardening than meets the eye. According to the ACGA, the advantages of community gardens to the city surrounding it are remarkable. Community gardening …

- Improves the gardeners' quality of life.
- Encourages social interaction between neighbors.
- Provides a catalyst for neighborhood and community development.

- Makes your neighborhoods beautiful.

- Reduces crime in the community.

- Conserves natural (and all) resources.

- Creates opportunities for income and economic development.

- Encourages self-reliance and community reliance.

- Preserves the green spaces in the community.

- Produces nutritious food for gardeners and their families.

- Saves money for families.

- Reduces city heat from the streets and parking lots.

- Can become a food source for local food banks.

- Offers opportunity for exercise, recreation, education and therapy for residents.

- Encourages intergenerational and cross-cultural connections.

Community Garden Rules

Usually there will be a place at the gardens to post rules, classes, and other information for gardeners. Community-garden policies vary widely, of course, but they usually include similar rules along these lines:

- Only organic gardening practices are permitted. No pesticides or herbicides can be used to help your gardening endeavor.

- Plot renters may be required to volunteer for general garden maintenance, including assigning each gardener an adjacent path to maintain.

- Specific areas will be designated for weed disposal.

- Consideration of neighbors is usually spelled out. Placement of tall crops, for instance, is sometimes limited.

- Planting timelines are sometimes established to ensure that the plots are being used.

- Child supervision requests may be posted to ensure that others' plots are undisturbed.

- There will most certainly be some type of plot fencing restrictions—usually it refers to height.

- There may be a time frame on watering plots.

- Usually there will be guidelines on community hose and tool care.

- Community gardens encourage their members to attend community meetings to keep abreast of current garden news.

Finding a Community Garden

To find a community garden in your area, check out the website for the American Community Gardening Association (ACGA) at www.communitygarden.org. If you can't locate one at their site, call your city offices; the gardens in your area may just not be on the ACGA list yet.

If you still come up empty, consider starting up a community garden in your area yourself. Chances are you'll find many like-minded gardeners who would jump at the chance to have one nearby. Find those gardeners at your local garden shops or garden clubs, and find master gardeners through the Cooperative Extension Office in your county.

According to the American Community Gardening Association, some of the beginning considerations include the following:

- Forming a planning committee
- Choosing a site
- Insurance
- Zoning laws
- Preparing the site
- Organizing the garden
- Budgeting
- Possible fundraising

There's much more that goes into planning a garden from start to finish. But that shouldn't stop you and your gardening cohorts. People put gardens together all the time, and when you have an entire group working on the details, it can come together surprisingly fast.

Yard Sharing

Yard sharing is very similar to a community garden but has different technical parameters. If there isn't already a yard-sharing community in your town, it's an excellent growing alternative for both suburbanites and city people.

Generally speaking, most yard shares are about growing home vegetables and fruits for healthier eating and saving money. But as far as I'm concerned, yard sharing can just as easily be about chickens (eggs), flowers, and other plants, as well.

TIP THYME

Part of yard sharing success is to combine garden effort with partners who have similar energy and goals. The idea is to have everyone sharing the garden maintenance equally and harvesting food that everyone will enjoy.

There are as many variations to yard sharing as there are gardeners. A yard-share project could be three neighbors maintaining a single garden at one person's home. This person may not have the time or the physical capabilities to garden alone, but has the land for such a project. It might also be one family or a couple gardening in their next-door neighbor's backyard. In both of these cases, the exchange for use of the land would be a share of the garden bounty.

Another example is three neighborhood families, each with a garden at their home. Instead of all of the families planting the same vegetables, each garden is assigned specific fruits and vegetables. One family may devote their entire garden to herbs, while another has tomatoes, green beans, and onions, and the last one may have squash, lettuce, and potatoes.

Garden Where You Work

In the last few years, mini–community gardens are slowly gaining popularity in the workplace. Along with monthly massages on company time and walking trails outside office buildings, savvy employers are embracing unique practices in order to keep their employees happy and healthy. One of these practices includes providing a garden for employees to grow and tend food and flowers.

The workplace garden re-energizes and destresses employees and encourages healthy eating. Co-workers maintaining and harvesting in the garden feel encouraged to spend some recreational time together outside of the more serious work environment.

In fact, some health-care providers actually pave the way for the workplace garden by providing materials and information for workplace gardens. If your employer doesn't offer one now, you could inquire about having a garden incorporated—but be sure your co-workers are on board, unless you're okay with maintaining the garden by yourself.

Guerrilla Gardening—Legally

Guerrilla gardening began when Richard Reynolds embarked on what he describes as his "illicit cultivation" around London. Looking for places of neglect and the occasional empty concrete planter, he got to work turning the neglected and drab areas into spaces of beauty or food. During the night hours, the guerrillas would gather their plants, seeds, shovels, and water containers and work their magic. And the early morning light would show off the amazing transformation to passersby.

Soon after came the technique of rolling native plant seeds with soil and compost—creating seed bombs—to be tossed over fences into abandoned fields. After the winter rains there would be flowers where there had been barrenness.

Wikipedia defines guerilla gardening as

> *"gardening on another person's land without permission. The land that is guerrilla gardened is usually abandoned or neglected by its legal owner and the guerrilla gardeners take it over ("squat") to grow plants. Guerrilla gardeners believe in reconsidering land ownership in order to reclaim land from perceived neglect or misuse and assign a new purpose to it."*

Because traditionally the guerrilla strategy tends to ask for forgiveness as opposed to permission, realistically guerrilla gardening is indulging in a bit of the naughty. But it's entirely possible to guerrilla garden in spaces where this random act of beautification will not only be accepted but applauded. You can start by looking for ignored hell strips (that's what we call the strip of ground between the sidewalk and the street) and asking the homeowner if you can beautify it.

TIP THYME

The key to success for guerilla gardeners is cheap or free plants. Ask local garden centers or hardware stores for any special deals they may have on close-out plants. Ask local gardening clubs if they can offer cuttings, or take cuttings from your own plants.

Places with high public traffic make the most sense because that's where the improvements will be the most noticed and welcomed. Look for places that aren't being developed and those with natural water run-off. Neglected public spaces are your best bet for guerrilla gardening, but I wouldn't rule out private property.

Whether you're asking the owner of the property or not, be sure to mention that you'll be planting drought-tolerant plants (when established), or offer to plant native species. Assure them that invasive species are never even considered for guerrilla gardening. College campuses are good candidates, and you'll more than likely glean some extra guerrillas if you chose a site there.

Even though I only participate in legal guerrilla gardening, I still prefer to do so in the cover of night. It's a part of the ritual that I like to keep alive, and it gives the process that edginess that the early guerilla gardeners had.

The Least You Need to Know

- Whether you're gardening in urban or suburban areas, the same small-gardening practices and principles apply.
- Community gardens offer more gardening space, education, and friendship, and they provide food for gardeners and the community.
- Yard sharing is similar to a community gardens, but is practiced in a more intimate setting.
- There are legal ways to practice guerrilla gardening.

The Lay of the Land

In This Chapter

- What is your growing zone?
- Making basic blueprints
- How to work with your microclimates
- How are cold frames, hoop houses, and row covers used?
- Discover the handy greenhouse

This second chapter is going to get right down in the dirt. We'll explain growing zones, heat maps, and microclimates. We'll explain how to use them to your advantage with cold frames, hoop houses, and small greenhouses. Don't worry if you already feel lost in the weeds—by the time you finish, you'll understand all these gardening terms and techniques. We've also got a couple of easy applications for you to work with in order to become familiar with your garden area.

In the Zone

Have you ever purchased a plant that you've seen in a friend or relative's yard, only to have it struggle to stay alive in your own garden? One reason the plant may not be doing well is that you may live in a different growing zone than your friend does.

Growing zones have been outlined by the United States Department of Agriculture (USDA) on a zone hardiness map. The map is a general guideline to let gardeners know which plant will tolerate which climate. Basically, plants are assigned numbers that correspond to zones on the map, to give you an idea of the lowest temperatures that a plant can tolerate without dying. You can look up the hardiness number of plants in books or online, and you'll also find this information on the plant's container or marker. This is also true for seed packets.

These are general guides and they're fairly accurate, but no map can guess at what your specific *microclimate* may be in your city, neighborhood, or yard. We'll get into microclimates later on in this chapter.

DEFINITION

Microclimates are specific local atmospheric zones where the climate differs from the larger, surrounding area. Think of it as a zone within a zone.

The USDA hardiness zone map will be the most helpful to you when you're thinking about planting perennial plants. A flowering annual can be grown in almost any zone as long as you have enough warm days for that plant variety to reach its blooming time. It's the same with vegetable crops.

Most vegetables are treated as annuals and, as long as your zone provides the right amount of warm days for that vegetable variety to fruit and be harvested, you're good to go. The hardiness in terms of cool temperatures won't apply here. It's the perennials, shrubs, and trees that you're interested in overwintering.

GARDEN GOSPEL

Hard frosts or "killing frosts" are when temperatures fall below 28° for a few hours or longer. With temperatures this low, the chances of tender plants and semihardy plants sustaining foliage damage or worse are high.

This is also known as a radiational freeze; signs of an impending hard frost are a cloudless sky, dry air, and no wind during late fall and winter. You may notice that there's no condensation on your car windshield. If it's 10 P.M. and the temperatures are already below 45°, your best bet is to cover your tender plants.

It's in your best interest to know your growing zone right from the get-go. It's generally pretty easy to find your zone on the USDA hardiness map. In fact, there are many places online where you can simply type in your zip code and it'll generate the zone number for you. Individual zones are defined by the lowest temperatures in your area, so it's easy to see for yourself what zone you're in even if you just have the number scale and can't see the color-coded map. If your area drops down to between 10° and 20°, then you're in Zone 7; if temperatures hover down in the -30°

to -20° area, you're in Zone 4, and so on. You can also contact your local Cooperative Extension office if you're unsure.

There are some versions of the map, where you'll find each zone divided even further into "a" and "b" regions. This breakdown reflects a 10° difference between zones that are otherwise very close in temperatures. These more extensively divided zones define some microclimates.

USDA Hardiness Zone Map

This most basic version of the USDA zone map will give you a solid beginning as far as where your garden's climate stands.

- Zone 1: Below -50°F
- Zone 2: -50°F– -40°F
- Zone 3: -40°F– -30°F
- Zone 4: -30°F– -20°F
- Zone 5: -20°F– -10°F
- Zone 6: -10°F–0°F
- Zone 7: 10°F–20°F
- Zone 8: 20°F–30°F
- Zone 9: 30°F–40°F
- Zone 10: 40°F–50°F
- Zone 11: 50°–60°F

The AHS Heat Map

The American Horticultural Society's (AHS) heat zone map is another general growing guide that can be especially helpful when you're growing vegetables. This is because this map focuses on the average highs in your zone, rather than the lows. More specifically, the heat map gives you the average number of days that temperatures in your zone are at 86°F and above.

I particularly like this map for choosing vegetable varieties. For instance, say you live in Zone 7. You can take a look at the AHS heat map and see that Zone 7 has about 60 to 90 days of 86 and above temperatures. You have a vegetable seed catalog and you're about to order seeds. If you're interested in growing watermelon (a sun worshipper), you'll be looking for a variety that matures within that time frame once you plant the seeds. This lets you focus on your real options, and you're less apt to be disappointed.

As far as ornamental plants, the heat map will help you decide if a plant can tolerate the temperatures within your growing zone. Like the USDA hardiness label, many ornamental plants are coded for their heat tolerance.

Here are the AHS plant heat zones, showing the number of days the thermometer will reach 86°:

- Zone 1: 1 day
- Zone 2: 1–7 days
- Zone 3: 7–14 days
- Zone 4: 14–30 days
- Zone 5: 30–45 days
- Zone 6: 45–60 days
- Zone 7: 60–90 days
- Zone 8: 90–120 days
- Zone 9: 120–150 days
- Zone 10: 150–180 days
- Zone 11: 180–210 days
- Zone 12: 210 days and up

Take a Walk and Get It on Paper

Of course it's exciting to get out there and actually purchase and plant because planting brings you closer to the finished product: your dream garden. But do some simple planning before you break soil or load the back of the car with plants. Besides, dreaming and planning are some of the best parts—so savor them.

You now have some general information on your gardening space, using the USDA growing zone and where you fall on the AHS heat map. Next you need to go out to the yard or garden area. And don't go empty-handed: Bring a spiral notebook (or journal), something sturdy to write on, and a pencil with an eraser. Walk around your entire home—every nook and cranny should be considered. Don't discount any space—you could be ignoring perfectly good and usable space.

You don't have to draw well to get the lay of the land on paper. In fact, I find that what I can do with a space becomes clearer with a simple drawing as opposed to one with a ton of detail. (Of course, you probably won't hear a landscape architect say that.) I start with a basic site map: the general shape and location of the places where I can plant things. You want to draw an outline of your whole property, whether it's an "L", rectangle, "U", square, whatever—just draw the general shape and make it take up most of the paper.

TIP THYME

Looking for a faster way to create a site map? Instead of drawing your property on paper, take pictures of each area. Get shots from different angles to get an accurate image of the space you have. Get one from above if you have a balcony or a tree—but don't break your leg.

If you live in an urban or suburban home that has usable yards in both front and back, draw the shape of your home inside that space. Draw garden beds and pots onto this map as you plant your garden, including the names of the plants and the date you planted them.

Again, you're not looking for perfection. If you live in an apartment or condo that has only a balcony or small front or back area, just draw that gardening space. Add paths, sidewalks, driveways, outbuildings, swimming pool, and existing trees and shrubs. Make a little icon for where you have water spigots and downspouts, too. Not only do you want to be reminded of water sources, but also potential rain barrel placements.

Taking measurements is a good idea, but not necessary. You may want to measure your property lines, the walls of your home, and the distance between your home and the fence or property line.

On a separate sheet of paper, I write notes to myself such as "south garden area but neighbor's tree blocks a lot of direct sun." I'll note any slopes I have in the yard, or tiny corners. If you live in a two-story building with space that you view from above, such as from a bedroom balcony, make note of that, as well. This may be an area that you aren't physically in much, but you could plant as a lovely area for viewing from above.

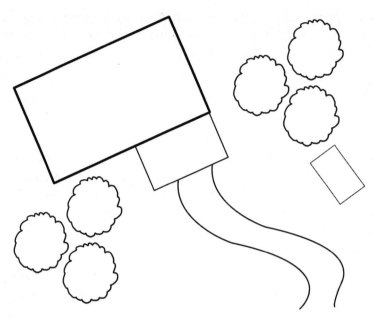

Drawing a basic site map of your property makes it easier to see what you're working with.

TIP THYME

If you love the idea of delving deeper into landscape design, there are kits for the amateur home landscaper on the market. Peruse bookstores, garden catalogs, and Amazon.com.

I also write down other details, such as places that are noticeably supershady or ideas I may have for a spot. I include the date and the weather in these notes. This first garden journal with your observations and site map becomes extremely valuable as you keep adding to it throughout the seasons and the years.

Stop and Get Directions

What direction does your garden face? Finding your garden or yard direction will give you the first indication of what types of plants you can use in that particular garden. Direction is a major indication of the garden climate.

If you have more than one garden space, such as the front and back of your condo or around your yard in the suburbs, figure out the direction each one faces. Some people have been blessed to be born with an internal compass, but I'm not one of them. I have a simple handheld compass that I purchased at a local sports store.

A garden that faces north will have a lot of shade, so the soil will stay damp longer. If you have plants in the middle of a north-facing garden, they won't get much sun. The plants at either end of a north-facing garden will see a little sun in the morning or the evening.

If your space faces south, you'll have lots of sun exposure and some very dry soil. It's perfect for sun-worshipping plants, because you certainly have full sun in a garden in this position.

A garden facing east is exceptionally versatile. You get wonderful sun in the morning, then shade in the afternoon. Most plants that like sun yet don't need full sun will love it here. It can also be ideal for plants that can't take the most direct afternoon sun, and require a little shade. This is the simplest garden space to plant, unless you want a summer vegetable garden; most summer vegetables need more sun, but many herbs will thrive here.

A garden facing the west seems to be the most awkward in terms of plants. The sun is sneaky over on this side. Plants find themselves in the shade all morning long until—wham!—the long, strong afternoon sun is beating down on them. One solution is to plant a shade tree to offer some dappled afternoon sun and plant part-shade lovers. Your house will appreciate it, too.

Defining Full Sun to Full Shade

Gardeners refer to full sun as six to eight hours of direct sunlight, or no less than seven hours. An area that sees five hours of sun is considered strong sun, but not full. What I've found is that two hours in either direction doesn't usually make a difference unless we're talking about certain vegetables such as tomatoes, pumpkins, and melons. These plants need a full six to eight hours to mature and produce.

After that, areas can be described in terms of less sun, more shade, dappled sun, or what-have-you. Full shade is three hours of sun or less. There are many charts to describe all of the various levels between full sun and full shade. The next section will have my descriptions.

How Shady Is Shady?

As you spot the shady places around your home, you may notice that those areas have shade for different lengths of time. Very observant! Indeed, not all shade is equal. By all means, don't be afraid to garden in shady places; just be aware of the amount of shade. You'll be amazed at the variety of plants that you can grow there.

Keep in mind that, just like the sunny areas of your yard or garden, the light will change with the seasons. For example, you may have full shade under a tree in the summer. However, during the spring under the same tree, you could have light shade or even full sun. In this case you'd want to have plants under that tree that need full shade in the summer, but in the spring, you could have plants that will grow in light shade.

These three basic levels of shade could be broken down further, but for the sake of clarity we'll stick with these three:

Full shade receives three (or fewer) hours of sun per day. Whether there's dappled sun or even some direct sun for less than three hours, it's referred to as full shade. The best plants for this area are those that will thrive in the shade as opposed to those that can take part shade. It'll be hard for a part-shade lover to bloom here, and they'll also end up getting leggy (have abnormally long, and weak stems due to lack of sufficient light) and bent as they reach for the light. Better to stick with those that shy away from the sun.

Part shade receives four to six hours of sun (either direct or dappled all day). This is often a place where you have some great morning sun, but by noon or soon after the area is shaded. This can also be a spot under open-branched or high-trimmed trees that let in good light. Shade plants are often appropriate here, as well as some light-shade types, but they may not give you much in flowers (remember, flowers aren't everything). For the most part, vegetables are out of the question here, but there are exceptions, such as lettuces as well as some herbs.

Light shade gets six to eight hours of sunshine, but the conditions can really vary. A garden area with light shade usually gets some fabulous morning sun and gentle or dappled afternoon light. The area can even be described more as "full sun" if you have a lot of afternoon sun, because that kind of light is intense.

Light shade is where even some full sun lovers can thrive, but we're still talking about plants other than full sun-loving vegetables. Plant branches may develop a looser structure than if they had been planted in true full sun, but the result isn't typically disappointing.

We'll talk more about shade in the sections "Seriously Shady Spaces" in Chapter 6 and "A Woodland Garden" in Chapter 12. In Chapter 18, you'll find annuals and perennials for the shade in your yard.

Caveman Sun Blueprint

Among the different ways to figure out exactly which areas have full sun, this technique is my favorite. It's simple to do and easy to understand. I certainly didn't come up with the technique, but it's so basic that I've dubbed it the "Caveman Sun Blueprint," because it's the most basic and rough guide you can create. There are plenty of reasons for figuring out the sunniest places in your yard and garden. You may want to plant some sun-loving perennials or herbs, or you may be looking for that sweet spot to start a summer vegetable bed.

So grab a paper and pencil, and plan to be home at specific intervals during the day to create your Caveman Sun Blueprints. You may think you know exactly where the sun is; on the southern side of your house, right? That's true, theoretically, but in reality other structures may be shading your otherwise sunny spot. It could be another building, tall trees, or a fence.

The best time to create your Caveman Garden Blueprint is on a cloudless day in the early to middle spring. Draw an outline of the area on your paper. Add anything that could produce shade: large trees, walls, or a neighbor's fence.

At 8 A.M., draw a circle that includes all of the space that has sun. At noon, make another circle that shows what areas are getting sun. Make another circle at 4 P.M. Now look at the space where the three circles intersect one another. This is the place that receives the most sunlight during the day.

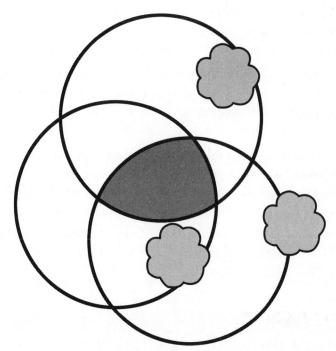

Making caveman blueprints of your yard is a simple technique, yet incredibly eye-opening.

Manage with Microclimates

A microclimate is an area within a region whose growing climate differs from the general zone for some reason, such as physical structures, extra windy areas, topography, or large bodies of water. For instance, if you have a large body of water nearby, such as a lake or the ocean, it'll tend to moderate the surrounding air temperatures. Your zone may be known for its heavy frost, but your plants may rarely freeze.

GARDEN GOSPEL

Raised beds and containers create microclimates. The soil in a raised bed heats up faster than the soil in the earth, giving plants a head start on the growing season in the spring and lengthening the growing season in the fall.

It's a beautiful thing when you realize that you don't have to rely on Mother Mature for these variables in your growing zone. Indeed, gardeners can use and manipulate them, and they should be in your gardening bag of tricks. You may not be able to control the weather, but you can alter your microclimate.

Using Walls and Buildings

Anyone can use their microclimates, but urban and suburban gardeners usually have a little more to work with. It's where small-space gardens can really shine.

Urban and suburban gardeners can take advantage of the very things that seem to be in the way: walls, houses, and other buildings. Buildings can have a huge effect on their immediate area. They may act as wind barriers or create wind tunnels. Walls or buildings made of brick, cement, or stucco will hold and radiate heat.

If you have heat lovers for plants, be sure to plant them on the south side of your house or any other wall. If you need a cooler place with less sun, go for the north side. Using the sun exposure can also be the difference between a perennial over-wintering or not. This is yet another way to enjoy a plant variety that's just outside the boundaries of your growing zone. For instance, bougainvillea plants don't usually make it through the winter in a temperate zone like they do in southern California gardens. But I know a northern California gardener who keeps her bougainvillea alive through the winter because it's on a wall with a southern exposure.

PLANTING PITFALL

Don't place heat-sensitive plants against a wall with a southern exposure. They'll need to be supplemented with extra water to combat heat stress.

Walls have a leeward (downwind) and a windward (upwind) side. The windward side is the place for water-loving plants, since it will receive more rain than the leeward side. Put plants you want to protect from driving rains on the leeward side.

The north side of your house might be the best place for early flowering fruit trees like cherries or peaches. A late spring frost can set the fruit production back, but if you plant it where there's a northern exposure, it can help suspend blossoming until the frost date has passed.

Because morning sun is gentler than the rest of the day, plant tender varieties on the eastern side of any structure. Heat lovers like roses are perfect for the west side.

Mountains and Canyons

Topography has a major effect on microclimates. Do you live on a hill? The top of a hill is going to get the most wind. Along with having fast drainage, the wind dries both the soil and the plants themselves. You want drought-tolerant plants here as well as those that can take a windy beating.

Do you live in a valley? Warm air is lighter than cold air, and valleys have more frost than areas higher up. Plants that like moisture do best in valleys.

Which side of the hill are you on? A northern slope is slower to see the sun and warm up. On the other hand, the southern side warms up faster, but if plants begin to bloom, they could be set back if a sudden frost hits.

Additional factors that can affect microclimates are rainfall, soil types, mulching practices, paved surfaces, fences, balconies, and rooftops. Don't let a number on a map dictate your garden plans. Clever gardeners will manipulate their growing zone by using any microclimate resources they have.

Cold Frames, Hoop Houses, and Row Covers

Cold frames and hoop houses are basically very short greenhouses sans the heat. They're most often used to get a head start on a vegetable garden in the spring, as well as extending the growing season into the fall or even winter. In climates with mild winters, some cool-weather crops can be grown all winter long in a hoop house or cold frame.

A cold frame is a handy gardening tool that will extend the growing seasons
in both spring and fall.
(Courtesy of Teresa Soule)

The names of these structures refer to the construction rather than the function. Cold frames are bottomless, box-type structures that have a lid or door on the top that can be raised to different levels. The lid is made of glass or clear plastic, which lets in light and collects heat while keeping off the frost. Old windows are handy to recycle to make a cold frame, as are entire glass doors. Cold frames can be permanent or portable, depending on your garden needs.

Gardeners use cold frames to "harden off" (toughen up) the vegetable seedlings they so lovingly raised indoors during the winter. I've also used mine to grow my lettuce all fall and winter. Trust me, once you have a cold frame around, you won't ever want to do without one again.

TIP THYME

Place seedlings under the cold frame outside for a couple of hours, then bring them back inside. Increase their time in the cold frame over a few days so they become adjusted to the outdoors. Once they've been out all day for a few days, you can leave them in the frame overnight until it's time to plant them in their permanent place in the garden.

The terms *row cover* and *hoop house* are often used interchangeably, but there are some subtle differences. Hoop houses are usually built with PVC pipe or another flexible material, and then bent over an entire garden bed. Several hoops are placed at even intervals. This way, all you have to do to protect plants in a hurry is to toss some plastic sheeting or plant fabric over the hoops. Plant roots aren't disturbed and you can take advantage of the good soil that you've created in the garden beds. You can make portable hoop houses to place over garden beds that are planted directly into in the earth (as opposed to a raised bed), as well.

Row covers are just miniature hoop houses used to cover specific rows of vegetables rather than the entire bed. Row covers are more often used to keep out insects while allowing water to get through. Of course, the fabric helps warm the soil, too.

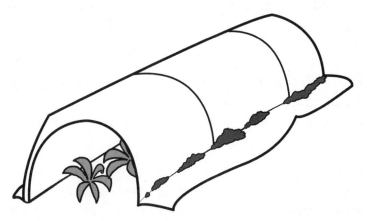

Think of row covers as transportable, miniature greenhouses.

Sometimes heavy-gauge wire is used to hold a light, synthetic plant material over the row, but a "floating" row cover can just be fabric placed lightly over the plants with the bottom edge of the fabric held down with small rocks or boards.

You can leave the hoophouse frame attached to a raised garden bed all year long and simply toss plastic sheeting or plant fabric over it when you expect a temperature drop.

The Cloche

Cloches are portable, miniature cold greenhouses, for lack of a better term. They're used to protect individual plants and seedlings from the spring frost. Back in the 1800s, cloches or bell jars were made of glass. As pretty as they are functional, bell jars are currently coming back into vogue as they're especially practical in small gardens.

PLANTING PITFALL

Don't forget to remove the cloche as the day grows warmer! Just as these handy devices can protect seedlings, they can wilt them just as fast if it becomes sauna-like inside.

You don't have to purchase a particular cloche in order to take advantage of this type of protection. Feel free to recycle plastic water bottle and milk containers. Cut off the bottom and place them over tender seedlings. You can add ventilation by taking the cap off of the top of the container.

If you have some small terra-cotta flower pots, you can turn them upside down over a sturdy seedling, being sure to stuff the inside with some straw for insulation.

Greenhouses: The Ultimate Microclimate

We can't leave this chapter without discussing the ultimate in climate control: the greenhouse. If you're lucky enough to have a greenhouse (and I mean *any* greenhouse), you probably already realize how versatile they are for the plant lover.

A greenhouse can be heated or not. A heated one may be more versatile in growing zones that have harsh winters, but even a "cold" greenhouse—one without any added heat—comes in extremely handy.

What You Can Do with a Greenhouse

People often think of a tropical paradise when they think of greenhouses. This is what's known as a hothouse. Indeed, they're wonderful for housing plants that like to winter in Florida. But a greenhouse is so much more, and it's fairly simple to regulate the temperature within. With the smaller ones, you can slide open the plastic cover or leave the door ajar.

- You can start seeds in late winter to prepare for spring planting. The seedlings grown for a couple of months in the garden will end up in a permanent garden bed later.

- You can also harden off seedlings that you may have started under lights in your house just before you plant them outdoors.

- Depending on your climate and whether your greenhouse has heat, you can overwinter houseplants in a greenhouse. Because I have quite a few houseplants and not enough light indoors for every plant, I like to overwinter some of my houseplants in the greenhouse. Come spring, I hang them under my back porch roof until fall.

- Greenhouses are excellent for propagating plants. If you've taken cuttings from perennial plants, this is the perfect place to have the new plants take root before you bring them outdoors into the real world.

- It's the right place to "hold" mature plant specimens for the winter. These parent plants can be used to start more plants come spring.

- Greenhouses are perfect for growing small winter vegetables such as lettuce, carrots, radishes, and peas. In reality, food crops can be grown in a greenhouse year-round.

You Have Plenty of Room

Greenhouses come in all shapes and sizes. They range all the way from bread box cute—perfect for an apartment patio—to giant structures grand enough to make my entire house look ridiculous in comparison. Most small-space gardeners will have one of the more modest varieties, and that's really all you need.

TIP THYME

If you have a few tender plants that you'd like to keep warm, but don't want to heat a large greenhouse, create a minigreenhouse inside the bigger one. Put up a couple of temporary walls with bubble wrap to act as insulation attached to them, then use an electric space heater with a thermostat to keep just that space warm.

The simplest greenhouses are basically shelves with plastic covers that slide over the entire four-shelf unit. They're approximately 62" tall, 27" wide, and 19" deep. Of course, the size and style will depend on the company that makes it, but you get the idea. You can't actually walk into these little greenhouses, but there's usually a zipper so you can reach inside and arrange plants and seedling. They'll run you anywhere from $65 to $120.

The next size up (in general) is a greenhouse that has shelves on two sides of a walkway. These houses may be 4' × 4' or 5' × 5', with a big plastic cover that slides over the top. But with this one, you can actually step inside after unzipping the doorway. They'll run anywhere from $150 to $240 or higher.

Up from there are 6' × 8' structures made with a simple metal frame and covered entirely with polycarbonate panels. They're roomy enough to walk around in and, at around $400, won't break the bank.

Another greenhouse that's less expensive than the permanent buildings are the type that are semipermanent. These could be moved, but it's not all that easy. These are made of metal much like a common storage shed, but they have fiberglass *glazing*. I have one that's 6' × 8' and it even comes with an automatic vent opener, which is a nice feature because the vents allow the hot air to escape and let in fresh air. This sturdy little greenhouse runs about $800 and up. The stronger greenhouses that have more bells and whistles and better glazing and so on can range from $1,500 on up very quickly.

 DEFINITION

Glazing is the walls or part of the walls that let the light into a greenhouse. Glass, fiberglass, or plastic are used for greenhouse glazing.

Insulate a "Cold" Greenhouse

Here's a great idea for cheap insulation: bubble wrap—the stuff you wrap the good crystal with and can't resist popping with your fingers. In a heated greenhouse, it works as added insulation and frost protection, but it's also smart to put up if you don't run electricity to the greenhouse. Bubble wrap is very effective for holding heat and is very cost-effective. In milder climates, bubble wrap is fairly impressive for keeping off that kill-chill for many plants. Extremely tender plants may still need to be brought indoors for the winter, but plants that are almost winter hardy may be able to hang around the greenhouse during the cold months without any heat.

TIP THYME

Take advantage of every bit of space inside your greenhouse. Hang plants in baskets from the frame at the top of the greenhouse. Attach hanging shelves onto the side frames, too.

There are several ways to hold bubble wrap against the walls and roof. If the greenhouse has a wood frame, you can use push pins. If you have one made with metal framing, there are special fasteners that twist into the grooves of the frame. If your glazing happens to be glass, suction cups can be moistened and pressed against it to hold the bubble wrap.

PLANTING PITFALL

It's fine to add humidity to the greenhouse by wetting the floor or by misting plants during the warmer months. But if you add humidity this way during the winter, you may invite fungal disease problems due to condensation on the glass.

When you have the wrap hung on the walls and roof, seal the seams with clear adhesive tape to keep as much heat as you can inside. Don't forget you'll need ventilation inside the greenhouse, so line the vents (at least one) separately to allow it to open. You can also cover windows with the bubble wrap. If you take it down carefully, you can store the wrap for the following winter.

The Best Place for a Greenhouse

If you have a choice in where you place your greenhouse, there are better spots than others. Place it on the most level spot possible. You also want an area that receives the most winter light you can get for as many hours as possible.

TIP THYME

If you'd like your greenhouse to receive the maximum amount of sunlight all year long, then ideally you'd place it so that a long side is facing 20 degrees due south (the shorter ends will be facing east and west).

Don't forget that structures or trees in the area could cast shadows onto your greenhouse. If you have very young trees near your chosen greenhouse location, will they end up shading it when they're fully mature? Of course, you may get away with a few nearby deciduous trees, since they won't have leaves in the winter so light will get through. This may not be a bad plan, especially if you live where the summers are scorching, as those same trees when leafed out might protect it from too much sun. On a final note, don't forget that the winter sun angles are a lot lower than summer sun angles.

Another thing to consider is easy access to water, potting supplies, and so on. You might also want to be sure that you can get a small wheelbarrow to your greenhouse.

If you don't have a choice in where you put a greenhouse, don't turn a free or cheap one down. You can adjust, and any greenhouse is worth it.

If you'd like to dig deeper into more greenhouse specifics (and I encourage you to do so), I have listed greenhouse information sources in the resources appendix of this book.

The Least You Need to Know

- Getting a basic layout on paper will tell you what you need to know about your garden space.
- Caveman Sun Blueprints can tell you exactly where the most sun is in your yard or garden.
- You can adjust your "official" growing zone by using your microclimates.
- Cold frames, hoop houses, and row covers can extend the growing season by allowing you to start your garden earlier and make the harvest last longer.
- Greenhouses don't have to be big or heated to be useful for small-space gardeners.

Big Thoughts on Small-Space Design

In This Chapter

- Ideas for personal expression in the garden
- Brainstorming garden themes
- Thoughts on repetition, scale, and shape in a small garden
- Leaf size and garden effects
- What makes for good garden bones?

In this chapter, we offer some basic design principles that are useful for any size garden, as well as specific strategies for smaller ones. We'll talk about what gives a garden a formal or more casual look, and offer ideas for garden themes to get your creative juices flowing. We'll also discuss what good garden bones are all about.

Express Yourself

Before gathering any ideas, and certainly before breaking ground or purchasing plants, you should have a good idea of what excites you in a garden. Like the rooms in your home, your garden or yard should be a place that makes you want to step outside with your morning coffee and enjoy the space. The best way to become the number one fan of your garden is to have it reflect your personality and style.

Here are some places to look to find personal garden inspiration:

- Books
- Magazines
- Garden catalogs
- Neighbors' yards

- Local public gardens

- Local plant nurseries

- Public parks

- Movies and television

PLANTING PITFALL

It's fine to keep an eye open for a style you like on the big screen, but don't be fooled by professional sets. The garden seen in the movie *It's Complicated* was an uber-staged Garden of Eden. Those greenhouse-grown cabbage heads were hand chosen from a variety of potted plants then carefully placed, and those amazing tomatoes were artificially wired to the plants. This isn't an example of an honest-to-goodness garden.

You may also find yourself turning for inspiration to the first garden that impressed you. The warm memories of our grandmother's cottage garden or our aunt's vegetable *potager* that we played in as children often steers us toward our final design.

DEFINITION

A **potager** is the French version of a kitchen vegetable garden. What gives the potager its style and appeal is its blend of vegetables, herbs, and cutting flowers. Such a kitchen garden is quite ornamental and visually charming, often designed with repetitive geometric patterns.

Another good way to get your mind going the right direction is noticing what types of plants thrive in other people's gardens. You may have a penchant for roses, or perhaps you dream of growing cutting flowers that can be enjoyed in vases in your home. Some people enjoy a formal setting they can use for entertaining; others wouldn't dream of planting anything that isn't fragrant. Vegetable gardens have become incredibly popular and can easily be incorporated into small garden spaces.

Formal Designs

I don't think there's any limit to garden plans and ideas, but there are some standard blueprints, and some tried-and-true themes within those categories. If you revel in clean lines and symmetrical shapes, then you may prefer a more formal look. Plants used in a formal setting are not allowed to grow out in what would be their natural form, but rather are trimmed and shaped.

Sometimes this look was inadvertently created when the housing developer poured your driveway and made sidewalks as well as other straight paths. It may just be easier to work within the shape that you have, but if formality isn't your style, don't think for one minute that you're simply stuck with it. Garden styles that lend themselves well to formal design are …

- **Traditional foundation plantings:** You'll see this garden or yard style all over suburbia. It may be something you really like, or it may be something that you'd like to change. But there's usually a rectangular flower (perennial) border along the front of the house—probably two. The lawn is grown in a rectangle or square—and certainly edged after it's mowed.

- **Raised-bed gardens:** Raised beds can be placed anywhere. You may see them on a front lawn, backyard, or a courtyard. Rectangles make up the majority of raised beds and because the geometric shape is raised up it stands out all the more. They fit in perfectly in a formal setting, but they can also be used in a cottage garden setting with a more loose design.

- **Herb gardens:** Herb gardens are wonderfully versatile. Because of some of the woody perennials like thyme and rosemary, herb gardens can be very formal, indeed. On the other hand, if you use the more airy plants such as dill and chives, they can be planted informally, too. We'll talk more about herb gardens in Chapter 12.

- **Knot gardens:** Low-growing hedges or herbs are used to create the strong geometric shapes in a knot garden. Originally, these sixteenth-century formal, shaped gardens were planted so that they could be viewed from upper-story windows of French and Italian mansions. In a small garden setting, miniature versions can still be beautifully created, albeit on a much smaller scale.

- **Rose gardens:** Many rose varieties themselves grow with a rather natural, formal look to them. Roses tend to have a formal feel just by virtue of being planted in the yard, and when they're grouped into their own garden space, they tend to look all the more regal. But for the most part, rose gardens are created within a geometrical shape. There's more on roses in Chapter 11.

TIP THYME

Remember that a formal look will require more maintenance than nearly any other design. Formality relies on perennial beds and lawns having neat corners and edges, which can be extremely time-consuming.

Keeping It Casual

When you're trying to create an informal garden, often buildings and fences pop into the picture too quickly and make the eye come to a full stop that breaks the flow of a casual garden. Growing plants up the fence or other structure will help hide the structures and help create the illusion that the casual garden goes on and on.

- **Cottage gardens:** Old-fashioned perennials and reseeding annuals are popular for creating a cottage garden. Vegetables and herbs are often added, too. Although a cottage garden should have a tousled, free-flowing feel to it, some calculated pruning will help give it some gentle shape. Brick, crushed granite, and stepping stones used for pathways help to give a garden that cottage feel.

- **Wildlife gardens:** Many people believe wildlife gardens have to be "messy" and overgrown. That isn't true in the least. All plants can be pruned back so that they can be admired by both you and the butterflies. The plants in this case would provide food or nectar for insects, birds, and other wildlife. This would include native plant varieties, as well. We'll get more into wildlife gardens in Chapter 12.

- **Woodland gardens:** Woodland gardens can utilize both evergreen and deciduous trees, azaleas, heuchera, wood anemones, ferns, bulbs, and more. A woodland garden needs a bit more space than you'll find in apartments or condo-sized gardens. If you live in a suburban neighborhood, you can pull off this style well. In fact, many yards that are already shaded by larger trees or are situated in part shade almost beg for woodland gardens.

- **Meadow gardens:** Okay, in a small-space garden, you probably won't be creating a full meadow. But it is possible to create a meadow effect. Soften the edge of a lawn by planting low-growing border plants, shrubs, and feathery grasses with a sweeping feel along the grass's edge.

- **Tropical gardens:** A tropical influence can be right at home—for example, in planters around a pool. To grow tropical plants outdoors, you do need to live in an incredibly warm climate such as southern California or Florida, or you can go for some tropical-looking plants that are hardier than they seem, such as a hardy yucca. Creating a tropical feel has much more to do with plant choice than the actual layout.

- **Rock gardens:** Rock gardens are very natural looking and can be an excellent choice for sloped areas. Of course, they also look their best covering a large space. But small-space gardeners can successfully create a rock garden by creating a raised garden complete with rocks that have been halfway sunken into the garden area. They're also well suited for gravel areas, as well as "islands" like the carved-out beds often seen in the center of lawns.

What's great about making this type of garden is that alpines (rock plants) are wonderfully small. It's exciting because the plant fanatics can have a vast array of alpine varieties within extremely tiny gardening areas. Another way to use alpines in rock gardens is to plant them in what's referred to as a "sink garden," which we'll talk about in Chapter 12.

Creative Theme Garden Ideas

These garden-style suggestions aren't even close to exhaustive. Even if you never talk to a landscape designer in your life, the design ideas are endless. A clever way to incorporate your personality into your garden is to use plants that reflect some of your other interests by using a theme garden. Below is a list of ideas to adopt as your own or simply to get your creative juices flowing.

- **Color combinations:** Plan a theme, such as blue and white. Don't forget that flowers aren't your only source of color. For instance, you could add white using the foliage from a plant such as Lamb's Ears.

- **Claude Monet's garden:** Plant the flowers that were painted by the famous artist such as sunflowers, water-lilies, tulips, chrysanthemums, and dahlias.

- **Biblical garden:** Grow plants found in the Bible. Your list might include bay tree, laurel, olive, mallow, coriander, myrtle, and pomegranate.

- **Shakespearean garden:** This would include plants that Shakespeare addresses in his works. Some flowers mentioned in his works are roses, violets, daisies, cowslips, and primroses.

- **Family garden:** Research plants and flowers that have the same name as your family members; roses are a great place to start for this type of theme.

- **Scented garden:** It's very often the gardens planted for scent that will be romantically remembered. But you do have to use a light hand when planting, taking into consideration how strong the scent of the plant species (or variety) is as well as how close to a walkway you plant them.

- **Period gardens:** Old-world garden themes might include an Elizabethan garden, formal and elegant and planted specifically to appeal to the senses; a medieval medicinal garden with plants grown specifically for their healing properties; or a Colonial garden like those of seventeenth-century New England, entirely utilitarian and comprised of small crops, herbs, medicinal plants, and plants for making dyes.

- **Heritage garden:** Maybe you have strong ties to an old-world country such as Italy or Ireland. Or maybe you just like Mexican food. If you have a penchant for a specific ethnic food, grow a garden filled with vegetables native to that country.

- **Sports garden:** If you're a diehard sports fan, consider planting some garden space with your favorite team's colors. Don't forget to add a few accent colors to help the team's primary color stand out.

Basic Garden Design Principles

There are somewhere around 400,000 flowering plant species in the world. They're all wonderful in their own right, but let's get something straight: they aren't all going to fit in your garden. Putting every concept you've ever admired into your garden usually ends up as a visual train wreck.

One landscape architect told me that she has many clients who are dead set on recreating plant collections they may have seen at public sites, such as botanical gardens. Once the design is actually installed, they realize that their theory was much more attractive than the reality. Big public gardens often use a wider variety of colors. This can work for broad, sweeping spaces, but in a small home garden may look unplanned or gaudy. She also mentioned that she now tries much harder to talk them into choosing a specific theme or setting from the beginning. If you'd like a visually attractive yard or garden, some restraint is in order.

I'm going to tell you up front that garden designers and landscape architects don't always agree on certain aspects of what works best in a small-space garden. I've tried to figure out why their views differ so widely and I can only conclude that it just depends—on many different levels.

It depends on the size of the yard or garden. It depends on the shape, the style, and what structures surround it. It also depends—quite simply—on the eye of the beholder. There has to be room for personal taste. In other words, there are no absolutes and there's always more than one right answer. That said, there are some general principles that work for most people and will certainly guide you down the path to your dream garden.

Repetition

First of all, repeating a plant variety, color, or shape is good design practice in any garden, large or small. But it's key for petite plots, and here's why: when there's too much going on in a garden, it becomes overpowering. The eye doesn't like overpowering; it loves balance and repeated patterns. Repetition pulls the garden together by bringing a sense of unity, organization, and calmness.

Say you have an area that's 12' × 3' that you're going to use as an annual border. You could create a lovely contrasting yet unified border with 11 rudbeckia (yellow), 5 ageratum (blue, pink, or white), 3 coreopsis (yellow), 3 coleus "golden wizards" (lime green), and 3 lacinata or dinosaur kale (blue).

You can use repetition with container plantings. Say that you have three terra-cotta pots in the corner of a patio. The grouping will look best if all of the pots are either all the same color even if they're different shapes, or all the same shape yet in different colors—just as long as there's something tying them together. You could connect container plantings together by arranging those plants that have the same overall shape.

You may have a couple of boxwoods trimmed into a box shape and a tea tree trimmed into the same shape. You can keep things interesting in two border beds that are on either side of a walkway. Simply unify the beds with color while still keeping some contrasting texture by having long-stemmed lavender (blue) in the left border and shorter, fluffier salvia (blue) on the right.

Another way to use repetition is to connect your elements with garden decorations or structures. Furniture, paving stones, garden art, fabrics, walls, arbors, trellises, statuary, containers, foliage, and flowers can all be used to connect elements with one another. For instance, you can use yellow furniture cushions to compliment nearby blue salvia flowers.

Scale

When we're discussing scale, we're talking about a size compared to another size. But exactly what are we comparing the sizes to? We normally walk around comparing the size of things to ourselves. That makes sense, because everything we see is from our own point of view.

When we plant a yard or garden, we typically compare (or measure) everything to the size of the largest (and perpetual) thing in the garden. Usually, that would be the house. If you move to a space that's away from the house, you'll automatically compare things to whatever is closest.

The principal of scale stands out as one of the biggest priorities if you're looking to create an attractive garden, large or small. But it stands to reason that you can get away with more in a large area than in a small one. The first thing that comes to mind when considering scale in a small space is the size of the plants. If standard plant varieties are all you plant, they'll simply overwhelm the small garden (and possibly shade out any other plants).

You may already realize that plant species often have a dwarf or semidwarf variety that's well suited to little gardens and yards. I completely encourage people to make use of the miniature plant varieties. But if they're overused, it won't be satisfying to the eye because you'll feel like you're living in a dollhouse garden. This will create an out-of-scale effect, just as using too many over-sized plants does. That's not what you're after—unless, of course, you're actually trying to create a dollhouse garden.

What you're really reaching for is the feel and ambiance of a bigger garden, adjusted to, well, a smaller space. You want to make your garden feel as large as it can by using the space you have effectively. The best way to achieve this is to use medium-sized plants, one to three larger specimen plants (to serve as the focal points), and a smattering of the dwarf varieties. This blend will give your garden balance and structure.

Think along the same lines when you add garden structures—and I wouldn't add many. Depending on the area you're working with, things can get crowded, ruining any design very quickly. Stick with medium to small rocks, unless you're using one large one as a *focal point*. For example, in a petite urban garden, keep a trellis or pavers on the modest side, and furniture to a minimum.

One garden design trick is to use medium-sized plants that happen to have large leaves such as cannas, small elephant ear varieties, and hostas. This offers the feel of larger scale without overwhelming the small space.

 DEFINITION

Focal points are pleasant-looking structures that are put into the garden design specifically to stop the eye. A focal point can be an interesting plant, but it can also be other man-made elements such as boulders, garden art, statuary, gates, trellises, ponds, arbors, and fountains.

Leaf Size

Texture, in terms of plants in garden design, refers to visual texture as opposed to the tactile texture. So it's about look, not feel. In garden design, plants are primarily in one of three categories: fine, medium, or coarse (bold). Many plants we use are basically medium in texture. So to give a garden a little pizzazz, the gardener may want to be sure to introduce some fine-textured plants as well as some coarse- or bold-textured plants.

Although it's true that things like shape and distance can play a role in describing plant texture, it's mostly about the leaves. Plants that have small leaves, like spirea or maidenhair fern, are referred to as finely textured; plants that have large leaves, such as cannas and hostas, are coarsely textured. All other plants fall into the middle.

If you want your space to have a soft feel, both small and medium leaves will create that for you. Finely textured plants play a key role in small-space gardens, as smaller leaves make a space look bigger by encouraging your eye to follow these plants. The medium-textured ones work the same way. Coarse plants tend to stop the eye. Small leaves tend to fade into the view, while the larger leaves make a bigger visual impact. Bold plants can serve you well as the focal points of a garden, and they add interest and perspective.

A garden appears larger when a coarsely textured plant or two is placed at the head (front) of the garden. Plant medium to finely textured varieties down the sight line after that—say, as you walk down a path. This will give the illusion of a larger and deeper garden than you actually have.

The idea isn't to decide which plant texture is superior, but which combination and location of textures works best. Plants with long, thin, straplike leaves like agapanthus can be either fine or coarse depending on the plant variety. Those with thin strappy leaves are fine, while the ones with big straps are bold.

Ornamental grasses are fabulous for adding texture and they work well in small settings. Mexican feather grass, maiden grass, fountain grass, bamboo muhly, and gulf muhly are all great grasses to consider.

What's the (Focal) Point?

As we just said, focal points are placed in a garden to draw and stop the eye at a certain part of the garden. Strategically placed focal points can draw the viewer's eyes all around the garden to the farthest end, once again making the garden appear larger. We like that.

The first focal points I always try to go for are plants. Remember, the idea is to lead the viewer up to a focal point that will stop the eye. One way to pull this off is to have some finely textured plants lead the way to a coarsely textured plant as a focal point.

You can also fool the eye by using something that, when you're up close, is a finely textured plant, like a pine tree. To make it look coarse, plant it way in the back of the yard. The needles will blur together and look solid, creating the illusion of being big leafed.

Overusing nonplant focal points will look cluttered and make your eyes jumpy. But you can certainly get away with a single man-made focal point in the vicinity of several plant focal points. In fact, I think utilizing focal points in this manner makes the biggest statement in a big or small garden.

In a small garden, you want to use focal points sparingly. You can also use plants that don't grow as large as their standard cousins. Maybe try a dwarf conifer on a balcony or courtyard as opposed to a full-sized fir tree.

> **TIP THYME**
>
> Focal points help make for great garden design, but too many ornament-type structures end up looking messy in a small space. How many man-made focal points should you have in a garden? You can't go wrong if you can only see one nonplant focal point at a time from any point of view.

Nonplant elements that can be focal points are walls, boulders, garden art, statuary, birdbaths, gates, trellises, ponds, arbors, and fountains. One plus to using hardscaping as a focal point is that it's going to look good through every season. Of course, an evergreen does, too.

> **PLANTING PITFALL**
>
> When planting to hide an unattractive view such as a meter or air-conditioning unit, be careful not to use plants that are pokey or spiky. Meter readers and anyone servicing these units won't be able to get to them easily without getting injured. Think grasses and other "soft" plants.

You can and should use focal points to distract viewers from less attractive things such as the air conditioning unit. For instance, you may have your garbage can area on one side of a walkway, and a lovely shade garden with ferns and heuchura on the other side. Encourage visitors to see the shade garden before they ever notice the garbage cans by planting a shade plant with bold texture on the shade garden side.

Get into Shape

In this section I'm referring to the shape of the garden itself, not the shape of the plants. Urban and suburban gardens and yards are usually rectangular and square shaped, bounded by straight lines. It's what the housing developer left us to work with, and since there are also buildings or structures on the neighboring properties, it makes sense.

TIP THYME

Remember that curves throughout the garden will carry the eye, and a focal point will hold it. If you're using curves in your garden design, give the flowing shape a purpose by bringing the eye to a focal point.

You can use the shapes that you were given, or you can create the shapes that make you happy. One word of advice: when working with shapes in a small garden, stay with one type throughout. Larger areas can have enough space between sections to pull off a mix of shapes, but you're much better off sticking with either straight lines or circles and curves.

Curves are my favorite shapes to work with in my suburban yard. When I say "curves," I mean broad and sweeping, not short and squiggly. These are messy, distract the eye, and create maintenance issues such as trying to mow or edge a lawn.

Sweeping curves are satisfying to me because I enjoy a meandering feel, and they casually lead the eye throughout the garden. Curves make a garden or yard feel larger because they suggest movement. I like to take my curvy creations down a path to just outside of view. It's a great way to trick the mind into thinking that there's much more right around the proverbial corner.

You can also use straight lines to lead the eye if you're using sharp geometrical shapes. If you're working with a very tiny space, it can be difficult to pull off the curves, so stick with straight lines if it will allow you to have more plants.

TIP THYME

If you're not working with curvy shapes, walls and paths created on the diagonal (slanted angle) will make a small space look bigger. For instance, when using tiles or bricks for a patio, placing them on the diagonal will "open up" the space.

To soften straight lines, arrange a group of containers in a deep corner or an outside corner. Don't forget to use plant varieties to soften a strict feel. Fine-textured and airy plants such as ferns, ornamental grasses, and loose cottage flowers are a great fix.

Keep in mind that plants throughout the season (and the years) are going to change shape—and can also be pruned to take on a different shape—whereas shapes created by cement, raised beds, walls, and so on, are permanent and constant.

Good Garden Bones

You may have heard of looking for good garden "bones." That means looking for—or creating—permanent fixtures that give the garden its basic foundation and structure. Picture a garden in the summertime. It's full, filled out, and leafy. Now picture the same garden under snow. Most plants are dormant and have disappeared. All that's left is a garden skeleton, the permanent man-made or natural focal points.

Garden bones might be stable structures, such as small outbuildings, fountains, gazebos, statuary, walkways, ponds, trellises, arbors, and even benches or tables. Because evergreen trees and shrubs keep their leaves or needles all year long, they add wonderful bones and bring permanent structure to a yard or garden.

They're the perfect place to start when you're considering the plants you'd like to grow, because they are the anchor for the plants surrounding them. Of course, deciduous trees make terrific garden bones, too, but just remember that in the winter, they'll be naked bones.

Trees and Shrubs in the Small Garden

Trees and shrubs are not only useful as structures in a garden, but they can also add form, texture, color, height, and shade. In a small-space garden, you may not be planting a forest, but there are plenty of reasons to bring in a couple of small trees, as well as some shrubs. If you'd like to get a couple more shrubs into a little space, go for some climbing, shrub-type plants such as star jasmine.

Make your tree and shrub choice count. Because you have limited space, choose trees and shrubs that will have added value to the landscape. Your garden will benefit the most from plants that provide great color in the fall or winter months. Some have particularly attractive bark, such as manzanita shrubs or birch trees. Some varieties will bring fragrance or flowers to your yard, such as lilac and mock orange.

Dwarf trees and shrubs (and other plant species) can offer you the look of a large tree without swallowing up all the space. "Dwarf" simply describes a plant or tree variety that's smaller than the standard specimen. It doesn't necessarily mean that it remains thimble sized when it's mature. So be sure to get information on the height and width of a dwarf variety before you purchase.

Trees and large shrubs can also hide something you'd rather not see in your yard. The electric company's control box that often sits in a front yard isn't attractive. Neither is the neighbor's flag pole or an old fixer-upper car that's permanently parked next door. Some good trees and shrubs for blocking the view in a small garden setting are American holly, small dogwoods, compact maple trees, and viburnums.

Consider Tree Shapes

When you're considering adding interest to a garden, don't forget to think about tree shape. Trees come in a variety of shapes (or habits), including round, weeping, columnar, clump, vase, pyramidal, conical, and oval. As you're gathering information on a young tree—growing zone, height and width at maturity—look at a picture of a mature specimen to see the final shape. Some trees grow in one habit but take on another shape when they're fully grown.

Tree shapes can bring different feels to the yard design. If yours is a formal garden, trees with a columnar shape will fit in beautifully. They're dramatic as vertical accents, especially along a long driveway or at the back of a garden lining a fence. The smaller columnar-shaped varieties make good container plants.

Maybe you'd like a plain old shade tree. These come in various shapes, too. Shade trees come in habits of vase shaped, pyramidal, oval, round, weeping, or clumped. Conical evergreens make good winter windbreaks because they're of good mass and keep their needles.

Graceful, weeping trees usually add big impact to a garden. Small gardens may be best left with only one such specimen, but there are many to choose from, including willows, flowering cherries, Atlas cedar, and birches. So take a good look around and choose what tree shape excites you. Even narrow spots can give a tree a home. Try the slender Italian cypress, Japanese Sky Pencil holly, and clumping bamboo—all of these are evergreens, too!

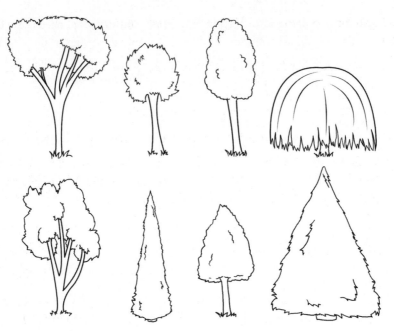

The shape of a tree can help define the "feel" of a yard.

Dwarf Conifers

These evergreens are easily identifiable by their needle or scale-type leaves and the cones on their branches. Exceptions include yew and junipers, which produce berry-like fruit as opposed to cones, and come fall, cypress will actually drop their leaves. Pine trees are easy conifers to spot, but there are many in this class, such as firs, spruces, redwoods, cedars, cypresses, junipers, yews, and hemlock.

Conifers offer year-round landscape interest, as many of them perform seasonal color changes. Various shades of green, orange, blue, yellow, lavender, and purple aren't unusual. Some varieties have *variegated* leaves or patterned leaves, or are bicolored.

DEFINITION

Variegated, in botanical terms, refers to the leaves or stems of a plant having more than one color on them. Plants with variegated leaves are especially useful for bringing light to shady areas.

You may only be picturing a Christmas tree, but conifers offer much more varieties of shapes:

- **Prostrate:** These are plants that hug the ground like a carpet (and stay that way).

- **Globose:** These have a round, globe shape to them.

- **Narrow upright:** These plants grow taller than they do wide.

- **Pendulous:** These plants grow upright with branches that hang down or have a downward curving leader and require staking. Or they can have strictly descending branches from a central leader.

- **Spreading:** While these are upright, they grow wider than they do tall.

- **Broad upright:** These are all of the plants that grow upright but aren't in the globose, narrow upright, or pendulous categories. Generally, these grow broader rather than tall.

- **Irregular:** These guys grow erratically without much pattern.

- **Culturally altered:** This means that someone made their own shape(s) with some pruning shears. Think topiary shapes.

So how do you fit a conifer tree or shrub into a small-space garden? Enter one of my favorite garden bone plants: the dwarf conifer. They're compact, versatile, and container friendly—which makes them perfect for small gardens.

Dwarf conifers reproduce asexually either by grafting or rooted cuttings. But they're not grafted onto dwarfed rootstock. They're cultivars originating from *sports*, mutations, or seedling selections.

DEFINITION

Sport isn't a genetic term, but rather one used by gardeners to describe an offset, a plant that deviates from the rest of the plant.

Unlike other plants that are grafted onto a smaller plant's roots or "dwarf rootstock," dwarf conifers (also called dwarf evergreens) are simply extremely slow-growing evergreen tree or shrub varieties. These little jewels aren't dwarfs in the sense that they've been bred to stop growing at a certain height; they just don't grow as quickly as their standard counterparts.

Miniconifers usually start as a bud that can be found anywhere on a regular conifer. Sometimes a bud's genes will mutate, which produces a clump of growth that's dwarfed. These are called "witches' brooms." They're harvested from the parent plant and more plants are propagated from the brooms, all creating dwarf specimens.

GARDEN GOSPEL

Did you know that there are over 500 conifer species in the world? According to the American Conifer Society, conifers hold the record for many titles, such as the largest, smallest, and oldest living woody plants on the planet.

Dwarf conifers dawdle so much that, according to conifer nurseries, a dwarf variety of native hemlock in 20 years grows to only 2'; in the same amount of time, a standard hemlock will grow 25' to 30' tall. This is fantastic news for small-space gardeners who want to plant some naturally lovely garden bones.

If all of this conifer talk is piquing your interest, you might be interested to check out the rest of the conifer sizes. The American Conifer Society's chart reads:

Type	Yearly Growth	Approx. Size in 10 Years
Miniature conifer	1"	1' tall
Dwarf conifer	1"–6"	1'–6' tall
Intermediate conifer	6"–12"	6'–15' tall
Large conifer	12" and up	15' and up

You'll notice a decent range of growth rates within these categories. This is because there has to be room for the differences in growing zones, climate, and cultural practices.

The Least You Need to Know

- You can find garden inspiration from books, magazines, garden catalogs, neighbors' yards, local public gardens, local plant nurseries, public parks, movies, and television.
- Before you start digging or planting, know what style and what type of garden you want. Garden options include entertaining, vegetable, perennial, wildlife, scented, rose, and cottage—just to name a few!

- For unity in the garden, try to choose either shapes with straight lines or ones with curves throughout the garden.

- To keep the garden interesting, have a combination of all three leaf textures in the garden: fine, medium, and coarse textured (bold).

- Garden bones can be created with small outbuildings, fountains, gazebos, statuary, walkways, ponds, trellises, arbors, benches, tables, trees, and shrubs.

A Feast for the Senses

In This Chapter

- How to create a garden view
- What colors do for the garden
- How to fool the eye
- Planting for all the senses
- Garden fencing options

No matter what your favorite garden style is, it's rather obvious that gardens should be visually appealing. In fact, many times the gardener is so focused on the view that the rest of the senses are inadvertently left out. There are pretty gardens and there are fabulous gardens. The ones that fall into the fabulous category are usually those that engage us not only visually, but through scent and touch, as well.

A Room with a View

One way of creating a garden view is to think of it just as you would a room in your house. Look at it as having a floor, walls, and a ceiling. Small-space gardens lend themselves well to this technique because this technique allows you to design the garden as a whole, which can give the garden a warmth and coziness.

The idea of creating a garden view this way has less to do with what's technically in the picture as it does with what creates the walls, floor, and ceiling. So we're not talking about outdoor furniture yet or even specific plant varieties, just what we want to have in general to hold the scene together.

Gather up your garden magazines and catalogs (which should be properly dog-eared by now) and bring them to a table where you have room to spread out. Break out some paper and colored pencils and make some sketches. That's right—don't just draw the first room design or idea that comes to mind; draw a few that feel completely different.

When we talk about the "floor" of the room (or view), we're talking about paths, stepping stones, grass, or low-growing plants, concrete, pavers, and so on, like carpeting or hardwood flooring in a bedroom. Now draw what you'd like to see on your garden floor. Draw some intriguing things that you saw in magazines, catalogs, or in your neighbor's yard.

> **TIP THYME**
>
> Don't ignore the floor of an apartment balcony. Outdoor carpeting and woven straw or jute mats can be used to create a "floor" with an outdoor look.

Be sure to create another with something that you'd never put in your garden. You may dislike that floor design as much as you thought you would, but then again, you may be surprised. In any case, open your mind to a variety of possibilities.

Next draw some "walls." They don't have to be solid like house walls; in fact, the idea of the walls in this context isn't about solid, it's about framing. Walls can be created with fencing, trees, shrubs, trellis, arbors, and flowers. You're just giving life to the sides of the room. Like the floor sketches above, draw a few ideas—give yourself room to consider things you hadn't thought of before.

The "ceiling" is much simpler and certainly doesn't have to be entirely filled in. A good example of a ceiling is a vase-shaped shade tree. The trunk stands as a wall and the canopy of the tree as the ceiling. This tree may be the only structure you have to fill that bill, and in no way do I mean to imply that it should cover the entire area over your head and between the walls. Ceilings in the garden can just be a hint or a feeling.

Keep in mind that sometimes you may not provide the ceiling at all. Look "behind" your immediate view. Are there open hillsides or another view you can borrow? Those borrowed views may be the perfect frame that holds your room together. When you have some ideas that excite you, look through the magazines for specific plants and structures that will fit into your design.

You can create as many views as you'd like from any point of view you have. There might be one point of view from the back garden (or more), one from the front, and one from each side yard of your home if you're in the suburbs. Or you may have only one point of view if you're in an apartment.

Create a sketch of your garden as if it were a room inside your home; complete with a floor, walls, and ceiling.

 GARDEN GOSPEL

When deciding how many plants to use of one variety, it's best to use the "Rule of Odd Numbers." Plants look the most natural when planted in odd numbers, like three and five. If you don't have room for that, try planting each color in odd numbers. Three different plant species that bloom in the same season in the same color will have the same continuous effect.

In Living Color

The impact that color has on the senses is undeniable. Color affects the mood of the garden, which can't help but affect the people who view it. Choosing flower and leaf colors is easier if you have a garden style in mind before you add the plants. Color principles are basically the same, no matter what size the garden, but there are a few things to keep in mind when working with the small-scale variety.

As we discussed earlier, repetition creates unity throughout the garden. So repeat your colors to tie the picture together. Don't forget that this doesn't have to mean that you only use the same plant varieties. You may have a group of yellow yarrow in one area; it isn't necessary to plant more yarrow a few plants down. Coreopsis or yellow lilies will work the same way.

TIP THYME

If you want your color scheme to stand out, this is where annuals truly shine. Use them to fill in areas between perennials to give bigger punch, or to add color to an area where the blossoms of other plants have finished for the season.

As far as color goes, honestly, less is more. Most professionals suggest using only two to three colors in a small-space garden because more than this can be distracting. This doesn't include the green leaves and stems of the plants, so there's that. Go for groups such as blue, pink, and white, or maybe yellow, orange, and red. You can also create a gorgeous garden if you go the easy route and simply plant all cool or all warm colors. Planting in one basic color scheme such as purple or white brings instant elegance to a small garden.

PLANTING PITFALL

Don't ignore what's behind the blossoms! Often there's a backdrop of some sort, such as wooden house siding, brick, or cement. Sometimes people can't figure out why a planting doesn't quite look right. Many times it's because the backdrop doesn't work with the plant or flower color. For instance, is your brick a salmon color? Try planting purple or blue flowers in front of it as opposed to pink or yellow.

Whatever you feel works best for the mood in your garden is fine; just try to keep it on the simple side. It also bears repeating that, although we're discussing three colors, we're not suggesting using only three plant species. Feel free to mix up different plant types while staying within the color scheme. Lastly, and as always, these are basic design guidelines, not hard and fast rules. I encourage you to play around with any plant color that excites you.

Introducing the Color Wheel

Here's the painless, short version of what constitutes the color wheel:

- **Primary colors:** The wheel starts with the three primary colors: red, yellow, and blue. These colors are pure in that no other combination of colors can create them, yet every other color under the sun comes from some combination of these three.

- **Secondary colors:** The colors green, orange, and purple are created my mixing combinations of the primary colors:
  blue + yellow = green
  red + yellow = orange
  red + blue = purple

- **Tertiary colors:** These colors are labeled with a hyphenated name because they're created by mixing a primary color with a secondary color: yellow-orange, red-purple, blue-green, yellow-green, red-orange, or blue-purple.

Anything you want to color will benefit from a glance or two at the color wheel, whether it's your family-room walls, playhouses, or your garden. In fact, I find them so handy that I like to have a couple lying around in strategic places like my kitchen and desk drawers. Hardware stores usually have color wheels made of sturdy material.

TIP THYME

It's easy to focus on flowers to brighten a yard or garden, but they aren't the only source of color. Use shrubs, grasses, and leaves such as the silver-white lamb's ears and blue hostas. Other ways to bring in color are with bark, berries, and fall foliage.

The wheel makes it easy to figure out which color combinations are attractive to you. Colors that are opposite each other on the wheel are called complimentary colors. A good example are Christmas colors—green and red. Orange would be the complimentary color to blue. Complimentary colors stand out by making each other brighter. These colors are often used to create a dramatic feel.

Monochromatic colors are the same basic color but in different tones or shades. They work especially well in formal garden designs (classic), such as using whites on whites. Often this garden will have not only white flowers such as peony and aquilegias, but silver leaves like lamb's ears incorporated, as well. Use monochromatic colors if you want an elegant, classic look.

The colors that lie next to each other on the wheel are called *analogous*. When closely related colors are used together in the garden, they create a harmonious, bright, and cheerful effect.

DEFINITION

Analogous colors are those that are closely related such as yellow, orange, and yellow-orange.

Small spaces can get crowded with the most vibrant colors, but it's not necessarily a bad thing. If you have a flair for the dramatic and can't resist fiery red or vivid orange flowers, you can temper them with white colors or lighter shades, such as a light yellow next to a bright orange.

Keeping It Cool

If you want to create an atmosphere of tranquility, the cool colors are for you. Blue, lavender, violet, green, and periwinkle are relaxing and soothing to the soul. Pastels like baby blue, mauves, and pink have the same calming effect, but can sometimes feel dull in mass plantings. It's easy to liven them up by accenting them with deep purple.

TIP THYME

Purple and blue flowers will be noticed best if you combine them with a few plants that bloom in bright yellow or cool white. Also, plant dark, cool colors in full sunlight.

To make an impact in a cool-colored garden, you'll need to plant a few more. But because the cool colors recede, which make them appear as if they're off in the distance, they make a garden appear larger. Another plus to the cool colors is that they can "cool down" an otherwise hot spot in the yard. White is a cool color that can be used to link other colors in the garden, and it's extremely useful for bringing light to shady places.

Classic Cool-Blue Border

Blue and white colors make for one very classy border. Do you have a narrow border next to your lawn or along the driveway? Here's one example of how to make a narrow garden bed of 1½' wide by 6' long into a lovely space using only three plant species. This planting offers a crisp and clean look due to the simplicity of using just two colors—okay, three colors if you count the green (which I don't).

<u>**Plant List**</u>

- Bluebeard

- Candytuft or bacopa

- Lobelia

The bluebeard is a drought-tolerant perennial that grows 3' to 4' tall by 4' to 6' wide. It'll bloom for you around midspring to midsummer and is hardy in zones 6 through 9. The plant is reminiscent of one that's commonly referred to as California lilac.

Candytuft is one of my favorite low-growing perennial plants. It's a survivor and versatile, so I find it superhandy in the garden; it's excellent for rock gardens, too. Its white blooms show up from late winter to early summer and it's hardy in zones 3 through 8. Look for the varieties Purity or the bigger-blossomed Snowflake. If this border were in a raised bed, I might use bacopa in place of the candytuft so the white would cascade down the side of the bed wall. Lobelia is an annual that blooms midsummer to early winter. This species flowers in a few different colors, so look for a blue variety such as Crystal Palace or Riviera Midnight. It's hardy in all zones.

All three of these plants will tolerate areas of part shade, and none of them enjoy being overwatered. Use the sketch that follows as a planting guide.

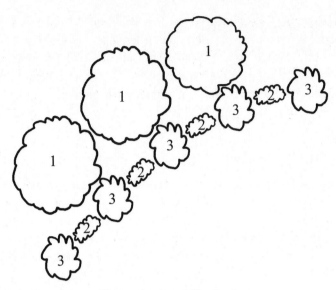

Plant a classic cool-blue border.

A Warm Welcome

Use warm colors in the garden if you want to create a pick-me-up mood. Red, yellow, orange, red-violet, and the like are warm colors. The bright yellows are attention grabbers and full of excitement. The energy of a warm-colored garden can make the temperature of the area feel higher and tend to bring the garden to the forefront.

> **TIP THYME**
>
> Inverted triangles make the best use of color, and in a small garden give the illusion of more plants than are actually there. This is done by making the widest part of the planting triangle (or the bottom) be closest to the viewer, while the tip of the triangle is the farthest away.

Use red flowers judiciously, as they scream so loud for attention that they can make a garden appear smaller. Pale yellows are versatile ladies and are relaxing when placed next to purple and lilac. They'll also soften an otherwise intense color scheme.

Create a Sunny Garden Path

Here's an easy planting that's perfect for small yards that have a short 6' × 6' walkway somewhere in the yard. Although this small garden view changes from summer to fall, it only takes six plants to create this bitty English garden.

<u>**Plant List**</u>

- Peony
- Mexican sage
- Chives
- Rose mallow
- Russian sage
- Rudbeckia

Peonies are a garden classic, and for good reason. If anything can rival roses as the queens of the garden, it's the charming peony. Blossoms come in various colors and both single and double petaled. Peonies come in both herbaceous (bush) and tree forms. The herbaceous type have tender green stems, and the trees are more like trees or shrubs with woody stems. Either type works for this garden plan. They love rich soil and full sun to light shade.

Mexican sage is a perennial shrub in zones 8 through 11 and otherwise can be grown as an annual. It blooms with purple, velvety flowers in the summer and fall. They're drought tolerant, and butterflies love them.

Chives are compact-looking characters that bloom light purple in the summer and can take the sun or light shade. Their flowers are often saved and used in dried arrangements. Don't resist giving these little guys a haircut every once in a while to bring to the kitchen.

Rose mallow is a summer-to-early fall blooming perennial that enjoys its soil moist with a little acidity. Its zones are 5 to 10, and the showy flowers can be white, red, or pink.

Russian sage grows well even in poor soils and blooms with mostly pinkish to blue-purple flowers in the midsummer to fall. Russian sage is a woody *subshrub* that's hardy in zones 3 through 9.

Rudbeckia is hardy in zones 4 to 8, and has vivid yellow flowers that bloom in the summer. It's a full sun worshipper, but will tolerate light shade. Rudbeckia is hugely drought tolerant and likes its soil well drained.

> **DEFINITION**
>
> A **subshrub** is a low-growing perennial whose woody stems are near the base of the plant, with the tips being more herbaceous. More examples are lavender, rosemary, and thyme.

Use the sketch below as a planting guide.

Plant a sunny garden path.

Become an Illusionist

Using smoke and mirrors to trick the eye is one of the most creative parts of small-space gardening. Optical illusions can bring interest and value to a garden. They'll literally flirt with the viewer, piquing their curiosity. The false imagery brazenly says, "Come hither …," leading the viewer to believe that there's more to the garden than is actually there. And we small-space gardeners applaud that type of deception.

Clever Color

Remember when we talked about the flower color? How cool colors (blue, green, mauves, purples) recede from view, while the warm or hot ones (orange, yellow, red, bright pink) jump forward? You can use colors to plan illusions both in a permanent bed or with porch containers.

Think about this: in a naturally big landscape, plants and objects in the distance are rather shadowed, which makes them appear gray (or bluish). Our mind's eye is used to seeing distant objects in these colors.

So let's say you have a small garden bed about 6' long but only 4' wide (deep), and you're planting flowers but you'd like to make it feel bigger (deeper). Plant your brightest (hot) colors at the front of the garden and the cooler colors toward the back. This will imitate what your mind already knows it should see in the distance. Your little bed now feels bigger.

TIP THYME

Flowers in blurred pastel or bi-colored shades can be used to blend the edges of garden boundaries, which leads the mind to believe that it doesn't end there.

Similarly, if you'd like planted containers against a wall on your front porch, use pale, cool, and pastel colors as opposed to hot-colored plants in the containers—it'll make the area look like it's longer or deeper. You can make the most of this by arranging the plant containers so that they are at short, medium, and tall heights. Obscuring the definition of the wall will make the illusion complete.

However, if your goal is to showcase blue and purple flowers by making them the focal point of the garden, you'll need to place them at the front, where their colors will be noticed and appreciated.

Practical Perspectives

Let's go back to the perspective of cool and shaded colors in the distance. What else happens to objects that are far away? Yep, they look smaller, even if they're not. Let's say that you have a path from the back door to the fence that ends up at a garden bed. I'm using the back door as a reference point because that's often the main view in a small space, but the viewpoint could start from anywhere. Maybe at the head of this path (the beginning that's closest to you) you have two big planters placed on either side.

You can take two more planters that are exactly the same as the first two, only smaller. It doesn't matter how long that path is; if you place the two smaller twin containers on the same line but at the far end of the path, it's going to make the path look longer than it is. You could really milk it by getting two more matching planters that are a size in between the others and place them down the same line but halfway between the tallest and the smallest.

This same perspective works when creating a meandering path to anywhere. The path can start out wide, while gradually tapering down to look as if it travels for quite a distance. Remember that if you're using color near the path or in the containers above, save the brightest for the entrance of the path. Savvy gardeners have been known to use the "sides" of a garden in the same way. They'll trim the tops of hedges so that they get shorter the farther they are from the viewer.

The same thing can be done with fencing, especially if you're on a sloped lot. In this case, the average preconstructed fence panels can be used in a graduated way down the slope—more illusion. Pathways that wind through small gardens give the feeling that you're walking farther. You can boost that feeling by giving them visual definition by lining the path with large stones, a short brick wall, or a low hedge.

Try borrowing the view from a neighbor or your front yard. Utilize a gap or hole in your fence or wall by placing a see-through trellis or wrought-iron piece there. It'll bring a more open feeling to the area while giving a glimpse to another garden next door. It may not be truly accessible, but your eyes and brain aren't that picky.

Deceptive Doorways

False doorways make me dance inside. In fact, even if I installed the fake entrance myself, I end up convinced that another garden lies beyond—that's how well they work. False doorways often end up adding some of the best character to the yard, as well.

They can be created with old wooden doors attached to a wall or fence; make the deception complete by adding a doorknob. You could use gates, arches, or even paint a false door (trompe l'oeil). Be bold—lead people right to the sham door with a path.

Trompe l'oeil

The Romans and Greeks first practiced trompe l'oeil images, and later the Italian artists of the Renaissance brought their masterful work to the mainstream. I'm in awe of today's painters who grasp the theatrical concept of this deception-with-a-brush. Trompe l'oeil means to "trick the eye," and when it's done right the illusion is second to none. The three-dimensional quality makes for extremely realistic images.

If you're good with paint, tap into your talent by painting a door, a window (or open windows), a scene, or an entire vista on a garden wall or the one attached to your home. If you're like me and have no painting talent whatsoever, it's worth it to pay an artist to do it for you. If that artist just happens to be a young Italian, so much the better!

Mirror Image

Mirrors are fabulous in the garden because they reflect everything that's planted around them—which gives you more garden. And sometimes more is just more. While they're reflecting the garden space, they're also reflecting light, which can brighten up dark places.

Be sure to place a mirror so that the viewer isn't reflected—that would kind of blow the trick, right? Be strategic by setting it up and then stepping back to be sure you have a pleasing angle (which is usually at the far end and on the diagonal) and you can't see yourself.

Whether or not to hide frame edges is a matter of style. "Burying" the frame edges in the flora and fauna works extremely well, but to hide a gorgeous frame can be downright blasphemous. If you use a wrought-iron gate as a false doorway, make the trick more convincing by placing a mirror behind it. It'll reproduce the image of your garden, which will look like ... yet more garden.

The Fragrance Factor

There's no good reason not to include at least a little scent in the garden no matter how small the space. Fragrance makes all the difference between seeing a beautiful garden or experiencing it. Scent is to the garden what salt is in the kitchen.

Something to keep in mind when you're considering fragrant plants is that most plants have a specific season for scent. The plants whose scent comes from their blossoms are most certainly seasonal, whereas some—such as rosemary—rely on their scented foliage instead. If you want to perfume your garden throughout the seasons, plant flower-scented varieties for each season.

There are also plants that perfume the air in the evening as opposed to the daytime. Night-scented flowers include sweet rocket and flowering tobacco. You also have both annual and perennial choices. Which flowers have the best scent? There's no right answer because, as with most things in life, we all have our preferences. However, I'd put stocks (annual), pink jasmine, and honeysuckle vines at the top of my list.

Along with plants that let their perfume go as their blossoms open, others release scent anytime they're gently stroked or brushed past. These aromatic plants produce volatile oils that are released by the heat of the sun and being touched. Plants like these include rosemary, lavender, santolina, and southernwood.

Fragrance is personal and can be therapeutic as we make our own associations with each one. Some scents are easily identifiable and may be described within the name of a plant variety, such as Chocolate Cosmos, Lemon Verbena, or Rose and Peppermint Geranium. Then there are those general scents, like that of roses, gardenias, or paperwhites, that evoke a feeling or a memory.

Be careful not to plant an overabundance of one variety too close to the area where people hang out. A couple of scented plants nearby is fine, but too much of a good thing can be exactly that. Also, if you like several different fragrances, plant them several plants over from one another so they don't compete with each other. If you have no choice but to plant close together, choose plants that bloom in different seasons so the fragrances aren't compromised.

You can strategically place pots and containers near windows and doorways to take full advantage of the plants. One of my favorite places to plant for scent is by windows. I have a large honeysuckle outside of our master bedroom window that perfumes my room when the windows are open. I also have a pink jasmine planted outside the kitchen window for the same reason. You can also plant aromatic plants, like creeping thyme, in between pavers that make a pathway. You'll enjoy a little aromatherapy every time you take a stroll!

Touch and Sound

I think that touch and sound are probably the last senses that we gardeners plant for, and it's really a shame. It isn't just kids who enjoy feeling what's in front of them. Every plant is touchable, and some stand out as nearly irresistible. This is as it should be; our gardens can and should be a feast for the senses.

Plants that fall into the touchable category may have extremely soft leaves, such as lamb's ears or silky gladiolus flowers. It might just as well be a giant sunflower head full of seeds, silky corn tassels, or smooth manzanita bark.

The sounds of the garden speak to us somewhere down deep. They aren't the same sound that we're so used to hearing in the busy work part of our lives: humming computers, engines, beeping, and ringing. No, the sounds of the garden are things like the splash of water hitting soil, buzzing bees, birds, rustling leaves, wind blowing through grasses and trees, and gravel crunching under our feet. These are natural sounds that calm and ground us. With a little thought, you can intentionally plant for these natural sounds.

Other plants that make great sounds are those plants like love-in-a-mist, which develop seed pods that hold tiny seeds like inside a shaker. Or honesty, which develop gorgeous silvery seed heads that rustle in the wind.

Hardscaping Hints

The term "hardscape" generally refers to any man-made accents added to the yard or garden. It may be what's on the ground, such as the paving, or it might be walls or other stonework. It can refer to decks, fountains, arbors, walkways, garden decor, light fixtures, and patios. Basically, when someone refers to the hardscaping, they're talking about anything that isn't plants (which are, not surprisingly, referred to as "softscape").

TIP THYME

When choosing accent pieces for your garden, keep uniformity in mind. If you have a stone pathway, some stone statuary will be a natural fit and pull everything together.

When a garden starts out as a clean slate, the better part of the hardscaping (what I call "major" hardscaping), is usually put in first. The major stuff—walls, decks, big fountains, and the like—is for the most part permanent or unmovable. Softscaping is then planted around these anchored structures.

After both the major hardscaping and the softscaping are in place, you can arrange the minor hardscaping. These are the final touches or accessories, such as light fixtures, small arbors, trellises, and garden decorations. Many garden designers consider this order of hardscaping, plants, and accessories very important. Of course, if you're renovating an existing garden or yard, a change of order may be unavoidable.

Have a Seat

You have to have seating. You didn't go to all of this trouble only to skip the part where you can sit comfortably and enjoy. But you also have to consider that every square inch in a small-space garden is prime real estate, so choose only what you love and remember, in this case, less is more.

Keeping decorations and furnishings at a minimum is truly valuable for a spacious feel, so add decorations that really bring something to the table: style, color, punch, or utility. As many of those five attributes as possible would be the goal. For maintenance sake, keep cleanablity and weatherablity in mind when choosing furniture.

Also, keep your eyes open for two small garden chairs that have been orphaned from their table. For some reason, there seems to be a million and one ways to use them. You can situate them into the coziest little areas in between planted containers. Try a plant shelf to place onto one of your bigger pots to hold your iced tea.

A plant shelf that attaches to a large container is especially handy in super-small spaces.

Built-in seating—for example, around the base of a tree—makes good use of space, as does a flat bench situated on top of (or built into) a retaining wall of a raised bed. Always have some portable seating tucked away somewhere, too. Folding chairs can be brought out and tucked away easily, and you'll never be without a seat for others to enjoy your garden.

TIP THYME

Purchase solid-colored chairs; when you want to change the look or the theme of your garden, just switch out the chair cushions.

Decorative Pieces

If you have a theme in your garden or if it's particularly formal or informal, the decorative pieces that you add should do their best to mimic that style. Again, no hard-and-fast rules here, but ornaments that reflect a garden's mood can be just the right detail. For instance, a Grecian ceramic statue is a natural fit for a formal rose garden. A woodpecker whirly-gig? Not so much. But, hey, far be it from anyone to dictate the right accents for your personal space, especially if the whirly-gig was a gift from your granddaughter.

One last thing about accents in the garden: go for the lighting. Nothing shows the garden off at night like the light and shadows of well-placed lighting. You'll need to experiment with the lights to capture just the right nuance, but you can't go wrong if you start with highlighting the bones of the garden first, like major hardscaping such as walkways, and uplighting large trees or plants. Another lovely finishing effect is to place a light high up in a tree so the light is facing down creating "moonlight". You can enjoy the highlighting and downlighting even in the winter when the green has gone.

PLANTING PITFALL

Beware the urge to "over-light" pathways. Solar lights sticking up don't present a pretty picture and it aren't necessary anyway.

Garden Fences and Walls

Since you're gardening in a small space, it's probably safe to assume that there will be fencing or walls. If you're in an apartment, it'll be in the form of railing. Fences and walls can be limiting, but they can also be useful and add personality to a yard or garden.

Walls and fencing not only clarify boundaries, they give us the framework to create the personal space to make our gardens—no matter how small—a reflection of our own personal bliss. On the other hand, walls and fencing aren't only used for boundary demarcation. Both of these can be used as artistic additions to the yard, and to create a garden within the larger garden. Walls can hold soil back (as with a retaining wall), or form an edge of a raised bed.

Solid Fencing

Many small-space gardeners will have a solid fencing of some sort, referred to as paneled or close-board fencing. Truth be told, they can be boring by themselves, but the beauty is that they're usually sturdy enough to be used for vertical plant support. They can be dressed up with wrought iron or wood trellises that can support flowering vines or sprawling vegetables. They're the perfect backdrop for espaliered trees and shrubs, too. Some plain-wood fences have added latticework on the top, which makes them more attractive and lends extra view.

TIP THYME

If you don't like the fencing you have, you're not necessarily stuck with it. However, if it's also your neighbor's boundary, the decision to replace it may fall on both parties. A good rule of thumb is that if the posts are visible on your side of the fence, then the fencing is theirs even if it's on the property line. Even if the fence is yours, it's a good idea to mention your plans to the neighbors—if not for consultation, then as a prewarning that their view is about to change. It's always in your best interest to consider the neighbors.

Fence companies usually erect the general fencing in suburban areas. But if you want to create another spot in your yard—say, to hide your garbage cans—sold fencing can be purchased in panels and installed by the homeowner. They're an instant boundary, as opposed to growing living fences, and they're cheaper and easier to construct than a wall.

Even (maybe especially) with fencing small spaces, every choice counts, so explore your options before you install your boundary fence. One made of horizontal boards is better than the traditional vertical privacy fence. If you would like to keep a great view such as a greenbelt, park, or golf course, try deer-panel fencing, which is more attractive and leaves your view intact. Wattle fences have a framework of stakes or poles that have twigs or reeds intertwined and woven to create a very natural-looking barrier. Plants are right at home against a backdrop of wattle fencing, but it's best used in informal gardens.

This is the situation with using bamboo screens in the garden. They work best in a natural or woodland setting. When bamboo fences are constructed from crossed larger bamboo poles, they often work as open fencing because the pattern shows up with square "holes." However, more common are the skinnier bamboo rolls that can be put up in minutes and are visually solid.

Walls

Talk about bringing style and warmth to the garden. Garden walls are my favorite hardscaping for adding personality and anchoring the view. Unless your yard came with high walls to begin with, it's generally not a great idea to add tall walls to the small-space garden on purpose. Low walls (1'–2' tall) are much more suited to those of us with little areas. If you're interested in something more hedge-height and you have some decent space, 3' to 4' tall can work, too.

You can create walls using any number of materials—brick, stone with mortar, dry stone, concrete, cement blocks. The most creative of us will find a way to blend a couple of these materials and come up with something special. The options for wall design are unlimited. They can be a solid brick-and-mortar (or stone) type, or they can have cavities in the top or in the sides in which you can plant herbs, alpine, or other plants. Some cement blocks are designed so that when they're placed together, they have natural spaces and you can have a boundary without total visual obstruction to the other side.

Open Fencing

Open fencing styles include ranch style, made by using wide horizontal boards (or rails) affixed to upright posts. Ranch style is popular because it makes property boundaries clear and leaves an open view. Manufactured wood boards are traditionally used for this type of fencing, but plastic is gaining popularity. Plastic ranch-style fencing is handy because it's easy to maintain (just wipe it down) and it's generally easy for anyone to install. Another ranch or country look is a split-rail fence, which works the same way as the ranch style but raw split logs are used instead of straight, manufactured wood boards.

Picket fences are a sort of hybrid, as it's a fairly solid fence yet has good space between the pickets. The landscape beyond is easily viewed with a picket fence. So it can function as an animal-proof fence as long as the animal isn't terribly skinny. They can be left in their raw state or painted any color you like. Of course, you can't go wrong with a white picket fence if you like a cottage or casual effect.

TIP THYME

If you have chain-link fencing and can't afford to replace it with something more attractive, spray paint it black or dark green to help it "disappear."

Chain-link fences are a conflict for gardeners. They walk the line between "undesirable" and "rather useful." Oh, sure, they're ugly—there's no question about that. But that's about the only bad thing about them. Think about it. Chain-link fences are extremely secure for keeping pets or chickens in, while keeping wandering dogs and other varmints out. Plus, they make wonderful supports for climbing ornamentals as well as vegetables. In fact, if you want to make your otherwise open fencing "solid," you can plant fast-growing vines at the base and have a wall before you know it. Or you could leave it as a see-through fence. Then again, it is ugly.

Living Fences

Living fences are wonderful to use for a boundary line because they're, well … living. All that means is more plants, and it's hard to beat that. The most obvious living fence would be the traditional hedge plants, such as a formally clipped box hedge. Before purchasing what you've seen everywhere, consider the vast number of other choices first.

TIP THYME

If you're shearing your hedge in the traditional formal pattern, trim it so that the base of the hedge is wider than the top. This allows sun to reach the bottom branches so the shrub remains full.

Don't forget that the "formal" hedges that you've seen clipped take on a completely different look if they're left to their own devices. Don't get me wrong, they can still be pruned to maintain size, but they won't have the same formal and geometric feel. Hedges kept like this will have a shrubby feel, and many, such as laurustinus, have lovely blossoms.

Roses can be used very effectively as living fencing. That may strike you as a bit "off" if you're picturing tea roses, but some nice shrub rose species make excellent additions as walls to the flower garden. Fair warning: because they're deciduous, you're going to have a naked fence in the winter. This is something to think about if it's a focal point in your front yard.

On the upside, you can count on shrub roses to provide continuous blooms for an extended length of time *without* dead-heading. They'll also bring butterflies to the garden and flowers to cut and bring inside your home, too. Many varieties are disease resistant and come in a wide variety of colors. Some have fragrance and some don't. You'll want to plant them en masse to get the best effect as a living fence.

If your garden is informal, both rosemary and lavender make terrific flowering hedges. Glossy abelia is another unique option that also brings fragrant flowers. Dwarf conifers are a good substitute for their larger conifer cousins as hedges in the small-space garden.

The Least You Need to Know

- Create a view by thinking of it as a room in your home: floors, walls, and a ceiling.
- Plants look the most natural when planted in odd numbers, like three and five.
- Cool colors recede and give the impression of bigger space. Warm or bright colors bring everything forward.
- Master the twin arts of perspective and illusion to make your garden feel larger and more interesting.
- With minor hardscaping, such as garden ornaments and decorations, less is more.

Principles for Petite Plots

Part 2 offers ideas on specific problems that we gardeners with tiny plots may have due to wind, heat, or wet areas of the yard or garden. These challenges are especially important to us because a soggy, narrow, or seriously shady spot may be the only gardening spot we've got!

In this part, we share ideas on how to make every area beautiful and functional. We'll talk about the advantages of raised beds, and how to make one fast. This is the section for container gardening, and where the square-foot gardening technique is introduced—perfect for vegetable gardens. There's also the small-space gardener's favorite trick—vertical gardening. We'll discuss what to climb, where to climb, and which ones climb.

Every chapter in this part is designed to show you that no matter what your small-space challenge is, we have answers!

Container Gardening

In This Chapter

- Descriptions of various pots and containers available on the market and why you might want to use them
- The "right" type of soil for container planting
- The latest products on the market for the ultimate in small-space gardening
- Why you should consider planting trees in containers

Container gardening is the most versatile because you can rearrange your garden's style, color, theme—its entire design—within an hour or two. It's a perfect small-space solution because you can have a full-blown garden even if you have zero in-ground soil.

You can find creative (and free) container options around your house and at garage sales that will add personality to your small space. We'll also discuss why you may want to have some big tubs on hand, and we'll show you what makes potting soil different from regular garden soil. Finally, we'll get you excited about planting trees in containers.

Plenty of Pots

There's such a wide array of container choices available that you'll have no problem finding styles to fit beautifully within your garden scheme. Whether you're planting flowers, small trees and shrubs, or vegetables, containers are fun to collect and refresh with new ideas. When you're out there purchasing, remember that the biggest containers will offer the most space for roots, as well as for the rest of the plant. A large container will also hold water longer.

Pots with wide bases will stay put in a strong wind; tall, statuesque ones will be more likely to tip and may need to be situated in a more protected spot. Consider the weight of the container after soil and plants are added. If you're likely to do some random and regular rearranging, your best bet is to go for lighter-weight pots made of fiberglass or plastic.

TIP THYME

Indoor plants can add outdoor beauty when kept in a protected place in a garden container. Let them enjoy the outdoors during the warm months by acclimating them to the different environment first. After your last frost date, bring them to a sheltered area outside for the day, increasing the hours they're out there until they're outside overnight. Most tropical indoor plants can stay outside in the shade or part shade for the season, but some can eventually take the full sun.

The first place you'll probably look for containers is your local home-improvement center. You'll find a fair assortment of pots and the like there, but don't forget to check out every other local garden center and nursery that you can before you make your final purchases. The smaller shops are where you'll find original and fabulous gems. It's fun to have something different than all your neighbors.

Here are some clues to the assortment of containers you'll find and why you might want to use them:

- **Terra-cotta:** Probably the most well-known and well-used type of container anywhere, it's produced in an endless variety of shapes, sizes, and styles. Terra-cotta is also less expensive than many other containers. Make sure a terra-cotta container is frost resistant (check for labeling); otherwise, it could crack during the cold months. Be aware that terra-cotta tends to dry out faster than most other planting containers.

- **Plastic:** Plastic is rather a win-win. It's nonporous, so the soil tends to stay moist longer than in terra-cotta. These containers are also lightweight and therefore very easy to move around, even after being filled with soil and planted. However, you may have to really look around to find one that's honestly attractive.

- **Wood:** Wood is a great material that looks natural with vegetable plantings. There are small tubs, half-barrels, and troughs made of wood. They're typically not expensive, with the exception of the monster-sized half-barrels. I tend to like wood containers because I can paint them any color I want, year after year. They can also be varnished to help prolong their lives.

PLANTING PITFALL

If you're looking for outdoor garden containers, don't buy the ones without the drainage holes on the bottom! Unless you want to give yourself some more work by turning them over and draining the excess water out, leave those at the store. Pots without drainage holes are for decorating. They're primarily used for indoor houseplants as an outer "sleeve." The idea is to take them out of that sleeve, water them in a sink, and then slip them back into the decorative container.

- **Glazed stoneware:** I love the glazed stoneware pots for both ornamentals and vegetables. They're usually quite frost resistant and come in lovely shades. Typically the glazed pots are a basic round- or square-shaped container, but I've seen them in other shapes, as well. Because they're glazed, they hold in that precious moisture much better than terra-cotta.

- **Fiberglass:** Fiberglass containers also hold moisture well and their light weight makes them extremely easy to move around. Generally, they're shaped like other, more pricey containers (glazed, copper, stone, and so on)—which is a plus, aesthetically. The only downside is that they break or crack easier than the more expensive ones.

- **Metal:** This includes those containers made of copper and galvanized steel, too. Although it can be perfect for the right setting, pure metal is quite contemporary and isn't "warm" enough for me. If contemporary describes the style of your balcony or porch, it may be the right choice for you. Be careful, though. Roots will warm up extremely fast in this type of container and will freeze just as quickly in the winter.

- **Concrete and stone:** Natural stone and even concrete containers can be beautiful and house vegetables nicely. These are probably the most expensive type of containers to purchase. The only drawback is that, once they're filled with soil, planted, and then watered, you won't want to move them. So find a nice little spot for them to live for the entire season.

- **Recycled containers:** Nearly anything is fair game when looking for a container to recycle as a planter. All they need to have is drainage holes. Old wheelbarrows, kitchen sinks, shoes, plastic cat-litter containers, rusty buckets, tool boxes, BBQs, bicycle baskets, and Easter baskets are all fair game.

Handy Hanging Baskets

Hanging baskets are a method of gardening vertically and simply give you more space for plants, as well as a handy way to add quick color. Blossom-filled baskets at the door never fail to be festive. Other great places to consider are house eaves, fences, balconies, arbors, gazebos, trees, and cyclone fences.

TIP THYME

Remember that hanging baskets dry out fairly fast—especially if you've planted a sun-loving plant—and may need to be watered daily in hot summer weather. If you have succulents and cacti in your baskets, give them a drink about once a week.

If you want some color above another garden space, you can purchase hanging rods that stake into the ground called shepherd's hooks. Metal arms can be attached to walls and fences to display baskets, too.

There are unlimited sun-worshipping annuals that will be at home in a sunny basket spot, from geraniums (scented, too), Callibrachoa, bacopa, alyssum, marigolds, and pansies to plumbago, lobelia, daffodils, and verbena.

Anything that can be grown in any other containers can be grown in hanging baskets. Herbs, eggplant, strawberries, small peppers, cherry tomatoes, and lettuce are perfect food candidates for hanging baskets. For those living in areas with high temperatures, cacti and succulents make an absolutely handsome presentation. This is also the place to show off trailing plants such as dead nettle, sweet potato vine, and black-eyed Susan vine.

TIP THYME

If you're hanging several baskets in a row—say, under porch eaves—consider planting the same plant variety in each basket instead of a mixed collection for uniformity. Conversely, choosing different plant varieties that bloom in the same color will also unify the baskets.

Bring life (and light) to a shady area building that has an overhang. Many shade-loving plants thrive in hanging baskets, including fuchsias, impatiens, ferns, and begonias. In fact, the begonias in my baskets come back reliably for me year after year without any problem.

Hanging baskets come in several different styles. Some are traditionally bowl-shaped, wire frames lined with thick coconut shell. Others have a thin liner that can be pierced with scissors, allowing you to plant from the top, sides, and bottom of the basket.

This type of hanging basket display makes a bold and beautiful statement once the plants have filled in. You'll find that these wire frames come in many other shapes, such as conical and oblong. Check out Chapter 8 for more on vertical gardening.

These containers weren't specifically made to hang on fencing. I attached them to this wrought-iron fence with black zip ties. They're planted in full sun with Calibrachoa 'Million Bells'.

Big Tubs and Half-Barrels

Big tubs and half-barrels allow you to create more of a "scene" within one container. They also offer plenty of root room for plants that need it, such as dwarf fruit trees, camellias, roses, Japanese maples, and flowering perennials. Compact shrubs and flowering perennial plants can be kept in oversized containers year-round. Big containers are also the right thing to use for growing tomatoes.

Big tubs are usually made of wood, copper, or terra-cotta. The half-barrels are always made of wood, so they look best in a natural or otherwise informal setting. Needless to say, after they're filled with soil, planted, and watered, they become very heavy. To make the containers lighter, many gardeners will fill the tub about a third of the way with packing peanuts or other recyclables before adding soil. This is useful in some situations, but I tend to plant things in big tubs that need as much soil as they can get (for roots and nutrition), so I usually find a semipermanent place in my garden for these containers. That way I'm not struggling to move them around.

Creative Containers

If you'd like to plant a reusable or recycled container or you simply have a flair for the whimsical, container gardening leaves acres of room for creativity. Be on the lookout for containers that have adequate drainage. Baskets are a natural fit as planters, but there are ways to get the most out of them.

First of all, the weave is usually loose enough that when you're watering plants, you'll lose more soil than you'd like. Prevent this by lining the basket with any plastic you can find before you add your soil and plants. It needs to be thicker than the average sandwich wrap; the thicker, freezer baggies work extremely well. Many times you won't be able to see the plastic lining, but if it's visible, just line the inside of the basket with sphagnum moss and then add the plastic liner, soil, and plants.

There's no end to the reusable container possibilities:

- Old dressers
- Old watering cans
- Wheelbarrows
- Boots
- Easter baskets
- Buckets
- Painted tin cans
- Iron bathtubs
- Canoes
- Small wooden boats
- Cinder blocks

- Tires

- Hollow tree stumps

- Bicycle baskets

- Wagons

- Truck beds

- Wastebaskets

- Laundry baskets

- And, literally, the kitchen sink

Plant a Kitchen Colander

A kitchen colander is a unique and appropriate container for growing plants like lettuce, peppers, cherry tomatoes, chives, or strawberries. It would also make a wonderful hostess or housewarming gift. By the way, the plain silver colanders aren't the only ones out there.

You could match the colander to the recipient's kitchen or back porch. Keep your eyes open for brightly colored plastic and porcelain colanders, too. Watch for cheap ones at garage sales and flea markets. The colander below could also be planted entirely with strawberry plants or all herbs.

You'll need the following items:

- Colander of your choice

- Potting soil

- Plastic sheet or two large food-storage baggies

- Scissors

- Assortment of seedling plants—look for some food types

Take the plastic or the baggies and cut some slices in them with the scissors. Line the colander with the plastic or use the two baggies and spread them out so that they cover most of the inside of the colander. Clearly the colander has holes already in it, but I line it with the plastic so that I don't lose a lot of soil when I water. It also stays neater looking should you want to use it as a centerpiece or in a sunny kitchen window.

Next I take a few handfuls of potting soil and fill the colander about a third of the way. Don't add any more soil at this time, because the plants themselves have a lot of soil attached and you want to get them all into the container. Slide a plant out of its container and place it into the colander.

Do this with another plant until all of them are sitting in the colander. Then move them around until you're happy with the arrangement. Now, add soil by the handful between each plant, pressing gently. Add enough to reach the top of each plant's root ball, then water lightly.

Colander planters make great hostess or house-warming gifts.

Potting Soil

There are so many different soil-type products bagged up at the nursery, it's easy to get confused. You'll find bags marked "Garden Soil," "Top Soil," and "Potting Soil." For container gardening, you're after potting soil. You may not notice the difference, but potting soil is very different than garden soil.

GARDEN GOSPEL

If you check the ingredients on the bag, you'll find that most potting soils don't contain any actual soil like you would find in your garden. In this case, it's also referred to as a "soil-less mix." Soil-less mixes are usually a combination of something such as ground bark or peat that holds the plant roots in place, as well as water. This ingredient makes up the biggest percentage of the mix. Other ingredients such as vermiculite or perlite are added to keep the ground bark (or what-have-you) from clumping into a solid mass. A few more things may be added depending on the company that created the mix. Often there will be some form of synthetic time-release fertilizer, as well.

Your average garden's soil (both the kind found in your outdoor garden bed and in the bags) is much too dense for container gardening. It's extremely heavy, which has less to do with container weight than it does with drainage. Outdoor garden soils also become compacted rather quickly. This is bad news for container plants because their little roots will have a hard time penetrating the soil and receiving oxygen, both of which are necessary to absorb the nutrition in the soil. Potting soil is specially blended to have structure that's light enough for good drainage and wiggle room for roots, as well as the absorbency to retain water.

The fastest way to get container soil is to buy a bag at a nursery. The most time-consuming way is to make it yourself, but if you're big on experimenting then creating the entire mix yourself might be your thing. My favorite way to create container soil is to blend the two. I'll purchase a bag of potting soil and add about another quarter of that amount in compost. The compost will offer the best overall nutritional value to the soil. Yum!

At some point, you'll want to *amend* the soil in your container. One reason to amend soil is because you might have plants that prefer a pH level that falls more to one side (acidic) or to the other side (alkaline) of the *pH scale*, such as azaleas or blueberry bushes. Another reason is because when you water, plant roots are able to absorb the nutrients, but some of those nutrients are eventually washed away and you'll have to put them back in again. If you're using a soil-less mix—containing only peat, vermiculite, perlite, and the like—then you'll have to add either organic or synthetic fertilizer, because that's the only source the plants have for the nutrients (NPK) and micronutrients that they need. We'll talk more about soil amendments and pH in Chapter 15.

DEFINITION

To **amend** soil is to correct or improve it. It can refer to the nutrition available, or the organic matter, or when attempting to alter the pH balance.

The **pH scale** is drawn on a number line that ranges from 1 to 14, which measures the acidity or alkalinity of a soil. The lower the number is on the scale, the higher the acidity, and the higher the number is, the higher the alkalinity. The middle ground or neutral point of the scale is at 7.

Portable Raised Garden Beds

For those living with the smallest garden spaces (like apartments and condominiums), portable raised gardens can be the best answer. These convenient garden plots take the guesswork out of planting and focus on beginning gardener success.

Some portable raised systems are seriously less strenuous for the gardener. When the garden bed is higher, bending and reaching is reduced and sometimes eliminated. Product companies are aware that many of us are dealing with precious little space, which leaves less room for error. These companies are listening and they're coming up with some fabulous products.

The EarthBox

The EarthBox and products like it are becoming popular with gardeners everywhere, whether they have lots of gardening room or not. At first glance it looks like any ordinary, rectangular, plastic planter. I personally discovered that it's actually a pretty wonderful little self-watering growing system and was amazed at the results.

The EarthBox features a watering tube that fills a reservoir in the bottom of the box. This keeps the soils evenly moist. You end up actually watering this container less than other containers, but you need to check it as plants get large and begin to produce, because you'll need to give it a drink more often at that point.

When the soil is first added to the box, a slow-release fertilizer is also introduced, as is some dolomite. The dolomite is a calcium source for veggie plants, and it raises the pH. You place a cover over the entire EarthBox and then cut holes in it to add plants. Although you can use the system for anything from ornamentals to herbs to vegetables, the veggies simply go crazy in these. They certainly outperform the average container or pot any day of the week.

The EarthBox has accessories that you can add, such as wheels (which I love) and a staking system for growing climbing plants and vegetables. There's a plastic "sleeve" that resembles a white picket fence to change the style of your planter, and a white trellis to complete the picture.

Woolly Pockets

Woolly Pockets are terrific, portable, soft-sided containers that are made from 100 percent recycled materials. These little gems come in a couple of different designs. The Wally is used as a planter to hang on indoor or outdoor walls. We talk more about Wallys in Chapter 8. The Meadow version (for use indoors and out) functions as a portable raised garden bed.

Woolly Pockets come in smallish squares, 24" × 24" and in bigger squares, 48" × 48". The indoor version is heavily lined so that they're just as safe inside your house as they are out on your deck or patio. My favorite thing about them is that they're extremely easy for anyone to set up—no sawing, drilling, or screwing.

The Meadow Woolly Pocket.
(Courtesy of Woolly Pockets)

Eleanor's Garden

You can certainly take traditional wood, screws, brackets, and the like to come up with your own design for a portable raised bed—but why would you? Eleanor's Garden is proven, portable, and as handy as they come. From an economical standpoint, you couldn't build this any cheaper than this finished product. Besides, it has some impressive features all its own.

Its modular interlocking units adjust vertically to any height you need. In fact, the company is making the system adjustable for gardeners in wheelchairs, too. If you simply want more gardening room, you can add on container beds horizontally. This kit has everything you need to get a vegetable garden going, with a 24" × 24" container, soil, and vegetable seeds.

My favorite feature is that it has a unique drainage system. Plugs control the flow of the excess water through connector pipes, which allows you to collect the drained water and reuse it in the garden bed. Because the Eleanor's Garden drainage system collects water runoff, this portable raised garden bed can literally be placed anywhere, inside or out.

Eleanor's Garden is a completely self-contained raised garden bed system.
(Courtesy of Eleanor's Garden)

Make a Tri-Level Container Planter

Tri-level planters are vertical gardens that are easy to create using plain terra-cotta pots. It's a way to add color and interest to your small space in under an hour. Any garden theme will work for this planter, such as flowers, strawberries, lettuces, herbs, or a display of succulents. Here garden-designer extraordinaire, Jenny Peterson of J. Peterson Garden Design in Austin, Texas, shares her instructions for this project highlighting flowering annuals.

What you'll need:

3 terra-cotta pots of graduating sizes. In this case, the smallest pot is 16" in diameter. However, if you'd like a slightly smaller version, you could start with one that's 12" in diameter.

1 large bag of potting soil

1 large plastic nursery pot, cinderblock, or several bricks

A variety of annuals in 4" pots

1 larger plant for the top planter

Bagged sphagnum moss

What you'll do:

1. Place the large plastic nursery pot upside down in the largest pot. If you don't have a plastic nursery pot, use cinderblock or bricks. This will provide stability for the other two pots, and you'll avoid the expense of filling the largest pot with unnecessary potting soil.

2. Stack the second pot on top of the upside-down container (or block or bricks) and fill the bottom pot with soil up to 4" from the top of the rim.

3. Fill the second pot with soil about 4" from the top of the rim.

4. Fill the smallest pot with soil—again 4" from the top—and place it onto the soil surface of the middle pot.

5. Now here comes the fun part: Take your 4" annuals out of their pots and carefully place them on the soil in the rings created around the base of each pot. Pack them side-by-side, adding a bit of soil to make sure they're tucked in nicely. Finish off your creation with small handfuls of moss tucked in and around the plants.

You now have a stunning vertical planting that will look great for months!

Here's where extra used nursery containers come in handy.
(Photo courtesy of J. Peterson Garden Design)

This is what the tri-level planter will look like just before you add the plants.
(Photo courtesy of J. Peterson Garden Design)

In less than an hour, you have a beautiful plant display.
(Photo courtesy of J. Peterson Garden Design)

Keeping Trees in Containers

Keep in mind that some trees do well and even thrive in containers. Full-size, standard varieties may be out of the question, but dwarf specimens, including some fruit trees, make themselves right at home in containers. Large shrubs can also be pruned to take on the shape of a tree, and then there are always the dwarf conifers.

There are a few different ways that dwarf trees are created. Some are the top part of a standard-size tree that's been grafted onto a dwarf rootstock. Some are kept small by heavy pruning and training, such as bonsai. Dwarf conifers are a little different, as we talked about in Chapter 3.

Any way we get them, dwarf trees make it possible to create garden bones, texture, shape, winter interest, beauty, and fruit in a container garden setting. When choosing a container to house a tree, the first thing to look for is excellent drainage. Don't use terra-cotta—you won't be doing your back any favors if you decide to rearrange.

Most people purchase trees that have been grown in a nursery container or perhaps as a bare-root plant. The rule of thumb for a tree you brought home in a nursery pot is to transplant the tree into a container that's up just one size. If you brought home a bare-root specimen, the container should be as large as the roots are when they're spread out.

Growing trees in containers will naturally restrict the ultimate size of the plant, but you should be prepared for a tree to outgrow its container after a couple of years. You can handle this in one of two ways. The easiest way is to simply repot the tree in a larger container, but you could also perform a technique called *root pruning*, after which the tree can then be planted back in its original container.

Just like trees planted in the ground, trees in containers tend to make an area feel cooler, with the added benefit that container trees can be strategically placed—and replaced. They can also bring a permanent feel to even the smallest setting. And what gardener wouldn't enjoy harvesting his or her own lemons for the kitchen?

DEFINITION

Root pruning is the technique in which parts of a plant's root are cut off, which restricts the size of the plant or tree.

The biggest concern for container trees is that they dry out much faster than their earth-grown counterparts. Be aware of that from the start. Most people feel that a drip watering system is especially appropriate for trees in containers. Offer them a nutritional boost by removing some of the loose soil and adding in compost or other loamy soil each year. They'll also need a regular application of nutrients by way of fertilizer or other soil amendments.

The Least You Need to Know

- The biggest containers will offer the most root space for plants and the least amount of watering from you.
- Portable raised garden beds are the perfect solution for apartment gardening.
- Regular garden soil is too dense and heavy; use potting soil for containers.
- Container (dwarf) trees create garden bones, texture, shape, winter interest, beauty, and fruit.

Living on the Edge

In This Chapter

- Tips on balcony gardening
- What you need to know before gardening on the roof
- Working with challenging areas such as narrow, sloping, or windy garden spots
- Wind-tolerant plants
- Thoughts about hot, shady, and soggy gardens

This chapter will give an overview of those areas that may make you feel like giving up on gardening. People struggle to believe that an exceptionally small, sweltering, soggy, windy, or shady area can become a garden. It may surprise you to know that, just like people, individual plants have adapted to survive in every nook and cranny on earth. No matter what unusual situation you find yourself in, I promise you can have plants growing and thriving around you. Believe it!

Balconies and Fire Escapes

For the most part, if you're planting on a balcony or fire escape, you'll use containers and vertical container gardening almost exclusively. Balconies are interesting places to create a room or a scene because so many settings are possible without much time or effort. They can be transformed into an outdoor room in an instant.

With a space as small as a balcony, concentrating on the flooring can make all the difference as far as effect. Something on the floor really pulls the garden design or theme together. It could be as simple as a bamboo (or cloth) mat or outdoor carpeting. If your balcony floor is cement, you could place wood decking over it and change the look entirely. But remember, you can only change the flooring if you happen to own the apartment or condominium unit.

If you're less than handy with wood, modular decking is available. These handy, interlocking pieces go together just like a puzzle. Decking will keep the floor cooler than the cement in the summer, too. Another idea is to stain or paint over the cement and then throw a colored mat as an accent. Before you embark on this particular adventure, talk to someone in the know at a hardware store to be certain that you've purchased the correct materials for the look you want.

If you have plans to add large cement planters, gravel, or anything else that is exceptionally heavy, please get the advice of a structural engineer. No matter how slight they may appear, they can add up—and don't make any structural changes to a balcony (or a fire escape) unless you've obtained permission through permits or whatever is necessary for your building.

If you're shying away from balcony gardening because it's in full sun, make use of patio umbrellas, shade screens, and roll-up shades. If it's possible, attaching an awning to the building is not only useful for shade, it brings great character along with it. Do whatever it takes to make your balcony a pleasant place to hang out—or, even better, an escape.

Wall trellises are perfect for balcony gardens, as are other wall-type plantings such as the Woolly Pockets. You can use the Meadow Woolly Pockets as a raised bed on the balcony, as well as elevated gardens like Eleanor's Garden system. There's more on these gardening systems in Chapter 5.

TIP THYME

Add a little privacy to the see-through railing on your balcony by planting a line of dwarf conifers, climbers, or boxwood shrubs. Not only will they bring a little seclusion, but they make a great windbreak, too.

Always consider what's below you—your neighbors—when you're watering your balcony or fire escape garden. You'll be held responsible for anything that's damaged below, plus you'll have to live with unhappy neighbors, even if the "damage" is just water on their heads. You may have to take your containers to another spot where water runoff won't be a problem. Regardless, if you're gardening on the second level or higher of a building, you'll want to hone your watering skills and perhaps adopt a "less is more" attitude when soaking the soil.

You can plant fire escapes with containers on each step, as well as planters hung on railings. But the first thing you need to find out before you put anything on a fire escape is if you're allowed to do it. Call your local fire department and ask what the regulations are for placing objects on fire escapes. If the stairs have to remain clear, there's no harm in asking if you're allowed to hang plants on the rail on the opposite side of the stairs. If all else fails and fire-escape gardening is illegal where you live, then consider planting a window box or other wall-mounted planter at the front entrance of your apartment. Or this may be the right time to become part of a community garden, as discussed in Chapter 1.

Working with Window Boxes

Window boxes have been used by generations all over the world—and for good reasons. They not only give gardeners a place to grow, but they can hide a less-than-optimal view, or at least distract the eye from views such as the black iron railing of a fire escape or the faded paint on your neighbor's house. Sometimes your hands are tied as far as upgrading or renovating a home due to finances or renting. In any case, window boxes can give an instant but removable face-lift to any view.

These pint-sized gardens can be changed out and recostumed simply and inexpensively if you want to plant for seasonal color or alternate with vegetables. You may have pansies planted in your window box to herald the springtime, and switch it out for all herbs come summertime. It probably won't come as any surprise to know that the heat lovers of summer tend to grow extremely well in this garden situation, because window boxes tend to dry out quickly and there are heat-tolerant plants that won't mind at all. Do a little research on the plants that you're going to use because there are some heat-lovers such as sweet-potato vine, petunias, and mandevilla that won't tolerate completely dry soil for long.

TIP THYME

If water becomes trapped between the window box and your house siding, it could damage your home. Using brackets that are a little deeper than the box will prevent this from happening.

You can find window boxes that are made of more traditional materials such as wood, iron, cement, or terra-cotta. But plastic window boxes are becoming increasingly popular because they retain moisture better and they're lighter. Lighter not only means cheaper, but it means that, even after they're planted, they're easier to secure than the others.

Which material lasts the longest? Surprisingly, it can actually be a toss-up when you're comparing wood to plastic. At first glance it may seem that the plastic containers will hold up longer, but if they're positioned in the blazing sun for a few years, this isn't always true as the plastic will become brittle and crack. Eventually, it ends up in pieces.

Of course, we have to give the "lifelong" award to those made of cement. Wood scores another point for insulation; wood boxes offer the best root protection against heat and cold. To prevent the wood from warping, be sure that the box's boards are at least 1" thick.

TIP THYME

Instead of securing outside window boxes so that they sit even with the window sill, adjust them to sit lower by a few inches. This will give upright plants room to spread without blocking the view from inside the house. Keeping the boxes lower is especially important if your windows open outward.

Window boxes always make a fabulous statement in their traditional place on the ledge outside a window. Some houses will have ledges wide enough to support them alone. But more often than not, they need to be secured in some way—usually with brackets. This isn't the only way to use them, however. You can place a long window box on a bench, wall, balcony, or walkway.

If your window box is literally outside a window, be sure it's a window you can get to easily for watering and general care. These are containers like any other, so you want to fill them with a light potting soil. Because they aren't always in the most handy place for daily care, many gardeners will add a time-released fertilizer to the soil. Organic gardeners may want to use a slow-release organic product.

Choose your window plants the same way that you would for any garden area. Know the level of sun exposure so that your plants remain alive. Also consider whether you're borrowing the view from the window box, or making it the view. It's usually about the outside of the house when you're making the box the view. Think about the color of the window frame, as well as the house color and rest of trim. Another way to go about planting is to look at the window boxes from inside the room and borrow the view from the plantings. If you're more interested in how the window box looks from inside, your best bet would be to complement the room just inside the window.

Aside from the obvious flowers, try planting vegetables such as lettuces in shady areas, or succulents for sunny spots. And for Pete's sake, don't rule out the dwarf conifers or alpines, which can also make a unique statement and are in the easy-to-care-for category.

Because they're generally at a higher level than most containers, you may feel the urge to plant only trailing plants that hang down; resist. It's easy for planters that house only trailing plants to get rather lost. Adding some height with a few uprights will truly round out the scene.

Gardening on Your Roof

Rooftop gardens can make good sense for urban gardeners because they make terrific use of an otherwise unused space, they're environmentally friendly, and they usually have great sun. Roof gardening makes the most sense in an area that sees some decent rainfall. It's much harder to keep plants alive with nearly year-round blazing sun and drying winds—especially if you have to haul water up to the roof.

Many city gardeners take advantage of their space up top, but don't break out the soil just yet. There are a few things to consider before you start planting. You'll need to get permission from the building owner and get your hands on the building codes. Even if you're allowed to garden on the roof, you'll need information on fire regulations, roof access, and height restrictions. Check city ordinances.

You'll want professional guidance from a licensed structural engineer, who'll take a look at the site so that you're certain the roof can carry the burden of soil/water/plant-filled containers. This is especially true if you're looking at making an actual landscape complete with heavy planters, large raised garden beds, fountains, water gardens, rocks, furniture, and the like. Some buildings can take the weight without any problem and some won't support it at all. Many are somewhere in between and have limitations. You need to know what they are.

Other than structural considerations, strong winds are something to think about in such a high, open space. Your climate is of the highest importance when it comes to rooftop gardening. If you live in an arid area where there's little annual rainfall, it becomes a lot more challenging to keep a thriving garden. If you have your fair share of wind, consider using plants as a windbreak or implementing a fence or other structure. Don't forget about the heat. Even if you plant all sun-worshipping plants up there, you'll need somewhere to escape the sun while enjoying your little piece of heaven.

Here are a few more things to consider:

- **Barriers:** Do you need to construct some sort of barrier for visiting people, kids, or dogs? Check the regulations, because you may even be required to do so.

- **Roof access:** Be sure that you can get not only yourself and any guests to your garden, but also planting and maintenance supplies. You may legally need to have a couple of exits for emergencies—check those codes.

- **Water:** This should be high on the list. How are you going to water your Eden? If you rely solely on watering cans, you're going to have a long summer. Find out if you can run a hose to the roof or possibly a drip-irrigation system.

- **Money:** Exactly how much are you willing to part with? Now match it to your rooftop garden plans. It doesn't have to be an extremely expensive proposition, but the logistics of this type of garden may cost you more than a few pots on the terrace.

- **Electricity:** It's definitely not a requirement, but if there's any way to have good lighting up there, you're going to be really, really grateful. Not only so for evening gardening, but also so you can enjoy your garden at night.

- **Drainage:** Often the building engineer will have surface drains already installed for directing excess water. If this is the case, be careful that you don't cover or block them with planters!

Once you've done the research and been given the go-ahead to plant a rooftop garden, you'll have a blank canvas in one of the greatest spaces ever for sun-loving plants such as vegetables and herbs. Containers make the most sense for rooftop gardens because they're easy to move and inexpensive. However, you can also construct raised beds.

Again, be sure to double-check the maximum weight that can be placed on the roof before loading up on the soil. It isn't just the weight of the soil, but how heavy it becomes after it's been thoroughly watered—plus the plants and the lumber.

Placing containers closer to the edge of the roof is best because that's usually where you'll find the structural support. (It also makes a good boundary to keep guests and little ones away from the edge.) Lightweight paving or footing can turn a roof into a room. That, along with some strategic lighting, can give you living space for summer evenings, as well. For those living in the concrete jungle with the legal freedom, structural integrity, and good climate to create a rooftop oasis, the rewards are well worth the effort.

Challenging Spaces

Although small-space gardeners have some clear advantages, we also have our share of challenges. Have you ever looked at a spot in your yard and said, "What a waste of space"? You know, like those skinny areas in between the side of the house and the fence?

Most people fill this spot with garbage cans and plastic kiddie pools with holes in them. I'll admit that these awkward places need a little more thought to become great gardens, but the truth is that no space need ever be wasted. And what you now think of as a throwaway area just may pleasantly surprise you when well planted.

Narrow Places

First, put the garbage cans in the garage or set them outside the front gate and promise yourself that you'll make their own little area with some prefab fence panels. But get them out of your usable space. (If you have absolutely nowhere else to put the cans, leave them toward the front of the side yard, but make a separate space for them on this side of the main gate. There's no reason to keep them in view.)

Start with the path or walkway—create one if you don't already have a permanent one. Remember to use illusion and make it wind a little. If you're looking for cheap and easy, purchase some simple square pavers and place them in a staggered fashion along the center of the skinny space. Then fill the gaps between them with pea gravel.

First of all, a narrow path is just begging to be lined with fragrant plant varieties. It's perfect because the skinny walkway will encourage feet to step on a leaf or two, releasing some fabulous scents. Remember that we're still in a small space, so don't use too many varieties or the scents will compete or be too strong.

Go for the medium range in plant size. There isn't any one specific height, just not too tiny or the area will have zero visual impact. On the other hand, if you grow really tall plants in a skinny space, it'll be overwhelming. You're looking for a variety of plants between tall and small.

Tall and narrow plants can also work well in a skinny space such as Italian cypress, bamboo, Will Fleming yaupon holly, and Japanese Sky Pencil holly.

TIP THYME

You probably also have a bulky air-conditioning unit sitting outside on one side of a path. When it matches the color of a structure around it, the unit becomes less noticeable. If you can paint a nearby fence nearly the same color you'll notice the air-conditioning unit less. Or add a same-colored structure on the opposite side of a pathway.

It's hard to resist taking a narrow strip and making it all neat and uniform with perfectly shaped little plants. But a better idea is to use plants that are more free-form. Battle the boring with plants of differing heights.

Some side yards are shady and can be drafty and function as a wind tunnel. But a shady area can end up looking like a tropical forest by using hostas, ferns, and bleeding heart. Narrow passages naturally draw the eye all the way down to whatever happens to be at the end. Make this work for you by placing a focal point that you love at the end: a beautiful tree, a fountain (placed to one side), or a piece of garden art.

If there isn't much in the way of soil and you aren't inclined to bring any in (or maybe you're renting), use container plantings in the same way. Cover the entire area with whatever walkway material you're using, be it pavers, pea gravel, brick, or what have you.

If the area sees strong wind, choose plants and trees that are tough enough to take that type of treatment. Don't forget to consider using climbing plants in narrow spaces. Climbing plants add a lot of dimension and leave the impression that the space is bigger than it actually is.

Do you have a useless-looking rectangle of grass between your and your neighbor's driveways? Don't leave it barren and *don't plant grass*—now that would be a waste of space! Bring in some garden soil, amend with compost, and plant maybe three good-sized perennials there. Fill it in with the annuals of the season. Be sure to plant the taller annuals in the middle of the rectangle and the shortest ones on the outside edges. This way the complete picture can be viewed from either driveway.

PLANTING PITFALL

Don't plant extremely tall plants in a driveway area. Tall shrubs and perennials can hinder a driver's view as he or she is backing up or parking.

You may have a slender place that's only about a foot deep along a fence or wall. Don't just toss in some bark or mulch. Plant massive amounts of bright-colored plants such as dianthus (if it's sunny) or coleus or hostas (if it's shady). This is another place that would also benefit from climbing plants.

Dealing with Slopes

Because this book deals with small spaces, we're referring to the slopes that you might find in a suburban backyard or perhaps a terraced urban yard. If you have a drastic slope in your yard and you'd like to transform it into a garden, you may need to have a professional come out and give you an assessment. They may suggest that you add terraces to create gardening space or baffles. Terraces are basically cutting giant steps into the hillside. This creates flat spaces for planting. It's usually recommended that terraces be installed by a professional unless you've had experience.

Baffles, on the other hand, are mini versions of terracing. With gentle slopes, you can create baffles using lumber or plastic edging like that used to edge lawns. If you want baffles made of brick or stone, you may once again need a professional, unless you're good with masonry.

You don't have much of a problem if the slope is gradual, or less than 3 percent. But if you're working with a steeper slope, planting rows of plants up and down isn't the best way to go. You'll want to plant rows so that they run perpendicular (across) to the slope. When building a retaining wall or terraced area, the same rule applies. They should be constructed so that they follow the hillside's natural contours.

One of the biggest problems you're going to have with a slope is keeping the soil under the plants when you're watering. Soil-hugging ground covers are second to none for helping control soil erosion and slowing water evaporation on any slope. In fact, not only will these reliable fellows act as water retainers in the warm months, they're also impressive insulators in the cold. Ground covers also take up arms against weeds by blocking their seeds from sun, and refusing to share soil nutrition with them. For a list of some of the most useful ground-cover plants around, check out Chapter 19.

TIP THYME

Resist the urge to plant grass on steep slopes. Not only is it incredibly hard to mow, but it can actually be dangerous to navigate a heavy mower with spinning blades. An alternative to turf are ornamental grasses that you don't mow, such as blue fescue. These are left to grow into their natural mound shapes.

For crops such as grapes or fruit trees, your best bet is to install a drip irrigation system or soaker hoses to prevent water runoff. While these plants are trying to grow in and mature, you may want to cover the hill with a weed fabric or black plastic in order to keep soil in its place.

If you're at a loss for ideas for a sloped area, why not plant a rock garden? Rock gardens are naturals at looking their best on slopes. And the rock plants (or alpines) have no problem at all growing in this environment. Plus, you're looking at using minimal irrigation once the plants have established themselves. We have more on rock gardens in Chapter 12.

Windy Areas

One nice thing about urban and suburban settings is that you probably have fencing somewhere to help temper prevailing winds. If you deal with considerable wind, you'll want to use the widest and largest containers you can find to keep plants anchored to the ground. Tall, slender containers are easily blown over, as are top-heavy ones that are narrow at the bottom. Containers can also be anchored to a railing or wall using hooks and wire or even chain.

Remember that wind is extremely drying to plants and you'll need to keep those containers watered—even in the winter months. Evergreens are especially vulnerable to dry soil during the cold months, so leave yourself a note to keep them hydrated. If you've recently planted very young trees, you may have to protect their bark in high wind areas. Try wrapping them with burlap or check your local nursery for special tree wrap.

TIP THYME

The best way to use trees and shrubs as windbreaks is to plant them in two or three rows if you can. Start with the tallest plants such as evergreen or deciduous trees in the first row. Use the tall shrubs in the next row, and so on. Don't forget to plant flowering shrubs to get the most beauty out of your windbreak. For the most natural look, stagger the plantings—even if they're in containers.

The first goal is to block as much wind as possible, not only for the good of the plants but for the good of the people who want to enjoy the garden area. Sometimes solid windbreaks don't work the way you think they will because they can create blustering wind, which is just as annoying. If you have very little in the way of fencing, put up a barrier that actually lets the wind pass through it as opposed to a solid fence. This is where screens, trees, and tall shrubs come in to play. Windbreak netting is extremely useful and, although it isn't the most aesthetically pleasing, it does a lot to break the prevailing winds.

PLANTING PITFALL

If your area is known for its high winds, don't plant trees that break easily, such as silver maple, mimosa, willow, or poplar.

I enjoy using trees and shrubs as windbreaks because they just give me more with which to garden. If chosen carefully, they can offer year-round interest as well. Of course, certain plants are top-notch for handling the wind:

- Japanese barberry
- Forsythia
- Honeysuckle
- Yew
- Red cedar
- Viburnum
- Smoke bush
- White spruce
- Oregon grape
- Yucca
- Mountain ash
- Tree mallow
- Honey locust
- India Hawthorn
- Mock orange
- Japanese black pine
- Birch
- Tamarisk

- Bayberry

- Dogwood

- Japanese meadowsweet

- Firethorn

- Privet

- Russian olive

- Crabapple

Horrendously Hot Spots

It's a fact of garden life. Those of us with garden beds roasting in the blazing sun wish we had some cool shade, and those with only darker places to work with can barely conceal our jealously of those who have sun. I'm here to tell you that neither is better than the other. Both situations have their frustrating aspects and their admirable traits. Let's start with the hot spots.

For gardens that see a ton of sun, you want plants that don't fry easily and even thrive in the heat. Heat-tolerant plants are enjoying increased popularity because these species save water, which saves you money and natural resources. Environmentally friendly and a money saver—that's the definition of your sun-drenched garden spot. Using drought-tolerant plants in your garden or border (also called xeriscaping) makes for a landscape that's easy to care for.

Sometimes plants will leave clues about their heat-loving preferences. Lamb's ears, for instance, have the fuzzy leaves to catch any stray water drops that come their way. Succulents make it obvious that they're hoarding their water in their plump leaves. Not all of them are that obvious; penstemon, sunflowers, Mexican sage, lavender, and silver thyme are all happy in the sun. In fact, many common herbs are perfect for sunny borders, such as rosemary and sage.

Rock, herb, rose, cottage gardens, and summer vegetables are all excellent choices for hot places in the yard or garden. Rock gardens are especially suited for those sunny areas that are on a gradual slope. If you actually have some natural rocks poking through the soil, you've hit a jackpot for a great rock garden spot. If you don't have a natural rock outcropping, how about a short rock retaining wall? Rock plants (also referred to as alpines) are used for this style, but other sun-loving perennials are often mixed into this garden, as well. If you want to plant a rock garden, check out Chapter 12.

Herbs are a versatile plant group. An herb garden does well in both sun and semi-shade. The added perk is that this garden gives you food for the kitchen. Roses are the original sun worshippers and, once established, only need to be watered deeply about once a week to keep them happy. Rose gardens make a classic, formal bed. Create a cottage garden by planting a combination of perennials, roses, and herbs.

Another natural garden for full-sun gardening is a vegetable bed. Spring and summer vegetables will thrive in the sunshine, and you'll have fresh and delicious food for the dinner table. Most vegetables will need more watering than a rose or rock garden, at least while they're growing and beginning to produce fruit.

For the most part, hot places are all about choosing the right plant varieties. But even the sun worshippers appreciate good, *friable soil* if they can get it. It's important to add compost as well as mulch to the bed once in a while.

DEFINITION

Friable soil has an open structure that crumbles easily when handled. it's also referred to as "tilth." Friable soil is most desired by gardeners.

Not only will those materials add nutrition to the soil, but they'll also make the most of whatever water they get by retaining it much longer than soil that's bone dry and carries zero organic matter. There's more on compost and mulch in Chapter 15. In Part 5 of this book, you'll find excellent choices in plants for sunny garden areas.

Seriously Shady Spaces

Now we come to the shady places. I realize people tend to ignore the shadier areas of the yard, but I can't for the life of me figure out why. My guess is that they think they have very little choice in garden styles or plant varieties for darker spots. Nothing could be further from the truth. Whether your space is shaded only part of the time or all day, there are tons of plants for you to choose from. See Chapter 2 to figure out how much shade you have.

TIP THYME

Thin out the canopy of a tree by pruning off the lower branches. This will bring in more light and create dappled shade as opposed to full shade.

There's not only a variety of shade plants, but this is the environment that's necessary to pull off a woodland, wildlife, or lush, tropical-type garden. Shady plants also have some of the most vibrant-colored foliage of all. Not to mention that shade offers privacy and moderates the high temperatures of summer.

A shady garden can not only make enjoying the outdoors bearable, but in some cases entirely possible! If shade is what you have, make it work for you. You may even find that your shade garden is the envy of your sunny-gardening friends.

Many (but not all) shade dwellers have large leaves. The broader surface allows these plants to gather as much light as possible for *photosynthesis*. Some of them also have variegated leaves—which means they have white or cream on the leaves as well as green. They reflect any light around and serve well to brighten dark corners. Examples of these are dead nettle, coleus, and lungwort.

 DEFINITION

Photosynthesis is the process by which plants create their own food. Plants use energy from the sun to convert carbon dioxide and water into simple sugars (carbohydrates).

Leaves aren't the only bright thing found in the shade. Flowers also make their home there, such as impatiens, bleeding heart, and cyclamen. Scent isn't lost in the shade, either. For a thorough list of fabulous shade plants, check out Part 5.

Soggy or Boggy

Then there are those areas that never seem to dry out. They have almost nothing resembling drainage and seem to hold rainwater forever. Soggy and boggy areas may seem like the most hopeless places of all to plant a garden. But, as always, nature has her answers, and some plants actually thrive in wet conditions.

There are a couple of ways to deal with boggy places. The first thing you could consider is to continuously add organic matter in the form of compost and garden soil. Doing so will eventually transform the area to a place with drainage that would be adequate for whatever you'd like to plant.

But another way is faster and less bothersome: plant things that don't mind getting their feet wet. In fact, I actually suggest that you steer even more water to this site in order to maintain a soggy environment for these types of plants. Whatever drainage system you have near this area, direct it toward your boggy garden space. How's that for working with what you're given?

Japanese iris, astilbe, filipendula, snake's-head fritillaria, ferns, ligularia, and bee balm are a small sample of plants that enjoy their roots planted in damp areas.

On the other hand, sometimes the smallest lots (townhomes, condominiums, and so on) end up inheriting some less-than-desirable drainage due to a neighbor. If you're getting run-off from a neighbor, invite them over for drinks to discuss solutions!

> **TIP THYME**
>
> Don't have a bog garden and wish that you did? Make it yourself by digging out the soil in an area about 2" or 3" deep and as wide as you want. Punch a few holes into a thick sheet of plastic—not too many. The idea is to create slow drainage. Use the plastic to line the dug-out area and fill the soil back into the hole. You can add some peat moss to help retain moisture.

What I enjoy so much about garden spots that at first glance look like wasted space is that they're actually an opportunity to broaden your gardening world. Whether it's a bone-dry, shady, or soggy area, there are plant species that have adapted to those conditions. These places make for interesting gardens that are wonderful conversation pieces for you and the gardening folk around you. Bog-loving carnivorous plants are certain to get people talking! You can create small bogs for soggy-soil plants by using plastic planters and small kiddie pools.

The Least You Need to Know

- Don't forget to focus on the flooring of a balcony garden, as it can pull an entire look or theme together.
- Check with your fire department on the regulations in your city for gardening on fire escapes.
- The soil in window boxes tends to dry out quickly, so heat-loving plants tend to do the best in them.
- Think about using wind-tolerant trees and shrubs as natural windbreaks for the garden.
- Before planning a rooftop garden, you'll need to be aware of city ordinances, structural specifications, and roof access.
- Unlikely looking gardening spaces offer opportunities to get to know new plants and themes.

Raving Over Raised Beds

In This Chapter

- The benefits of gardening in a raised bed
- Materials for building a raised garden
- Making a quick and cheap raised bed in an afternoon
- Discovering square-foot gardening

In many ways, raised beds have it all over regular in-ground planting. Although you may not want to use them exclusively, there are good reasons to use them as often as you can. There's no limit on the materials that can be used to create them and they can save time, money, and water in the garden. Come see what raised beds can do for both you and your plants.

The What and Why of Raised Beds

Raised beds are gardens where the soil level has been built up several inches above the natural ground. Raised beds are heralded by seasoned gardeners, but they're perfectly suited for beginners, too.

There's no special way to make one, and getting creative may help you keep project expenses low. Giving some thought as to what's used as walls to hold in the soil will allow for stylistic creativity. For instance, if you live in a log home and plan to build up some soil for a perennial flower bed, consider using logs as a frame.

You'll often hear talk about raised beds in reference to vegetable gardening. For many people, the first image that comes to mind is evenly spaced, rectangular boxes with lettuce or tomatoes planted in them. There's good reason for this image—which we'll get to in a minute. But raised beds are used more often for foundation plantings around homes, for garden spaces under large trees, and so on. Raised beds are not only about vegetables, they're just as valuable for growing perennials, annuals, shrubs, and roses. In fact, containers are actually raised beds, even though they perform a little differently. Unless otherwise specified, raised beds imply that there's no barrier between the soil we've added to the raised bed and the original earth beneath. So plant roots have more wiggle room and can utilize the space and nutrition in the ground below the bed.

> **TIP THYME**
>
> Soil can also be built up without a frame to contain it, but you'll have soil erosion when you water. If you decide to make a raised bed without sides, using soaker hoses or a drip line for irrigation will help keep the soil where you want it.

If you have places where you'd like to plant and your soil isn't quite the loamy stuff of a gardener's dreams, go for a raised bed. Think of it as yet another way to create a microclimate. Fair warning: if you've never gardened in a raised bed—vegetables or otherwise—once you've done it, you'll be forever spoiled to the practice. But that's a risk worth taking, for many reasons:

- **Less weeds:** It's simple. When you bring soil and compost into a raised bed, the weed seeds that are dormant in the ground don't ever get the chance to see the light of day—literally. That isn't to say that you'll have zero weeds, but most gardeners find that weeding is extremely minimal in a raised bed.

- **Better water retention:** Prepared garden soil has a lot of organic matter creating good tilth, which holds on to water longer. This is especially good news for those of you living in an area that has super-sandy soil.

- **Better drainage:** Soil that's high in organic matter is free-draining. So while it'll stay moist, it won't stay sopping. This is a big plus for those with heavy clay soil.

- **More growing space:** Beds can be constructed where there was no previous garden space, such as on a lawn, rocky areas, or even cement.

- **No soil compaction from human feet:** The less soil compaction, the better, as far as plant roots are concerned.

- **Warm soil earlier in the season:** This is most useful for those growing vegetables in raised beds. Spring and summer vegetable seedlings are planted once the soil has warmed for the season. Raised beds offer a jump-start on planting time.

- **Warm soil for a longer season:** The soil in raised beds doesn't freeze as quickly as the bare earth, so some vegetable harvesting will be available for a longer period into the fall and winter.

- **Soil that has basically a neutral pH:** Prepared garden soil and compost basically have a neutral pH unless you've purchased a soil that's been amended for, say, acid-loving plants such as azaleas or blueberries. Because of this, if you have plants that prefer a higher or lower pH balance, you'll need to amend the soil for them.

- **Less or no soil erosion:** This refers to framed beds, as opposed to just built up. For the most part, the soil stays where it's put in a raised bed.

People think of vegetables in raised beds for all the reasons above, which are necessary for healthy and productive vegetable gardens. This makes raised vegetable beds extremely popular with the food-growing crowd.

Bed-Framing Materials

As I mentioned earlier, there are many ways to go about framing a raised bed, and potential materials are endless. You have just a few things to consider before you put one or two together: location, size, and materials.

The majority of raised beds are constructed from lumber. I'll talk about treated lumber from the get-go because, for many years, the CCA-treated wood was used until we discovered that the arsenic, chromium, and copper was leaching into soils. At that point, the EPA (Environmental Protection Agency) stopped arsenic from being used in the lumber. Pressure-treated wood is now processed in a more ecologically friendly way and it's deemed to have no ill effects on people or animals. The new treatments (ACQ or CA) have dropped the arsenic but are also higher in copper.

As with all chemically treated wood, you should still avoid the dust particles by wearing a mask when you're cutting it to size; you also still shouldn't burn any waste, taking it to a landfill instead. If you'd rather use a material without any chemicals, there are some great alternatives:

- **Raw lumber:** It's a little more expensive and it won't last as long as pressure-treated lumber, but there's something to be said about peace of mind. Both red cedar and redwood are naturally rot resistant.

- **Composite timber:** Made with a few different materials depending on the company, it's commonly made of polypropylene and wood fiber. Some are made from recycled materials and can have UV-ray protection to give it longer life. It's a little more expensive than raw lumber, but it lasts longer, too.

- **Recycled plastic:** Another long-lasting choice, and it's nice to know it puts old plastic to the very best use, in my opinion. Free (recycled) is as cheap as it gets.

- **Cinderblocks:** Okay, not as attractive as wood. But very inexpensive and fast!

- **Logs:** I've made a raised herb bed from some logs I had lying around about three years ago. It's still holding that bed together and the only part of the logs showing any sign of breaking down is the outside bark. Some of it has peeled away and broken off, but the structure is still sound. Talk about cheap.

- **Rock:** Maybe not the fastest way, considering the mortar and drying time involved, but raised beds made of rock are quite permanent—and beautiful.

- **Brick:** Brick beds turn out just as lovely as the rock kind, they just have a different look. These also last forever.

- **Concrete and concrete blocks:** Both of these offer a less formal look—but they're permanent, too. Regular concrete will take longer depending on your skill and drying time, but some concrete blocks are the interlocking type, which you can set up in no time.

TIP THYME

Don't make weeding and planting hard on yourself. Build your raised bed only as wide as you can reach to the middle from both sides. If the bed is up against a wall, you should be able to reach to the back without stepping into it.

Beds made of lumber are usually joined at the corners with galvanized or stainless steel screws or bolts. But some new products on the market allow you to join lumber together without digging into the tool bucket, such as corner brackets that allow you to slide the wood into position. Don't forget to look for this helpful hardware before you purchase.

Some (okay, all) of the best raised beds that I've seen feature a ledge or cap that's been mounted to the top board of the bed. It sits like a triangle at the corners. These sitting areas can keep you out in the garden longer by making garden chores like weeding, cutting flowers, or harvesting more comfortable for you. So keep that in the back of your mind.

How Tall Is Your Bed?

As far as how deep a bed needs to be, there's no magic number. I've made beds from 6" to 24" and they've all worked equally well. It depends on what I'm going to plant; a 6"- to 12"-deep bed works beautifully for most gardens, but you may want to make one that's 18" if you think you'd like the leeway for root crops such as carrots.

> **TIP THYME**
>
> If you're constructing raised beds on the lawn and are keeping grass paths, you should leave enough room for the lawn mower and weed eater. If you're building side-by-side beds, be sure that your paths have enough space for a small wheelbarrow to fit through.

In reality, I've never found an 18"-deep bed necessary—unless you like the fact that you don't have to bend down very far. That may sound like a good idea, but remember this: it's going to take a lot of (unnecessary) soil and compost to fill that bed.

Make a Fast Raised Bed with Cinderblocks

A small raised bed made of cinderblocks is easy to construct and will have you planting the same day. These instructions are for a little 4' × 5' bed. If you want to make it bigger or taller, just do the math. Also, if you do make it two cinderblocks high instead of one, staggering the blocks will make the structure more secure. Construction on this is just about as easy as it gets.

What you'll need:

- 12 cinderblocks
- Rocks, gravel, or sand
- A rake
- A shovel
- A level
- Blend of one half garden soil, one quarter compost, and one quarter manure to produce roughly half a cubic yard of soil.

hat you'd like to grow in the bed and choose a location based on
f those plants. Make sure there's a water source nearby.

the area where you want the bed and rake it flat. Be sure to remove any
eeds that are growing, as well.

3. Before laying the cinderblocks down, dig a bit of a depression into the soil
along the line where they will be placed. They'll be a little more stable sitting
in this groove. Make the depressions for each side of the rectangle as you go
along.

4. The bed will have four cinderblocks on each long side and two on the
short sides. You want to build the bed with the holes in the blocks facing
up. Starting with a long side, place four of the blocks end to end into their
groove.

5. Now do the same for a short side, being sure to place the first end block
against the inside of the last long side block.

6. Make the next long side and finish up the last short one.

7. Take your level and place it on top of each side of the bed to be sure that the
bed is as level as you can get it. That way you won't have water draining away
from one area and sitting in another after you've watered.

8. Now fill the holes with rocks, gravel, or sand.

9. If the bed is for growing root vegetables, this would be the moment to place
chicken wire at the bottom of the bed to ward off root-nibbling varmints like
gophers. You could also put landscape fabric or another mulch cloth at the
bottom to help deter weeds.

10. Fill the raised bed with the soil blend up to an inch or so from the top. In
taller garden beds, you wouldn't fill the soil up quite that high, but this bed
is short and it's nice to have as much in there as possible. Also, truth be told,
I tend to add even more compost into the mix.

11. Start planting!

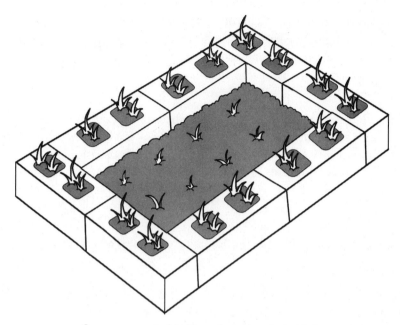

Construct a raised bed in a day using cinderblocks.

Make Your Bed on the Lawn

Suburban gardeners looking for more space need look no further than the front or back lawn. There's nothing wrong with having a lawn, but they are water guzzlers and, face it, most of us use very little of it if any at all.

Some of you may think of this as the ultimate sacrifice, and some of you may be relieved that someone finally gave you permission to have something other than grass in your front yard. In any case, it can make sense to take a little bit of the green carpet and use it for flowers, food, or both.

There are several ways to make a raised bed on the lawn, but this is my favorite way because it also happens to be the easiest. At the end of summer or early fall, I make way for a new garden bed by making what I call a "compost sandwich." It's also called sheet composting, and some loosely use the term "lasagna gardening."

TIP THYME

If you're an alpine aficionado, there's no better way to show them off than in a raised bed where their intricacies can be appreciated.

In reality, this isn't true lasagna gardening because with this technique, you're actually waiting until the following spring to plant the beds. Therefore, the organic matter in the beds will have already composted (for the most part) by the time you plant. Usually with lasagna gardening, the beds are planted right after the layers are created; that is, before everything breaks down into compost.

The reason it's a great idea to start a garden bed off as a compost sandwich is because it ends up with excellent water-holding capabilities—making terrific use of the winter rainfall. It'll have very few weed problems. If weeds do occasionally appear, they slide easily out of the crumbly soil. Best of all, it'll be pliable, nutritional, and ready for spring seeding.

What you'll need:

All kinds of cardboard—keep pizza boxes, cereal boxes, and so on, to have a collection

Newspaper

An assortment of carbon materials ("browns") such as leaves, straw, weedless grass hay, newspaper, shredded bark, shavings, and so on

An assortment of nitrogen materials ("greens") such as grass clippings, vegetable peelings, seedless weeds, perennial plant clippings, coffee, tea bags, and so on

Topsoil or garden soil

Manure from herbivores (chicken, rabbit, horse—no dog or cat poop)

Water

What you'll do:

1. Start with covering the entire garden area with cardboard, corrugated or whatever you have.

2. Next, take some newspaper and lay it over the cardboard. You'll want to make this layer about 2" thick, if possible. Don't get a ruler out—it doesn't need to be exactly 2", just make a solid layer. Have a hose nearby to water in between the layers to get everything moving toward decomposition.

3. The next layer you'll add will be a green—whatever green your heart desires, but if you choose grass clippings, keep the layer thinner as the grass seems to compact and not let air inside.

4. Next, you'll spread a manure layer, and then a thin layer of topsoil. At this point, you'll go back to your carbons; maybe this time you'll use straw instead of newspaper. You can also go back to newspaper.

I can't stress enough that composting of any kind is an art—not rocket science. While there's certainly a basic chemistry to it, you don't need to measure and get precise. Make your sandwich the best you can and use varying materials while creating.

5. Make as many layers as you can, switching between the browns and the greens, manures, and the topsoil. Don't stop until you run out of materials, even if the pile is higher than the bed; it won't be for long.

6. The last layer will be topsoil.

Be sure to water between the layers while you're building the sandwich. You're not trying to flood it, but the sandwich needs to be wet. Water the last layer of topsoil. Now, other than watering the sandwich if you have dry weather, leave it alone. Don't do a darned thing to it all winter. You're going to be so thrilled with the soil in your new bed next spring.

Now, if you were to build this sandwich in the spring, be sure to add quite a bit more topsoil into the layers and maybe some peat moss for good measure. You could plant it with veggies right then and grow a garden while everything is breaking down. The plants would do great—but next year's crop would do even better.

Also, if you do plant in the bed before the organic matter has broken down, it'll tend to rob some of the nitrogen from the soil that was there to begin with. So you can add extra greens to combat this, such as bone meal or grass blades.

Square-Foot Gardening

Square-foot gardening is based on general raised-bed concepts and old gardening practices, including those of the ancient Native Americans. The fabulous Mel Bartholomew has brought the technique up to the present and made it extremely easy for beginners by adding his own special twists. The resulting method has been amazingly popular.

You can apply the technique to herb, vegetable, flower, and fruit gardening, but it's predominantly used for vegetable gardens, since the basic premise is to rotate and harvest as many crops as possible. Of course, most gardeners will interplant flowers with their vegetables, as it should be.

Mel's garden method shows you how to have a much bigger harvest in a 4' × 4' bottomless bed than you could from the same amount of space planting in traditional rows. It's about using a short (6"-deep) raised bed filled with a soil blend of one third compost, one third peat moss, and one third vermiculite. To make the system obvious and to keep the square-foot vision, a grid is made on the top of the bed using *lath*.

> **DEFINITION**
>
> **Lath** is a thin strip of wood that's used to make latticework or patterns. It's routinely used for securing climbing plants to walls.

Mel has specific guidelines for how many of each vegetable can be planted inside the 1' squares created by the lathe. It's a great system for everyone trying their hand at vegetable gardening because it's very precise and detailed, with charts to guide you.

The benefits of the square-foot method are much the same as any raised bed. But by keeping the bed short, you save money and time on unnecessary soil and construction materials, and the soil blend is perfect for moisture retention. Mel declares that additional fertilizer is unnecessary. By keeping the bed in a 4' square, every side is easily accessible for tending.

In his book *All New Square-Foot Gardening*, Mel lists guides for building structures for your bed, such as a trellis for vertical vegetables or a protective frost cover, and how to keep unwanted critters out of your garden. Of course, one of the best things about Mel's method is that it's tailor-made for the small-space garden.

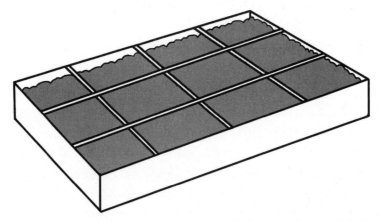

Square-foot gardening is a great system especially for those planting their first vegetable garden.

The Least You Need to Know

- Raised beds offer you fewer weeds, better drainage, less watering, longer growing seasons, less soil erosion, balanced pH, and more growing space.
- Raised beds are gardens where the soil level has been built up several inches above the natural ground.
- It can make sense to borrow some space from an unused lawn for a raised garden bed.
- Square-foot gardens are perfect for small spaces and vegetable gardens.

Vertical Thinking

In This Chapter

- Vertical gardening techniques
- How plants climb
- Using trellises, arbors, and pergolas
- Growing vegetables and fruit vertically
- Gardening "down" and other vertical variations

One of the biggest considerations when gardening in a small space is square footage. We're always looking for creative ways to get the most out of every inch of available space. Some of us may have small horizontal growing spaces, but that's not necessarily true of our vertical space. Growing plants vertically is one of the best space-saving techniques for everything from flowers to vegetables and fruit.

As a small-space gardener, one of the best habits you can get into is to practice vertical thinking. People have a natural tendency to plant all the earth they can until they run into a wall, fence, or tall tree. Let's get past the "I-ran-out-of-room" thinking and start growing up!

Why You Should Grow Up

Let's start with the first and most obvious reason to grow plants vertically. With an upright structure, you'll enjoy a lot of plants, flowers, or vegetables while using very little ground space. Other than saving prime horizontal real estate, there are other good reasons for gardening up. Plants grown vertically can be exposed to more air and sunlight, and, depending on the structure, vertical plants can offer shade to desired areas of the yard.

> **TIP THYME**
>
> If you'd like to plant some shade or semishade plants, growing vertical vines can create a shady space on the ground.

Hiding or disguising a view is an excellent reason to plant things that grow up. You may want to camouflage the swimming pool pump or an open compost pile. An air-conditioning unit or the place where the garbage cans are stored can also be obstructed by growing plants onto an upright structure of any kind. Climbing plants can soften the view of the chain-link fence that divides the neighbor's yard and yours. Speaking of neighbors, plants grown vertically can act as a privacy screen for your home.

In the vegetable garden, vining crops such as cucumbers, zucchini, tomatoes, mini pumpkins, and melons can be grown toward the back of the garden and trained up a trellis. This allows you to take full advantage of every inch in the vegetable garden bed.

> **PLANTING PITFALL**
>
> Resist the urge to plant a clinging vine against a wood-sided house or wooden fence. Moisture becomes trapped by the suction cup–like discs or aerial rootlets which will eventually cause the wood to deteriorate.

What's Your Vertical Goal?

Before you purchase climbing plants, it's always best to come up with some personalized guidelines. Even if it isn't incredibly detailed, it'll at least have you looking at the right plants in general. Before you borrow your brother-in-law's truck and head down to the nursery, ask yourself some questions first:

- Are you interested in great flowers, fabulous foliage, or food?
- Are you looking for an evergreen or will a *deciduous* plant do?
- Will the plant live through the off season in your zone?
- Does it need supporting? Pruning?
- Are you looking to cover or hide something quickly?

> **DEFINITION**
>
> **Deciduous** plants lose their leaves in the winter. Varieties include oak, maple, and birch trees and some honeysuckle shrubs.

How Plants Climb

Gardeners don't usually think about how plants climb until they realize their climbing rose needs some help. This can be confusing; something called a "climbing rose" should do exactly that, right? Well, not exactly. The term "climbing plant" casts a wide net, and before you choose a lovely-looking one from a glossy magazine, you should know the differences between the climbers.

Not all plants climb the same way. There are scramblers, climbers, and twining or tendril plants.
(Courtesy of Brenda Haas)

Scrambling Plants

Scrambling plants are also referred to as the leaners. This is the group that the climbing roses belong to, as well as bougainvillea and plumbago. Gardening purists will reject their dubious title as a climber, saying that they're actually an extremely open, prostrate shrub. That may be technically true, but we still tend to grow them as a climbing plant.

GARDEN GOSPEL

Leaners like climbing roses and bougainvillea have thorns that help hook them to their support. That doesn't contribute to actual climbing, but it does keep them from sliding backwards.

In any case, these guys will scramble up walls and trellises, and drape down the other side in a graceful cascade—sometimes. If you want to be sure that happens, you should offer them some mechanical support every so often. Usually this means some intentional pruning and tying of the canes (the long, climbing stems) at regular intervals.

Climbers That Cling

These climbers have truly earned their moniker; they climb by literally sticking to the structure they scale. Boston ivy and Virginia creeper cling to walls (and everything else) by using suction cups. Other clingers have aerial rootlets along their stems that allow them to get a firm grasp onto whatever happens to be nearby. English ivy and climbing hydrangea belong in this group.

TIP THYME

Clinging climbers are best used for growing up the flat surfaces of concrete, stone, or brick.

Twining and Tendril Plants

Some climbing plants will twine their entire stems around anything they touch. Depending on the species, their stems will either twine reliably clockwise or counterclockwise. Morning glories, honeysuckle, sweet peas, and pole beans belong to the twining group.

Other twiners have curly little side shoots off of their stems called tendrils. These tendrils work much like the twining stems; they wrap themselves around any support. Passionflower and grapes are examples of tendril climbers. A few climbers also have twining leaf stalks (petioles), such as clematis and climbing nasturtium. For a lovely and unique tendril climber, try the cup'n saucer vine. The only thing these beauties need from you is something to wrap themselves around.

TIP THYME

Give those with tendrils something like a chain link fence, railing, rope, or wire. The stem twiners will do well with lattice, arbors, and pergolas. After that, you can step aside and let them do what they do best.

Structures for Climbing Plants

Nothing brings vertical impact to a yard like a trellis, arbor, or pergola covered in greenery. Man-made structures add warmth when they're intertwined with nature. For many gardeners, plants grown overhead complete the landscaping picture. And for us small-space gardeners, those upright structures give us one more way to grow one more plant.

Permanent climbing structures are part of the foundation of the yard or garden. They're appropriate for climbing perennials or wisteria. Any other long-lived temporary structures should be used for supporting vegetables or annuals that are in a place that you might be revamping from season to season.

Trellises

Although trellises can be found in square, rectangle, and fan shapes, the latticework constructed in a diamond pattern is probably the most common. The wood used for a trellis is predominantly left in its natural state without any sealer or coating.

TIP THYME

Before you choose any trellis, arbor, or pergola, be sure you know which climbing plant you're interested in first. You need to know what a mature specimen of that plant is and just how strong the structure needs to be; some of these climbers become extremely heavy!

This works out fine as most of them are made of wood that is slow to deteriorate, such as cedar, redwood, and teak. Lattice also comes painted white and sometimes a blue-wash if you'd like some color. Some companies even make it in heavy plastic and wrought iron.

Mounting a trellis or lattice just a couple of feet away from a wall is a great way to get the soft, romantic look of vines climbing up the side of your house without risking damage. It also functions as a light and beautiful privacy wall between your yard and whomever you're seeking privacy from. Yet it's airy and gives you just a peek to the other side. Peruse a nursery, lumber yard, or hardware store for a variety of trellis options.

You know the old adage, "less is more"? Well, sometimes more is just more. Consider growing two vines up the same trellis; one could be a perennial that'll take time to mature and come into its own, while the other is an annual climber providing quick color and coverage for this season.

How to Attach Lattice to a Wall

Here's how to attach latticework or a trellis to the wood siding of your home.

What you'll need:

Six to eight $2\frac{1}{2}$" pieces of PVC pipe

Wood screws

Phillips screwdriver

What you'll do:

The short pieces of pipe will create space between the structure and the wall. The length of the screws will depend on the thickness of the lattice or trellis. They'll need to be long enough to go through the wood, through the PVC pipe, and secure into the siding. The screws are simply driven into the wood siding of the house.

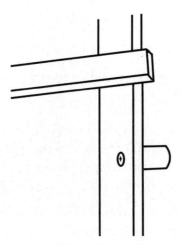

Attach lattice to a wall for extra vertical gardening space.

TIP THYME

Instead of attaching your lattice or other trellis to a wall with screws, use hooks and eyes. It makes for easy removal should the wall need to be painted or repaired.

If you are attaching the trellis to masonry or a brick wall, you'll need to add to the original hardware list above:

Masonry shields

Hammer

Vacuum or a piece of thick wire.

The masonry shields should be put into the wall before you use the (lag) screws. To do this, use a masonry bit that's the same size as the shields you purchased. Slowly drill holes into the masonry or brick that are $\frac{1}{4}''$ deeper than the shields.

You may have to take a break every so often so the bit or drill doesn't overheat. Clean the dust from the holes using a piece of wire or a vacuum. Use a hammer to tap the shields into the masonry until they're sunk to just past the wall surface. Now drive the lag screws into the wood through the pipe and into the shields in the wall.

*Trellis or lattice mounted just a couple of feet away from a wall is
a great way to get the soft, romantic look of vines climbing up
the side of your house without risking damage.*
(Courtesy of Teresa Soule)

Get Creative with Trellis

If you're a creative sort, you could come up with your own trellis design. As far as climbing materials, there's no need to stop at lattice. Almost anything climbable can be used to make a trellis. I've even used T-posts and chicken wire to make a trellis for vines. We sunk T-posts into the ground in the area in front of our swimming pool filter. We then pulled the chicken wire between the T-posts, and attached both ends of the wire to the posts.

I planted several pink jasmine vines along my chicken wire trellis. Low and behold, in just a couple of years, the entire structure was covered with a thick mass of tiny leaves with hundreds of pink-white blossoms perfuming the air in the spring and summer. Best of all, the ugly pool filter remains a secret behind the evergreen wall forever.

Other clever structures that can be used as trellis are ladders, old gates, fences, and doors. Willow and dogwood branches pruned off of trees can work, too.

Arbors

Most people use the terms "arbor" and "pergola" interchangeably. Technically, there's a difference. Arbors are smaller than pergolas and they usually have an arched, half-dome top, although some have a flat top. Arbors stand anywhere from $6\frac{1}{2}'$ to 9' tall at the very top. They're typically used over a gate entrance or the beginning of a walkway.

The thought of an arbor in a small garden may sound unusual. However, the arbor or pergolas are, in fact, small spaces in which you garden to create an effect. Both can add interest and shape to great and small spaces as well. They're also perfect for creating various "rooms" in a garden or yard. Arbors can also help to create the promise of more space on the other side—whether this is true or not.

Pergolas

Pergolas are a variation on that theme and are usually bigger structures. They can, indeed, be used over an entryway. But more often they'll cover the entire walkway and are wonderful for covering an entire patio. Pergolas have flat tops that are at right angles to their sides.

Pergolas can link gardens to each other, or the backyard to a front yard. When they're built as a strong and secure structure, pergolas can hold the lovely (and eventually heavy) wisteria. The dappled light underneath a pergola provides yet another microclimate for indoor tropicals on vacation for the season, semishade lovers, and, depending on how thick the climber grows, possibly shade plants.

TIP THYME

Check local zoning codes before starting construction on a large pergola or arbor. There may be some building regulations that you'll need to know about.

If you use the pergola as a simple cover structure for a patio, it becomes easy to reflect the inside of your home to the outside. Because pergolas are semiopen, they may not serve as a true outdoor room, but they tend to lower the height of open space and will provide that same cozy feeling.

To get that consistent look that works so well in a small-space garden, it's best to echo the shape of the buildings around it and keep it in proportion. You don't want the pergola to give the appearance of being larger than your home. Don't be afraid to use unusual materials and finishes in order to harmonize with your home or other buildings. Hardwood, softwood, and metal are all appropriate for a pergola structure. You can stain or paint it, as well.

Espalier

Espalier is the art of training (pruning) trees and shrubs in patterns flat against a wall fence or trellis. This is a technique that's often associated with fruit trees, making it possible for practically anyone to grow their own fruit.

Espalier does involve a little know-how, practice, and patience, as it takes years for the final pattern to emerge. But once it does, the results can be jaw-dropping. If you'd like immediate espalier gratification, many nurseries have started the process for you. These can be purchased at a hefty price, but it's an option.

Depending on the plant species, patterns include the diamond, espalier, and fan. They can also be pruned into X, U, V, and T shapes. I adore the beautifully formal look of espalier, and once again, the vertical space is used well. Not all espalier is done in geometric shapes; it can also be done free-form, which gives it a less formal look. We'll talk more about espalier in Chapter 10.

The espalier technique makes any small yard a fruit orchard.

The "U" is one of many shapes that can be used to esplaier.

Before choosing plants, confirm the amount of sun exposure the wall or fence receives, and whether you want plants that are evergreen or deciduous. Also consider espaliering fruit trees. Here are some espalier examples in each category:

- **Evergreens:** Holly, juniper, lilac, winter jasmine, yew, pyracantha, camellia, Southern magnolia

- **Fruit:** Apple, grape, lemon, pear, raspberry, blackberry, fig, persimmon, plum, quince, and nectarine

- **Deciduous plants:** Redbud, forsythia, mock orange, viburnum, dogwood, laburnum, rose, ornamental cherry

Climbing Plants on Trees and Shrubs

Gardeners often take sides about whether it's ever appropriate to use live trees as climbing structures for vining plants. The undeniable truth is that an aggressive climber such as ivy can suffocate a tree by eventually shading the crown of the tree from the sun. This is clearly not desirable.

There's some room for flexibility on this issue. I think if you choose a nonaggressive climber like a clematis, climbing hydrangea, or passion flower to shimmy up a mature tree-trunk, you can create a colorful canvas against a tree that's past its blooming season with no harm done. Be sure to prune away any vines that are coming close to the canopy of the tree.

By the way, climbers can be fantastic growing through shrubs, too. This tandem planting keeps blossoms around longer if you consider the bloom time of the shrub, as well as that of the flowering vine. Encourage vining plants to weave their way through by planting the vine on the shady side of the shrub. To be certain that the vine doesn't take over the entire shrub, feel free to prune the vine hard in the late winter to about 12" from the ground.

Climbers on Tree Snags

Snags, or dead trees, are a free-for-all. There's no fear of suffocating a tree that's no longer alive. If you've left an old snag standing for the wildlife, make it do double duty by using it for climbing vines.

> **PLANTING PITFALL**
>
> Eventually, snags do decay to the point of coming down. Be certain that any snag you leave standing won't hit something if or when it falls over.

Old trees, even those that are partially alive, make great vertical structures. You can hang wire baskets on the gnarled branches in a staggered fashion. The dappled shade from the heavy branches and leaves are perfect for planting begonias, impatiens, fuchsia, lettuce, and even string of pearls, creating a vertical garden view.

Vertical Vegetables

No matter how slight the area is where you garden, it shouldn't stop you from growing vegetables. In fact, more often than not, vegetables grown vertically have less pest and disease problems than their ground-dwelling counterparts. Veggies grown vertically are less likely to rot or be eaten by things other than your family.

Ripe vertical vegetables also have a better chance at being seen (and therefore harvested) on time. This is especially important for plants such as cucumbers, which send out the "stop-production" signal as soon as a cucumber or two reaches complete maturity.

Another advantage to growing vegetables up is that the crops are usually larger and the harvest can last longer. They get more sunlight and air circulation than ground growers.

Vegetable varieties that have a vining habit are perfect for vertical gardening: cucumbers, squash, grapes, kiwi, tomatoes, peppers, zucchini, and peas. All types of beans can be grown up, including green (snap), shelling (drying), lima (butterbean), fava (broad), and soy (edamame). There's more about growing vertical vegetables in Chapter 9.

Vertical Gardening Variations

Growing up doesn't have to be about climbing plants that cover an entire structure. Vertical gardening can also be about attaching containers or trough planters along the top of a fence and planting trailing plants among the others. It's often referred to as gardening "down" instead of "up." For instance, a trailing plant such as bacopa will hang down and soften the lines of the fence.

TIP THYME

Some lucky people have outside walls that have been constructed so that there's a hollow area built into the last section at the top, such as walls made of cinder-block. Take advantage of this natural planting space by filling it with potting soil and planting trailing plants. If this doesn't describe your wall and you own the place, you could always add cinder blocks (holes facing upward) to the top or use bricks to create the hollows that you need for planting.

Several different container styles are specially made for planting on fences. Some have hooking arms that are meant to hang on to the fence, which lets the planter face one direction. There's also the type that are made to actually perch on top of the fence so that there's equal container parts on either side of the fence. Hanging baskets, wall sconces, and other decorative pieces that might be planted and secured to walls are other options to consider for vertical gardening.

Woolly Pocket—Wallys

Here's a wonderful new wall-mounted product by Woolly Pockets. These handy wall containers are yet another way of gardening vertically. They're durable hinging containers that come in both indoor and outdoor variations. I love the fact that I can bring this special Wally inside my home so I can decorate my wall with plants.

You'll also feel good knowing that they're made of 100 percent recycled plastic water bottles. Wallys are no harder to hang than a framed picture, and you can plant anything in them, from houseplants to succulents, veggies, and herbs.

Wally Woolly Pockets are the fast way to a hanging garden.
(Courtesy of Woolly Pockets)

Mounting Pots

For those of you who like the look of terra-cotta—or happen to have a large collection—consider mounting them on an outdoor wall. You can mount pots by using special circular wall sconces that attach to the wall; the pot slips into a ring holder.

You can also screw wall mounts (clips) into a wall or other structure, and then clip the pot into them. You could also use these wall clips to attach terra-cotta pots to latticework that's mounted on a wall or house siding.

There are companies that make terra-cotta plant containers especially for wall mounting. They have a flat side that lies flush against the wall. This type of planter actually offers more root room for plants than the smaller, round pots.

The Least You Need to Know

- Thinking vertically brings new possibilities to what can be grown in a small space.
- To provide the right climbing structure, you should know what type of climbing plant you're purchasing.
- You can use a living tree as a climbing structure if you choose the vining plants carefully.
- Vegetables grown vertically are often healthier and have a higher yield than those growing on the ground.
- Vertical gardening isn't just about plants climbing "up." You can also garden "down" by using trailing plants. You can also attach nonclimbing plants to walls and fences. It's about getting creative about all vertical structures!

Small-Space Garden Themes

In this part we get to the heart of vegetables and great places to plant them. We've got instruction on how to make simple structures for growing your veggies up instead of out, as well as a chapter on fruit in your little landscape. This is also where we talk about flower gardens and borders and how to keep them interesting no matter what the season.

Small-space gardens are naturals for creating garden themes, and in Part 3 we get into some other themes we think you'll love.

We'll share with you some super-easy-care gardens like herb, rock, woodland, and wildlife gardens. If you need more gardening room, we'll show you how to remove some lawn or replace it entirely with something less labor and water intensive. We've included water features such as miniature ponds and wall fountains. Peruse this section for small-garden inspiration.

Small-Space Vegetables

In This Chapter

- Squeezing vegetables into a landscape
- Interplanting and succession planting
- Simple structures for vertical vegetables
- Dwarf vegetable varieties
- Grow a salsa garden in a strawberry jar

In our minds we tend to naturally separate vegetable crops and flower beds—probably because we imagine a commercial farm when we think of food crops. Well, we need to open up our imaginations! Urban and suburban gardeners everywhere are reevaluating what can be grown in small areas and planting everything and anything their hearts desire—including food.

The biggest difference between a traditional farming landscape and our own is that, to get the most out of our space, we have to let out plants intermingle. Many of us don't have room for separate flower and vegetable gardens. And even if we do, flowers and food make terrific small-space bedfellows.

In this chapter, we'll talk about growing food among your ornamentals, structures you can make to grow your vegetables vertically, and how even small spaces can flourish with fruit.

Eat Your Landscape

Edible plants are easily integrated into your existing landscaping. You can tuck edibles into every part of the yard, whether it's a perennial bed or under ornamental shrubs along the front of the house. Herbs are also natural candidates for edible landscaping. Below are examples of vegetables and herbs that'll fit easily into your landscape—and the list is by no means exhaustive.

Vegetables:

Lettuce	Collards	Peppers
Bulbing fennel	Peas	Rhubarb
Swiss chard	Parsnips	Garlic
Broccoli	Cabbage	Radishes
Carrots	Spinach	Beans
Artichoke	Eggplant	Leeks
Onions	Kale	Tomatoes

Herbs:

Lavender	Chives	Dill
Thyme	Oregano	Parsley
Rosemary	Thyme	Chamomile
Sage	Basil	Marjoram

Plant a Food and Flower Border

Here's an excellent solution for anyone who wants to grow flowers and food in a small area. It's easy to plant and easy to maintain. All you need is a 2' × 5' border that's in a lightly shaded area of the yard. It doesn't have to be that exact size. But I'm referring to a border that often runs alongside a cement driveway and the boundary fence or one that's been created with thin boards, brick, or other material next to the lawn. Head to your local nursery in early spring and pick up: six onion sets (baby onions already growing) and four butter-head lettuce plants. Also pick two 1-gallon pansies or impatiens, fifteen 4" Johnny-jump-ups, and five 4" sweet alyssums.

Before planting the border bed, add a little bit of fresh garden soil or compost. First plant the onion sets in the back, 6" apart. Then plant the two pansies or impatiens in the middle area, about 18" apart. Place the four lettuces at the front of the bed, 8" apart. Now fill in the rest of the bed by planting the Johnny-jump-ups in groups of five in random areas of the bed, and the alyssums spread out at one end of the bed 6" apart. You could also intersperse the alyssums throughout the bed if you'd like.

All of these plants grow well in light shade and enjoy the cooler temperatures of spring. Harvest the lettuce leaves by taking the outside leaves first, leaving a few in the middle to continue growing. Harvest time for the onions will be determined by your zone as well as the variety that's available in your area.

Who says you can't plant food in your flower border?

Get Intensive with Interplanting

Interplanting is another space-saving technique that follows along the same premise as stacking the garden in a flower border—but this time with vegetables. When you're interplanting crops, you want to keep some general principles in mind. You want to be sure that the crops need nearly the same amount of sunlight, water, and soil preference. Much later, you want to think about mixing shorter plants with taller ones, such as peas or runner beans (tall) and lettuce (short).

TIP THYME

Plants have different root growth patterns. They can be shallow rooted, medium rooted, or deep rooted. The idea is to plant them so they won't compete directly with each other by combining different root growth patterns.

Corn, broccoli, spinach, cabbage, and lettuce are all shallow-rooted plants. Cucumbers, turnips, beans, summer squash, carrots, and peas are medium rooted. Tomatoes, asparagus, winter squash (including pumpkin), and parsnips are deep rooted.

You can choose to bring in some color (and pollinating insects) by planting short annuals, like marigolds or nasturtiums, with the taller veggies. Another way to use this intensive technique is to grow fast-maturing crops in with slow-growing ones. For example, plant Brussels sprouts (slow growing) with radishes or beets (fast growing). Carrots interplanted with radishes is a popular combination.

PLANTING PITFALL

Plants that belong to the same family make for an easy target for plant-specific pests if they're located in the same area. For this reason, don't pair up tomatoes, potatoes, peppers, and eggplant. The Colorado potato beetle finds all of these delicious.

Plant your tomatoes and corn away from one another because the tomato fruitworm is also known as a corn earworm. And squash, cucumbers, pumpkins, and melons share the same enemy: the pickleworm.

Carrots are the turtles of the garden world and, just about the time that the radishes are ready to harvest, the carrots' sleepy little greens are ready to be thinned out. Combos like corn and beans make good sense because the beans fix nitrogen in their roots—bringing nutrition to the soil, while corn is a heavy feeder and is busy sucking the life out of the soil.

You could also plant a cool-season vegetable at the tail end of the early spring season with a warm-season vegetable. As the cool season is coming to an end and those crops are being harvested, the warm-season ones will be ramping up for the summer. Whether you interplant vegetables in a border, raised bed, or in containers, the basic principles remain the same. In all cases, you'll get the greatest amount of harvest in the smallest of spaces.

Succession Planting

Succession planting means two things. The first is my hands-down favorite vegetable growing plan. It assures you a steady, continuous harvest as opposed to everything maturing at once. Let's say it's early spring and you're planting lettuce. You plant the first row (or container, whatever) of seeds or seedlings. Then simply plant the next group about two weeks later. There isn't an exact time span in between; just play with it so the harvest becomes tailored to how often you're consuming the vegetables.

As the cool-season (spring) crops are harvested, plant some warm-season vegetables such as green beans in their place. Be sure to stagger that crop, as well. Then, as the summer comes to a close, plant lettuce once again for the fall.

The thing to remember is that not all vegetables are candidates for succession planting. This isn't a good technique for long-season crops that take a long time to mature, such as tomatoes, peppers, and eggplant. It's great for quick-maturing vegetables such as lettuce, radishes, cabbage, and bush beans.

Vegetables in Hanging Baskets

Like any container, hanging baskets can be excellent for growing vegetables. This is wonderful for urban gardeners using mostly containers, but suburbanites often have baskets hanging under the eaves of their home. Please take advantage of this extra vegetable space! Some vegetables are especially well suited to this environment.

Lettuce, for instance, not only thrives in baskets, but looks gorgeous to boot. Plant a couple of different varieties for color and add some flowers or an herb or two. Don't be afraid to plant it full. You can just plant the top of the basket or cut holes in the liner and plant in the side, too—it's a stunning effect. Most people will comment on its beauty but never realize the basket is loaded with vegetables.

TIP THYME

Vegetables that grow well in part shade are primarily those that are grown for their leaves, such as lettuce, spinach, and Swiss chard.

Cherry tomato plants, chives, mustard greens, cabbage, and many herbs are naturals for hanging baskets, as are the ever-popular strawberry plants. In fact, while those strawberry jars look interesting, I've never had much luck with them; they couldn't come close to the strawberries growing in my baskets.

Have your crops pull double duty both as food and as an ornamental plant.

Soil-Bag Planting

Here's one of my favorite ideas for getting started vegetable gardening in very little space. It's called soil-bag planting. This no-dig method is the fastest way to get a vegetable garden: a soil bag can be planted in under 60 seconds (I clocked it). Because you're planting directly into a bag of topsoil, it's easy, inexpensive, and temporary. You're not committed to anything but the season.

One reason to give this method a go is if you can't find the time to build a proper bed—or you're living in a temporary home. It's also a nice warm-up if you feel intimidated by the whole idea of figuring out the size and structure of a garden bed, or if finding the perfect spot in your yard seems beyond all hope at the moment.

A spot in your yard may be just right for growing veggies, but what passes for dirt in that spot gives garden soil a bad name. This is one of the best ideas for landscape areas that are filled with rock, such as that lava rock from the '70s. Just drop a couple of soil bags there and plant to your little heart's desire.

What you'll need:

1 large bag of garden soil

Vegetable seedlings

Scissors

Access to water

What you'll do:

1. With one of the broad sides of the bag facing up, make three, 12" slices into that side with the scissors—this will be the bottom of the planter so it'll have drainage.

2. Lay the soil bag sliced side down in the area that you want to make your vegetable bed.

3. Cut a large, rectangular piece of plastic off of the top of the soil bag.

4. Dig some holes in the soil the size of the seedling containers, place your plants into them, and water.

If you like, you can also start seeds in the bags this way instead of using plant starts. During the growing season, feel free to mulch the soil bag beds with compost, grass clippings, etc. The plants will benefit from a little spoiling and it'll help your bed in the long run. If you want to hide the soil bags for aesthetic or deceptive reasons, mulch the bags with enough straw or hay to cover them.

When planting tomato starts, use one bag per tomato plant to get the best results, or put several pepper plants in one bag. At the end of the growing season, pull the plastic out of the bedding area and arrange the soil (and the added amendments). This will help enhance any lousy soil that was underneath the bags in the first place.

The fastest raised bed in town.

Structures for Vertical Veggies

In reality, you can use any upright climbing structure for a climbing vegetable such as ladders, trellises, old gates, and fences. But because vegetables are typically grown as annuals (for just one season), they're often rotated with other vegetable varieties after they've been harvested. So it makes sense to use temporary structures that you can move and store depending on what you've got planted in the garden during any given season.

TIP THYME

Are you gardening on a balcony or another apartment-sized place? Plant your veggies in rectangular troughs or containers. Situate a simple trellis at the back of the trough to take advantage of the growing space above it.

There are many clever ways to grow vegetables vertically, such as using a tepee trellis, stakes, cages, fence trellis, and an A-frame trellis.

Make a Tepee Trellis

A tepee trellis is a stand-alone structure made of bamboo poles or another long, slender wood. It's especially handy for growing pole (runner) beans, whether they're a green bean variety such as Kentucky Wonder Pole or a shelling (drying) type such as Speckled Cranberry. You can also grow lima (butterbean), fava (broad), and soy (edamame) beans up a tepee trellis.

These beans are true vines—they love nothing more than to climb whatever you put in front of them. Garden peas, nasturtiums, black-eyed Susan vines, and fragrant sweet pea flowers are also good contenders for a tepee trellis.

This simple, upright structure is perfect for small, urban, and suburban gardens, and it's easily modified for apartment gardening by placing a shorter version inside a half wine barrel.

PLANTING PITFALL

Some beans come in both a bush and clinging variety, such as Kentucky Wonder Beans. When planting a trellis with beans, be certain that you have a climbing variety.

The tepee trellis is more than just a practical way to grow beans, peas, and other vining plants—they're always a hit with the kids. In fact, with a simple variation, a tepee trellis can be turned into a fort! And building the tepee structure is so easy that even kids can build one.

What you'll need:

6–8 poles of bamboo, thin scrap lumber, or thick branches, 6'-8' long

Roll of twine, thin rope, jute, or wire

Pole, runner bean seeds, or any other twining plant seeds.

What you'll do:

1. Lay all of the poles evenly on the ground.

2. Use the twine or jute to lash them together about 1' from the top of the poles.

3. Stand the poles up and spread them out individually and at even intervals—Indian tepee style. The structure should be standing on its own.

4. Sink the bottom of the poles about 4-6" deep into the ground for added stability. The tepee only has to be lightly secure as you won't be growing heavy vegetables up this structure.

5. Plant four to six of your choice of runner beans around the base of each pole.

Keep the planted area wet to encourage seeds sprouting. The beans then grow up the poles, forming a live cover around all the structure.

Other excellent plants to grow up the poles are peas, sweet pea flowers, miniature pumpkins, scarlet runner beans, and birdhouse gourds. By making a "door" between two of the poles, the trellis becomes an instant kid's garden fort. Just widen the gap between two of the poles *before* you plant any seeds at the bottom of the poles. Add some straw on the ground inside the tepee for a comfortable sitting area—and post a sign with a strict warning: NO WRESTLING. Yet it could make a great make-out place for the teenagers … just sayin'.

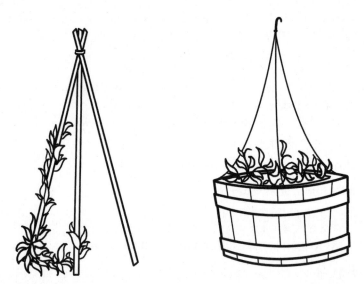

Tepees are perfect for garden beds, but containers can have trellises, too.

*A tepee trellis can become a simple kid's fort while
it's supporting your climbing veggies.*
(Courtesy of Brenda Haas)

Staking and Caging Tomatoes

Tomato plants generally fall into two categories: determinate and indeterminate. Determinate (bush) tomato plants are bred to stop growing usually somewhere around 3' to 4' tall. When flowers blossom at the tips of the branches, the plant has reached its full height.

The *fruit* of a determinate tomato plant ripens all at once. Because of this, this type of tomato plant is useful for those who want to grow tomatoes for canning. Since many determinate plants stay on the short side, they can be ideal for the small-space gardener.

GARDEN GOSPEL

Among the gardening crowd, the term "fruit" is often used interchangeably with "vegetable." In fact, vegetable isn't a botanical term, but rather a culinary one. Botanically speaking, if the food in question is the seed-bearing part of the plant, then it's the fruit—although it's true that the tomato, though technically a fruit, is considered a vegetable in the kitchen.

Indeterminate tomatoes continue to grow for what seems like an eternity. Depending on the variety, they can grow from 6' to 20' tall. This type continues to produce tomatoes all growing season until a hard frost hits and stops them in their tracks. These plants are particularly desirable if you want a continuous harvest of slicing or salad tomatoes. Indeterminate tomatoes can be used for canning just like the determinates, but you may need a few more indeterminate plants so that you have plenty to can at any one time.

GARDEN GOSPEL

Did you know that you can hasten the ripening of the season's last tomatoes on an indeterminate vine by simply pruning the top off the plant? This last pruning should be done at the end of the growing season—about a month before the first frost. This technique sends the sugars that the plant has produced to the unripe fruit and brings them to maturity faster.

Caging or staking with poles is the easiest and fastest way to provide structures for vertical veggies such as tomatoes or peppers. While these plants need something to "climb," they're not true vines and should have their branches supported by being tied periodically to keep them upright.

Caging is the simplest way to support tomato plants and is the perfect solution for determinate plants. Tomato cages work well for the indeterminate, too, but staking seems to offer the best support for the vining types. Staking tomato plants is an excellent way to keep the plants upright and the fruit off of the ground.

You can use scrap wood, bamboo, or metal as stakes. You'll need something with which to tie the plants to the stake at regular intervals while they're growing. You can make ties with torn fabric, twist-ties, or plastic ties.

TIP THYME

Peppers are easier to care for if in cages, too. Pepper cages look just like tomato cages, but in miniature.

Staked indeterminate tomatoes are typically pruned about once a week to keep them focused on fruit production rather than unnecessary leaf production. The nonflowering stems or "suckers" that are found between the main stem and the leaf crotches are pruned off of the plant.

Pruning tomato plants also keeps them from becoming unnecessarily wide. This is my preferred method of keeping my tomatoes vertical. I can plant more tomatoes in any given area when I use the staking and pruning method.

You can find prefabricated wire cages at nurseries from $3 for the lightest ones, to $5 for the cages made of a heavier and sturdier gauge wire. The new kids on the block are the commercially available "lifetime" cages. These hefty supports can run into the $20 to $30 range.

Whether you stake or cage tomatoes is a personal preference, but determinate tomato varieties are the ones most easily caged.
(Courtesy of Teresa Soule)

Make a Sturdy Tomato Cage

If you like the idea of lifetime cages but don't like the heavy price tag, make some super sturdy cages yourself. In reality, you could use nearly any fencing material to fabricate a tomato cage. But one of the strongest we've seen are those made of concrete reinforcing wire. Aside from durability, we like the fact that it'll have 6" mesh openings—the perfect size for easy tomato harvesting.

What you'll need:

Small bolt cutters

Work gloves

5'–6' of concrete reinforcing wire (5' will make an 18" cage; a 6' length will make a 2' cage)

You can find concrete reinforcing wire at your local home improvement center or hardware store. Word of warning: it's much easier to create these cages with a helper, if only because freshly unrolled wire likes to roll itself back up. If that wire snaps back while you're working with it, you're in for a bad day. So get someone to help out, and don your work gloves so you don't cut your hands.

What you'll do:

1. Have your helper stand on the end of the wire and roll a length of it out. Using the bolt cutters, cut a 5' or 6' piece of wire. Leave some individual strands sticking out so you can use them as hooks later.

2. Depending on your strength (this stuff is stiff), you may want to have your helper give you a hand bending the wire into a cylinder.

3. Bend the wires that you left sticking out over the wire on the opposite end to attach the ends together.

4. Be sure to cut off any extra wire that's protruding. You want to bend the point toward the inside of the cage and have the point end up facing down. You don't want to get cut arranging the cage over the plant or when you're harvesting tomatoes.

5. At this point, the cage isn't going to have the shape it should have. You need to work around the cage and just shape it with your hands until it's nicely cylindrical.

6. Okay, do you see the last circular wire that goes around the bottom of the cage horizontally? Cut that off so that there are long stakes at the bottom. Press the stakes deep into the ground for stability.

This wire is really strong and the stakes should be about 12" long, so you don't usually need to support it with anything else. But if you feel that you need to do so, after you've placed the cage over the tomato plant, drive some short stakes into the ground and use wire or twine to tie the stakes to the cage.

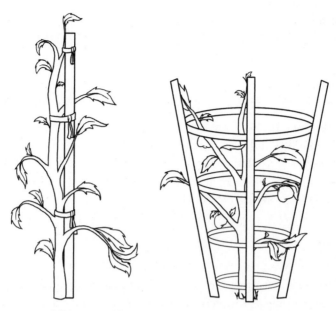

Make yourself a tomato cage that lasts a lifetime!

Make Your Own Fence Trellis

I use a couple of different types of fence trellising. The first one is one of my favorite ways to grow plants such as tomatoes, which are actually leaners as opposed to true climbers.

What you'll need:

Hammer

2 2' × 2' stakes or T-posts

Twine, heavy wire, strong netting, or fencing

Screw gun

Screws (any length)

What you'll do:

This fence trellis structure is created by using twine, wire, or fencing which attaches horizontally at both ends of two stakes hammered into the soil.

1. Hammer the stakes as support posts into the soil at 10' to 12' intervals. The number of stakes is up to you and how long you'd like to make the trellis. It can be as short as just two support posts and up from there.

2. Place the screws into the stakes at 4" to 6" intervals down the wood. Do this with each piece of wood that you hammered into the ground.

   The distance between the screws is going to depend on what will be growing up the trellis. If you're using twine or wire and want to support tomato plants, then stay within the 4"–6" range. If you're planting peas or beans, then netting would be your best choice and you can use fewer screws because you only need enough to secure the netting.

3. Attach your wire, netting, or twine to the screws on each supporting post. Then plant!

Leaner-type climbing veggies such as tomatoes will need to be physically secured to the wire or twine as they grow. Like everything else, you can modify this for vegetables such as garden peas, hops, and beans by using wire mesh or netting between the stakes. Since these plants will climb on their own, no attaching is required on your part. Just aim the seedlings in the right direction when they're a couple of inches tall.

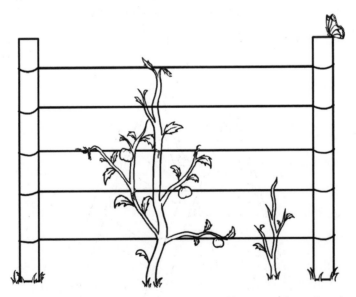

Using a fence trellis to support vertical vegetables is a gardener favorite.

A-Frame Structures

If you aren't familiar with an A-frame structure, it's the same design as a folding ladder. Now picture it shorter and wider. A-frame structures are used to support the heavier vegetable crops like melons, birdhouse gourds, cucumbers, zucchini, and small pumpkins. It does the work of two trellises because it has two sides for the plants to climb up and over.

TIP THYME

If you have a couple of garden beds with just a walkway between them, try placing one side of an A-frame trellis in one bed and the other side in the other bed. This makes use of the airspace above the walkway.

When planting vegetables such as small melons on an A-frame structure, at some point, the growing fruit will have to be supported or it'll detach from the vine before it's fully mature and ready to be harvested. The best way to do this is to use a piece of netting or pantyhose as a makeshift sling. The idea is to wrap the material under the immature fruit and gather the ends together and tie it to part of the A-frame.

An old wooden ladder is a wonderful garage sale find and makes an instant A-frame support for peas, cucumbers, and beans. Help the climbing plants along by wrapping wire, twine, or string up the ladder. It's a good idea to sink the legs into the ground several inches to help hold it in place.

Even small melons, small pumpkins, and other squash can be grown on an A-frame structure with the help of some creative slings to support growing fruit.

Warm-Season Vegetables

When we refer to "warm-season" vegetables, we're talking about those vegetables that grow all through the warm months. Warm-season vegetables find their sweet spot when temperatures are above 60 degrees. They're usually planted during the middle to late spring or the beginning of summer, depending on how many days it takes for the individual variety to mature. In any case, these are the plants that need to take advantage of the sunny, warm days of summer.

Choosing any warm-season vegetable variety isn't enough, though. While you're deciding on which tomato or eggplant to plant, be sure to check out how many days each variety needs for the vegetables to fully develop and become ready for harvest.

Here's where it's handy to know your growing zone (USDA Hardiness Zones) and heat zone (AHS Heat Map). If you still aren't sure how many warm days you have, contact your local cooperative extension office. Just be sure the vegetable's days to maturity are about the same number of warm days in your area.

Some vegetables are going to fall into a general category of warm or cool season. However, sometimes they'll overlap due to the variety, the USDA zone, or the micro-climate. Here are some examples of warm-season crops:

Peppers	Cucumbers	Sweet potatoes
Tomatoes	Melons	Pumpkin (winter squash)
Summer squash	Pole beans	Watermelon
Tomatillos	Bush beans	Cantaloupe
Corn	Zucchini	New Zealand spinach
Okra	Eggplant	

Cool-Season Vegetables

Cool-season crops can be grown during two seasons; spring and fall. They need temperatures to hang around 40 to 60 degrees. After you've experimented a season or three, you may find that your cool-weather lovers prefer one season to another in your zone.

Here in the San Francisco Bay Area, I have better luck with cilantro and broccoli not bolting when I plant them at the end of summer as a fall crop. I can certainly plant them in the late winter/early spring, but when our weather turns warm it usually does so with a vengeance, and I find that both of these crops bolt quickly in the spring.

Some varieties tolerate frost well, so not all cool-season vegetables are just for spring and fall. Some, like broccoli and Brussels sprouts, can grow well into—and even through—the winter, with a little help from cold frames, hoop houses, and mulch.

Cool-season vegetables include the following:

Carrots	Lettuce	Turnips
Endive	Swiss chard	Cilantro
Cauliflower	Peas	Kale
Kohlrabi	Beets	Brussels sprouts
Leeks	Radicchio	Rhubarb
Cabbage	Endive	Asparagus
Spinach	Radish	

Miniature Vegetable Varieties

Depending on how small your garden space is, you'll be able to grow many or any of these vegetables just in their regular size. Vertical gardening techniques or pruning will help grow some traditional varieties. Keep your eyes open for miniature (dwarf) vegetable varieties.

By no means am I suggesting that dwarfs are the only types you can grow in a small-space garden. In fact, if you want naturally compact snap beans, all you have to do is to look for the bush as opposed to the pole varieties. But planting some miniature or dwarf versions of these plants just might give you the room to squeeze in more vegetables. And I just happen to have handy some dwarf-sized vegetable suggestions:

Dwarf tomatoes:

- Early Girl Bush: 4" fruit, 63 days to harvest
- Better Bush Improved: 4" fruit, 68 days to harvest

- Small Fry: 1" fruit, 72 days to harvest

- Yellow Canary: $1\frac{1}{4}$" fruit, 55 days to harvest

- Red Robin: $1\frac{1}{2}$" fruit, 55 days to harvest

- Tiny Tim: 1" fruit, 45 days to harvest

- Patio Bush: $2\frac{1}{2}$" fruit, 65 days to harvest

- Cherry Gold: 1" fruit, 45 days to harvest

- Window Box Roma: 2–$2\frac{1}{2}$" fruit, 70 day to harvest

- Pixie Hybrid II: $1\frac{1}{4}$" fruit, 52 days to harvest

Dwarf cucumbers:

- Bush Pickle: 4" fruit, 45 days to harvest

- H-19 Little Leaf: 7" fruit, 60 days to harvest

- Bush Crop: 6–8" fruit, 55 days to harvest

- Spacemaster: 7–8" fruit, 60 days to harvest

- Salad Bush: 8" fruit, 57 days to harvest

Dwarf peppers:

- Mirasol (hot): 3" fruit, 90 days to harvest

- Jingle Bells (sweet): $1\frac{1}{4}$"–2" fruit, 60 days to harvest

- Bull Nose Bell (sweet): $2\frac{1}{2}$"–$3\frac{1}{2}$" fruit, 55–80 days to harvest

- Albino: $2\frac{1}{4}$" fruit, 75–80 days to harvest

- Baby Belle: 2–$2\frac{1}{2}$" fruit, 68 days to harvest

Dwarf pumpkin:

- Munchkin: 3"–4" fruit, 100 days to harvest

- Baby Boo: 2"–3" (white) fruit, 95 days to harvest

- Pumpkin Hooligan F1: 3"–4" fruit, 90 days to harvest

- Mini Jack: 2"–3" fruit, 95 days to harvest

- Lil Pump-Ke-Mon: $5\frac{1}{2}$" fruit, 100 days to harvest

Dwarf melons:

- Sugar Baby (watermelon): 6–10 pounds, 85 days to harvest

- Minnesota Midget (cantaloupe): 1–2 pounds, 60–75 days to harvest

- Golden Midget (watermelon): 3 pounds, 70 days to harvest

- Yellow Doll (watermelon): 7 pounds, 68 days to harvest

Dwarf summer squash:

- Gold Rush (zucchini): 8" fruit, 55 days to harvest

- Peter Pan (scallop): 4" fruit, 49 days to harvest

- Sunburst (scallop): 2"–3" fruit, 60 days to harvest

- Dwarf Summer Crookneck: 10" fruit, 50 days to harvest

Dwarf eggplant:

- Fairy Tale: 4"–6" fruit, 63 days to harvest

- Orlando: 4" fruit, 60 days to harvest

- Bambino (Baby Bell): 1" fruit, 50–60 days to harvest

- Bride Asian: 8" fruit, 75 days to harvest

Herbs

To be honest with you, I haven't found an herb yet that I haven't been able to grow both in containers and spaces with very little square footage. They're easygoing food plants and some of the most fragrant. To be certain that the fragrance is released, I purposefully plant them in areas near walkways and along bed edges so that people accidentally step on them. If your garden visitors don't seem to get any underfoot, just run your hand along them as you pass by.

Even if you have an herb garden elsewhere in your yard, it pays to have some of them potted up near the kitchen door so that you can easily step out and harvest fresh leaves for culinary dishes.

Herbs are pretty flexible when it comes to the sun. The majority of them, including rosemary, sage, and basil, thrive in full sun, but I've found that they tolerate light shade without a problem. This makes it a little easier to save some of the brightest areas of the yard for fruiting vegetables that truly need to soak up the sunshine. We'll get more into herb gardens in Chapter 12.

Grow a Salsa Garden in a Strawberry Jar

Strawberry jars are urn-shaped containers that have openings or "pockets" on the sides. Originally, they were made for growing strawberries as the jar structure allows the crown of the plant to stay above the soil line, which is important for the plant.

The design also keeps the fruit off of the ground. It turns out these handy jars are excellent for all kinds of planting themes such as growing a salsa garden on your patio or deck.

What you'll need:

1 strawberry jar (terra-cotta or plastic)—or a regular planting container as an alternative.

Potting soil

Hand trowel

1 bush tomato plant (a cherry or patio tomato)

1 jalapeño pepper plant

1 or 2 cilantro plants

1 or 2 chive plants

1 or 2 basil plants

You'll find that most strawberry jars are made of terra-cotta. As I mentioned earlier, while these containers are completely acceptable, they tend to dry out easily and you may have to stay on top of them as far as watering goes. If you can find strawberry jars made of plastic, you won't have to water as often because they retain moisture longer than their clay counterparts.

About the tomato plants: You're looking for a bush (determinate) variety as opposed to the vining (indeterminate) type. The cherry and patio varieties happen to stay a little smaller and like living in containers.

1. Fill the strawberry jar with potting soil until it reaches the first set of pockets. Tamp down the soil firmly with your hand.

2. Gently knock a few of your choice of herbs (or peppers) out of their little containers. Planting each herb one at a time, push each root ball through one of the pockets guiding it on the inside of the pot with your other hand.

3. Add more potting soil to the jar and fill it up to the next set of pockets. Plant more herbs and add more soil.

4. When the soil level is about three quarters of the way up the jar, you'll slide your patio tomato out of its container and plant it into the top of the strawberry jar.

5. Finish by filling up the rest of the jar and watering it gently, but thoroughly. Place your salsa garden in an area that receives six to eight hours of direct (full) sun.

Be sure to keep the soil in your newly planted garden moist for the first couple of weeks while the roots take hold. If you don't have a strawberry jar substitute it with a large, regular flower pot. Half barrels make exceptional containers for salsa gardens, too.

The Least You Need to Know

- You don't need a separate vegetable bed. Feel free to plant food in your ornamental landscaping, too.
- Use interplanting and succession-planting techniques to get the most harvest out of a small space.
- Knowing your zone and looking at the AHS heat map will go a long way in helping you decide when to plant vegetables in your area.
- Dwarf varieties make it super easy to grow vegetables in containers.

Fruit in Your Landscape

In This Chapter

- How fruit fits into small gardens
- Fruit for containers
- What is a fruit cocktail tree?
- Espalier basics

Have you fantasized about picking your own fruit and eating it fresh from the tree? Why dream about it when you can have a micro-orchard today? Like vegetables, fruit can be grown successfully in small spaces, especially when you plant the smaller varieties like columnar, dwarf, and double- or triple-grafted trees. Using space-saving techniques such as espalier and festooning will also allow you to squeeze in a special fruit here and there.

Micro-Orchards

When it comes to planting fruit trees, you have more choices than you think. Small gardens won't be able to handle standard-sized fruit trees, but there's always the semidwarf and dwarf varieties. The shorter versions are created by grafting standard cultivars on dwarfed rootstock.

Traditional fruit trees tend to grow to at least 20' tall. Semidwarf trees will reach about 15' tall, and a dwarf variety grows to a short 10'. So depending on just how small your small space is, you may be able to have a dwarf apple tree or two in your front or back yard. Or try a columnar apple that's tailor-made for the tiniest places, as well as containers.

There are various dwarf citrus available, as well as peaches, nectarines, and pomegranates. Other fruits grown in their standard form—such as grapes, blueberries, and cane berries—can often be kept in check with periodic pruning.

It bears repeating: before you purchase fruit trees, shrubs, or canes, be sure they're the right varieties for your area. This is especially important for those fruits (such as apples and peaches) that need some chilling time. For the most part, if you find them at your local nursery, they're the right ones. It doesn't hurt to double-check, though, especially if you're mail ordering from a catalog or online.

Columnar Apple Trees

God bless the experimenters. Just when you thought it couldn't get any better than the dwarf apple varieties, someone developed a willowy version: the columnar or colonnade. Columnar apple trees are the answer to micro–apple orchards.

These guys are smaller and thinner than the semidwarf apples trees—much thinner. They have some wonderful benefits over their full-size cousins. Columnars have a bottle brush shape, short branches, and grow straight up. Actually, the branches are more like "branch-lets" and fruiting spurs. This slender design allows plenty of opportunity to try every variety.

Because they only grow 8' to 10' tall and 2' wide, they can be grown in the smallest of yards. You can practically stack them! Apartment and condo dwellers will be happy to know they make perfect potted trees, as well.

Columnar apples are early producers and have the ability to grow fruit the first year. If that isn't enough, they bear normal-sized apples, and will produce fruit for about 20 years. When planted in a row, they can give a stately look to an otherwise boring good-neighbor fence or wall. These micro–fruit trees are an excellent complement to an edible landscape.

There are three things you should know about these trees. First, you may need to thin the apples a bit before they fully develop to help the tree support the weight of the maturing fruit.

Second, you're going to need two of them. Columnars will only produce fruit if they're cross-pollinated by two varieties of apple. So plant them about 2' apart or line them up in whisky barrels. Third, the price tag is a little heavier than for a regular dwarf or semidwarf apple tree. That said, like all trees, if you order them as bare-root plants in the winter, instead of purchasing them in containers during spring or summer, you'll save some dollars.

Small-space gardeners can actually have an apple orchard using columnar apple trees.

Columnars (Colonnade) apple tree varieties:

- Golden Sentinel: Yellow fruit, ripens in midseason
- Scarlet Sentinel: Green-yellow fruit, red blush, ripens in midseason
- Northpole: Red fruit, ripens early midseason
- Ultra Spire: Red fruit, yellow blush, ripens midseason
- Crimson Spire: Red fruit, ripens late midseason
- Emerald Spire: Green fruit, gold blush, ripens midseason

Citrus

Dwarf citrus trees are always popular, but many of them, such as oranges and lemons, won't do well year-round much after zone 9. That said, some citrus such as mandarins can take a little bite of frost. If your zone is below a 9, it's easy to plant citrus into containers and just pull it into the house for the winter. When planted in the ground, dwarf citrus might grow anywhere from 8' to 12' tall, but in a container they stay much smaller.

> **TIP THYME**
>
> For an organic boost, your used coffee grounds are a welcome addition to the container. Many coffee houses such as Starbucks will have used coffee grounds bagged up and ready for your plants.

If your dwarf has been soaking up the backyard sun for several months, it's best to bring it onto the porch under an overhang for a couple of weeks. This will let the dwarf citrus become used to a shady (and covered) environment gradually. Do the reverse about two weeks before you take it back outdoors in the spring.

All citrus love the sun, so if you bring your tree indoors, be sure to place it near a window that has a southern exposure (away from direct heat). The next best place would be a western exposure, but the more sun exposure it has, the better it'll grow and produce. Citrus want their soil on the acidic side, so use an appropriate fertilizer about every four to six weeks.

Popular citrus trees:

- Improved Meyer Lemon
- Kaffir Lime
- Blood Orange
- Key Lime
- Mandarin Oranges
- Kumquat

Peaches and Nectarines

Both dwarf peaches and nectarines grow about 5' to 6' tall and like to be situated in full sun. They dislike strong winds, so try to find a protected spot. They like their feet in loam or sandy-loam soil, so if your soil is clay, you're better off planting them in wine half-barrels or a raised bed. Peaches and nectarines produce an amazing amount of fruit, so when the new fruits are about 1 inch, remove some of them so that those remaining are around 8" to 10" apart.

Standard-sized peach and nectarine trees are pruned heavily, but the dwarf types can get away with less. That said, some good pruning will encourage the fruit to be produced all over the tree branches instead of just at the tips—which may cause them to break. Most (though not all) peach and nectarine trees have the additional benefit of being self-pollinating. Which means you can get away with planting one and still have fruit.

Dwarf peach varieties:

- Golden Glory: 5' tall
- Garden Pride: 4'–6' tall
- Garden Gold: 6' tall
- Southern Sweet: 4'–5' tall
- Honey Babe: 4'–6' tall
- El Dorado: 4–5' tall
- Bonanza II: 5' tall
- Pix Zee: 5–9' tall

Dwarf nectarine varieties:

- Nectar Babe: 5'–6' tall
- Garden Delight: 6' tall
- Golden Prolific: 5' tall
- Red Sunset: 5' tall
- Southern Belle: 4'–5' tall
- Goldmine: 3'–4' tall
- Necta Zee: 5' tall

Pomegranates

Look for dwarf pomegranate varieties State Fair and Nana that grow to a slight 3' tall, making them prime candidates for small spaces. If the fruit doesn't attract you, the tree's decorative features will. Pomegranate flowers are anywhere from orange-red, pink, and even coral striped—and stunning. New leaves come in bronze colored and turn bright green when they're mature. During the fall, the leaves change from bright green to yellow.

As sun worshippers, pomegranates like to be situated in full sun. They thrive in areas that have hot summers and short bursts of frost during winter. Like most plants, they appreciate good garden soil, but will survive just fine in soils that are less than perfect.

Pomegranate pruning should be done in either the early spring or late summer. If you plant pomegranates, bone up on how to prune them. Careful pruning is important because the blossoms and fruits form at the tip of the current year's growth. The fruit is usually harvested a little on the early side (when they turn red) because they tend to split if they're left on the branch until they're fully ripe.

Multigrafted Fruit Trees

You may be familiar with the fact that nurserymen and gardeners commonly graft branches of one type of tree to a different tree trunk. They do this for various reasons. Sometimes a sturdy rootstock is chosen along with a different plant that has desirable flowers or fruit. The *scion* cut from the desirable plant is then grafted onto the rootstock, which creates a sturdier or more versatile plant.

DEFINITION

The **scion** is a plant cutting that's selected to be the "top" or desirable half of the grafting set. It's the part that we've chosen to be the main focus of the end product. The other part of that unit is the rootstock, which is visually unimportant.

Multigrafting for a variety of fruit is a creative way to have several fruits produce on the same tree. These are sometimes referred to as "fruit cocktail" trees. For instance, you could have a four-in-one apple tree with Fuji, Gala, Golden Delicious, and Red Delicious apple branches grafted onto the same tree trunk. The same can be done with cherry, peach, plum, pear, and citrus.

The grafts are all created by using plants within the same genus. For instance, peaches and apricots belong to the same genus, *Prunus*, so they could be multigrafted. But did you know that plums and nectarines belong to this genus as well, so they could be grafted alongside the first two? You'll find fruit cocktail trees that have as little as two fruit varieties grafted on or as many as six.

We small-space gardeners are indebted to those who pioneered these trees, because we're prepared to take full advantage. Not only do they make it easier to have multiple fruit varieties in a compact space, but they allow for an extended harvest!

Grafted fruit trees mean you can have three pear varieties on one tree!
(Photo courtesy of Stark Bros Nurseries & Orchards Co.)

Entertaining Espalier

As we talked about in Chapter 8, espalier is a term that describes pruning techniques that train dwarf trees or shrubs into a shape not only for the sake of design, but to keep the tree flat against a wall or fence for small gardens. Technically, espalier describes an actual shape achieved by pruning and guiding main branches. But gardeners often refer to this pruning technique as espalier, even if the shape isn't that of a traditional form.

Fruit trees can be espaliered against a trellis or strung wires that are secured to the wall or fence. Horizontal wires or wood are spaced about 12" to 18" apart from each other. Specific branches are trained along the wires, and any extra growth that doesn't follow the guide is trimmed off.

There are other tree forms aside from the espalier, but the principle is the same. Aside from choosing a shape just because it tickles your fancy, you should know that some shapes work well for some fruits and not as well for others. You want a shape that's specific to how a particular fruit grows on that tree. For instance, the shapes espalier, cordon, palmette, and stepover are perfectly suited to apples and pears. The stone fruit trees, such as peaches, nectarines, and plums, should be pruned into a fan or bush shape.

If you're pruning your fruit into anything other than a bush (or other free-form shape), consider that forms such as espalier take some commitment to get the form right and can require pruning for several weeks as opposed to once a year. But if you're game, fruit trees pruned into classic shapes in the garden make unique and beautiful focal points.

But first things first. Before you purchase a tree and choose a shape, keep in mind that you may need more than one. Some fruits are self-pollinating and are perfectly happy living—and producing—all by themselves. But many of them need another tree or shrub in close proximity for cross-pollination to occur and for you to have some delicious fruit. You'll need to have that information on the tree(s) you'd like to plant to be sure that you have the space for more than one individual.

Blueberries

As far as fruiting shrubs go, blueberries are one of my favorite candidates for small-space gardening. They provide a tasty treat for pies, cakes, cookies, muffins, pancakes, and to top off ice cream. Due to their beautiful red or yellow fall foliage and sweet pink and white flowers, they pull double duty as an attractive landscape plant, too.

TIP THYME

Most blueberry shrubs are deciduous. But depending on the variety and your zone, some evergreen varieties such as Sunshine Blue remain clothed for the year.

Blueberries can hold their own as a single foundation plant in a border, or they can be allowed to grow together to create a hedge. Suburbanites may find that they can grow the Highbush varieties that grow to about 8' tall, while the Southern Highbush types may see 6'.

Most of you will be interested in the dwarf varieties, which are compact and nicely shaped—like any other ornamental shrub. They'll reach about 1½' to 3' high when they're mature, and these miniatures are just as valuable as short hedges. One of the blueberry's best qualities is that the dwarfs do just as well living their whole lives in containers.

The happiest home for blueberry bushes is in full sun with wet feet. They like their roots to be cool, so these fruits like their water. Remember to add a little acidic fertilizer once a year (spring)—and not until their second year.

Like conifers and azaleas, blueberries like their soil a little on the acidic side, so fill containers with an azalea potting mix. If you're growing them in the ground, plant them near other sour soil lovers for simplicity's sake. Whether they're in containers or the ground, you can add other amendments such as used coffee grounds or peat to keep the pH low. Some varieties are self-fruitful and some need to cross-pollinate.

In either case, most blueberry growers will tell you that, to be certain to have bigger berries and a large harvest, you should plant two or three different varieties. Whether fruit ripens early, midway, or late in the season will depend on the plant you choose, so be sure to get the specifics when you purchase your blueberries.

Pick the berries when they turn a deep blue and harvest them every day while the fruits are coming ripe. The bluer the berry, the riper it is—and, yes, you're going to need bird netting if you want to keep them for yourself.

Small-space blueberry varieties:

- Earliblue: 4'–6' tall, June harvest

- Chippewa: 3'–5' tall, early to midsummer harvest

- Patriot: 4' tall, July harvest

- Spartan: 5'–6' tall, July harvest

- Sunshine Blue (evergreen): 3'–4' tall, early August to early September harvest

- Top Hat: 1½' tall, all-summer harvest

- Bluegold: 4' tall, July harvest

- Polaris: 4' tall, July harvest

- Northcountry: 3'–4' tall, July harvest

- Dwarf Northsky: 2'–3' tall, July harvest

- Northblue: 2'–3' tall, mid-June harvest

Strawberries

Strawberries are the perfect fruit for growing in containers—especially hanging ones. Let's talk in a little more detail about the queen of small-space fruit. The first thing to know about these sweet berries is that each variety falls into one of three categories:

- **June-bearing:** The berries are harvested as one big crop in late spring or early summer.

- **Everbearing:** Offers a double harvest; once in early summer and again in the fall.

- **Day neutral:** Main (largest) harvest in the early summer, but continue to produce berries lightly all the way till fall.

Then there are the little Alpine strawberries, which are in their own group (*Fragaria vesca*) and bear a small crop of little but fragrant berries all summer long. These guys make pretty ground cover in ornamental beds, thus creating an edible landscape.

Strawberries like their soil to be rich in organic matter, slightly acidic, and well draining. Most varieties appreciate full sun, but the alpines will tolerate light shade with no problem. Truth be told, my Quinalts have done just fine in light shade, too. Still, sun is best.

You want to plant them so that their roots are under the soil, but the crown (where the leaves come out) is sitting slightly above the soil line. Don't plant them flush with the soil line because it encourages crown rot.

Typically you'd plant strawberry starts about 12" apart in a bed. But in a container, I plant them slightly closer together. Gardeners often mulch the bed in order to keep the fruit from touching the ground while they're ripening.

Many gardeners practice another strawberry-growing ritual that you may struggle with, but it can pay off big time. When newly planted strawberries begin to flower, pinch the blossoms off and don't let them become pollinated. This allows all of the plant's energy to go to building a strong root system instead of spending that same energy on making blossoms and fruit that first year. The proof will be in the years that follow: high strawberry production—*plus!*

I'm not saying that if you don't pinch off the flowers you won't have berries in subsequent years, just that you'll have more of them and stronger plants if you put on your big-girl panties in that first year and do what you have to.

If you plant your berry plants in containers, go for a hanging basket, window box, kitchen colander, or tub. As I mentioned in Chapter 9, the terra-cotta strawberry pots are cute, but they dry out too quickly for my taste. Choose a variety of strawberry types to harvest from late spring all the way to early fall.

June-bearing strawberries:

- Allstar
- Earliglow
- Shuksan
- Guardian
- Hood
- Firecracker
- Camarosa
- Chandler
- Pugent Reliance
- Ranier
- Sequoia
- Brunswick
- Jewel
- Cornwallis
- Cabot

Day-neutral strawberries:

- Seascape
- Tristar
- Selva
- Tribute
- Albion
- Alinta
- Evie 2

Everbearing strawberries:

- Fort Laramie
- Ozark Beauty
- Quinault
- Arapahoe
- Bolero
- Calypso
- Flamenco

Alpine strawberries:

- Alpine Yellow
- Alpine White
- Mignonette
- Baron Solemacher
- Alexandria
- Rugen

Grapes

It may not have crossed your mind that grapes could be grown anywhere other than a vineyard. They actually tend to fit neatly into small-space gardens much the way that espaliers do. Grapes can be easily trained against a wall or fence and, in fact, cover a short cyclone fence beautifully.

The bright-green leaves turn a cyclone boundary fence into a lovely, fruit-producing living wall. Grapes also do well in large, deep containers and make a handsome statement when underplanted with a ground-hugging annual or perennial plant.

If you live in a mild winter region (like California), grapes are planted during the winter. If you live in an area that's a cooler region (say, deep snow), you'll want to wait until about three weeks before your frost date. Typically you'll find year-old, bare-root grapes at your local garden center.

Most gardeners plant grapes against a support of some kind such as a fence or arbor. Dig holes a foot to a foot and a half away from the support structure. If there's any top growth on the plant, cut it back so that it has two or three buds. Plant them about 8-10 inches apart in full sun and well-draining soil. You want the plants to lean slightly toward the supports, so position them at an angle. Usually, they're planted as deep as they were in their original containers. However, check with a local nursery because depending on your area, they're often planted deeper. Gently tease (pull and straighten) the roots so that they'll spread out inside their planting hole.

Grapes aren't heavy feeders, so they don't necessarily need extremely rich soil, but they do appreciate a moderately fertile one. It's best to water grapes at the soil line because their leaves are prone to fungal diseases. Drip irrigation is your best bet.

You'll want to prune the vines every year, not only to restrict the plant's size but because the fruit is produced on the new growth. Pruning the old wood to two or three buds will stimulate new growth.

Nearly all grape varieties are self-fruitful, so go ahead and plant just one as a focal point if you'd like. Just be sure that you choose the right variety for your area. Grapes fall into these three categories: European, American, and American Hybrids (crosses between American and European grapes).

The Least You Need to Know

- Multigrafting makes it possible to have six different fruits on one tree.
- Columnar apple trees allow you to have a true micro-orchard.
- Multigrafted dwarf fruit trees offer variety and extended harvest.
- Fruit trees lend themselves to specific espalier shapes, depending on the fruit's growth habit.

Flower Gardens and Borders

In This Chapter

- The differences between annuals, biennials, and perennials
- Taking advantage of garden bulbs
- How to stack a garden
- Small-space rose gardening

Armed with the garden principals from the first chapters of this book to the small-plant profiles at the end, you can have blossoms and fascinating foliage every week through the spring, summer, and fall.

Small-space gardens offer an intimate setting that actually favors a flower garden because you get to enjoy them up close and personal. And if scented blossoms are involved, so much the better. In this chapter, the focus is on the flowers.

Annuals, Biennials, and Perennials

If you ever eavesdrop on a conversation between a couple of seasoned gardeners, you'll undoubtedly hear them singing the praises of perennial plants. I love perennials as much as the next plant freak, but I think annuals and especially biennials shouldn't be overlooked for their supporting role for the more permanent plants in the garden.

By definition, annuals are plants that complete their life cycle within a year. The seeds germinate, grow, flower, set seed, and die—all in a single season. This is excellent news for small-space gardeners. First, many annuals simply don't get very big. Second, annuals are in a big hurry to produce as many flowers as possible because going to seed ensures the survival of the plant species. We small-space gardeners applaud this habit because it fills our gardens with the blossoms we so crave.

You can take advantage of their need to seed and put it to work for you by routinely pinching off any spent flowers. Most annuals will react by continuing to blossom. They won't survive in your garden through the winter, but many annuals readily reseed themselves and their children take their parent's place the next season.

For the most part, annuals such as viola, alyssum, and lobelia are known as the "filler" plants. They can be tucked in here and there while perennials are waiting to bloom or have just finished their seasonal show. They can fill in places between nonflowering shrubs or in vegetable beds, too.

Some gardeners will use annuals in front of a trellis or arbor while waiting for permanent climbing plants to eventually cover the structure. In general, annuals are almost an afterthought in large gardens, but they're excellent as main plants in small spaces—especially in containers. Once annuals begin to flower, they're almost constantly in bloom, which makes them the number one plant choice when you're looking for fast color. Handy annuals also come in cool-weather and warm-weather varieties, so most gardeners can enjoy annual flowers from early spring to late fall.

Biennial plants grow stems and leaves their first year, but don't reach maturity until their second year, when they flower, go to seed, and die. They also tend to remain smaller as adult specimens than many perennials. Although you have to forego a season before biennials blossom, many gardeners wouldn't do without them. Foxglove, hollyhock, and canterbury bells are so lovely, their tardiness is easily forgiven.

Perennial plants are touted as the workhorses of the garden. They're the plants that flower and set seed for two or more seasons. Some are short-lived, like coreopsis, which live anywhere from three to five years, while others like bearded iris will live 15 years and longer. Then there's the peony, which will see 50 to 100 years in its lifetime.

Aside from the bigger plants such as trees and shrubs, the perennials help make up the bones of the garden by returning year after year without much help from the gardener. In reality, even trees and shrubs are perennial, if you will. However, when we talk in terms of perennials, we're talking about the soft-stemmed herbaceous perennials like balloon flower, phlox, and lantana.

Getting Them out There

The garden beds or containers where you'll plant annuals and biennials should be rich and nutritious—this usually means lots of added organic matter. Annuals, especially, will put out a tremendous amount of energy to complete their life cycle in one season, and offering them the nutrition that they need allows them to flower like crazy.

By the way, you're going to see the phrase "well-draining soil" over and over again, because it's the type that the vast majority of plants out there will appreciate. There are exceptions, of course, which we discussed in Chapter 6. But it's hard to go wrong if "well-draining" describes your soil type.

Plants can receive a lot of the nutrition they need from compost. You can also give them some plant food or organic or synthetic fertilizers, too. When fertilizing plants, you'll want to read the directions as far as how much to apply and how often. If you're predominately using compost as a side dressing, use it as often as you'd like. Compost or *manure teas* are usually applied every couple of weeks.

DEFINITION

Manure tea is made from taking composted manure and steeping it in water for a day. This technique is also done with compost to make "compost tea." This makes an organic liquid fertilizer that you can use to give your plants a nutritional boost.

Annuals are planted in the garden as new plants each year. "Starts" are plants that are started from seed in a nursery, brought to a garden center, and then sold to the public as baby plants. Purchasing plants as starts is the easiest way to get annuals into the garden with the least amount of casualties. In other words, most of them stay alive. Plus, it offers instant gratification for the gardener because they're already growing and getting close to flowering—indeed, some may already be doing exactly that.

But it's also the most expensive way to get annuals into the garden, so you'll have to decide what makes sense for you.

TIP THYME

It's difficult to resist the urge to choose those annuals that are already blooming—but do try. In reality, no matter now careful you are, their roots become disturbed when they're transplanted into the garden or container.

When first transplanted, you want your plants to concentrate their energy on growing strong roots, as opposed to the flowers. Choose annuals that have full and healthy-looking foliage and let the color come after they're established in the garden.

Although biennials can be started from seed, I prefer to purchase and plant them as second-year starts. Biennials are sometimes sold as first-year starts, which is nice because they're already well on their way to adulthood, but if you'd like to see flowers this season, you'll need to purchase those that are in their second year. Just be sure to ask at the garden center if they'll bloom this year. Of course, if the employee pauses after you ask this question, then he or she may have no idea and is just giving you a favorable answer. Ask someone else just to be certain.

TIP THYME

To avoid freezing your annuals to death, plant them out in the garden or border after the last frost date in your area has come and gone. Your local Cooperative Extension office will have the date for your zone.

You can start both annuals and perennials from seed at your home if you're so inclined. Don't be afraid to try it—it's not that hard, but it is more time-consuming. You should start your seeds earlier than they're available as starts in your garden center. Read the instructions on the individual packets for specific seed-starting dates.

Starting plants from seed remains the most inexpensive way to get your share of plants. In fact, once planted, many annuals and biennials will drop their seeds onto the soil and you'll have new plant babies by default next year.

Bulbs Offer Bounty

Bulbs are like that surprise $20 bill that you find in the pocket of an old coat. No matter how many times they come up, there's always that little element of surprise. That's a good enough reason for me to plant them. Of course, bulbs (and other bulbous structures) are fabulous in the garden in any case.

Generally speaking, the term "bulb" is tossed around loosely, which is okay with me and other gardeners. But there's some merit in at least knowing what we're referring to when we talk about planting bulbs or bulblike structures. You may, indeed, be planting true bulbs if they're tulips. But you might just as easily be planting tubers if they're caladiums, or corms if you have begonias.

TIP THYME

When planting bulbs, think in terms of planting them in groups as opposed to rows. They'll look more natural when they come up.

In horticultural terms, these bulbous-type structures may be different, but they all work under the same basic principle: they're underground, food-storing structures that keep plants alive with food reserves bundled inside. Depending on the bulb type, there are some differences in how they're planted and preserved from one season to the next.

Be sure that you know which one you have and get to know them, even if it's just reading the instructions that come with the package. Some should be left in the ground to overwinter because they need the deep cold to bloom again, but others may need to be dug up and replanted in the spring.

TIP THYME

For the most part, the top and the bottom of bulbs are easy to spot. But once in a while you'll run into one that isn't so obvious. So which way should you plant it? When in doubt, plant the bulb on its side as it'll be simple work for the shoot to reach for the sky and the roots to keep their feet in the ground.

Here are the bulbous-type structures that we usually refer to as simply "bulbs":

- **True bulbs:** These are covered with food-storing modified leaves called scales. The base of the bulb (basal plate) holds these scales together. Some bulbs have a papery skin covering them called a tunic. True bulb examples are onions, tulips, lilies, amaryllis, paper whites, snowdrops, hyacinths, and some irises.

- **Corms:** These may have a papery tunic as well, but they're different from true bulbs in that they have a solid stem base. Corm examples are crocus, gladiolus, freesia, and baboon flower.

- **Tubers:** These are swollen stem bases, but they're fleshy and have buds (eyes), which are growth points. Some tubers are cormlike but produce roots from all over. Tuber examples are many anemones, begonias, cyclamen, caladiums, and corydalis.

- **Rhizomes:** While they look like roots, in reality they're thickened horizontal stems. Leaves and flowers sprout from the top of the rhizome and the roots at the bottom. Rhizome examples are African lilies, many irises, canna, and lily of the valley.

- **Tuberous roots:** These true roots are fleshy and swollen. They have an upward-pointing bud with a cluster of swollen parts pointing down. Tuberous root examples are dahlias, rannunculus, gay feather, and daylilies.

Give yourself a break and skip the special little bulb planter that's made for planting bulbs one by one. Go for your spade and dig bigger holes so you can get a whole group into one hole. In fact, you can plant different bulb varieties in there for a succession of blooms.

Aside from planting them strategically among your perennial bed, bulbs are prefect candidates for planting in "drifts." Picture perfect vegetable garden rows. Well, a drift is the polar opposite of that. The amount of blossoming flowers should ebb and flow; big areas drifting into smaller areas and maybe into yet another larger area.

At this point you may be thinking that to achieve drifting you'd need an expanse of land. Not at all. You can plant perhaps 10 bulbs at one end of your perennial bed, plant fewer a little further down, and maybe 7 more at the other end. Or do what many of us lazy gardeners do: toss a handful onto the ground and plant them right where they fall. This is the epitome of creating a natural drift.

Bulbs in Pots

Container-planted bulbs aren't fussy, but two things can make all the difference: well-draining soil and a container that has adequate drainage. Bulbs don't like sopping soil and will soon be covered in mildew or rot under these conditions.

Don't forget that, although there's some variation in planting time (depending on the variety), most bulbs should be planted in their containers in the fall so that they have a chill period during winter. Another rule of thumb is to plant bulbs so they're not touching each other; give them a little space in between. Once again, get information on your particular variety.

Because bulbs are usually planted before winter arrives, containers can be exposed to hard frosts that can break or crack them. Combat this by insulating them with bubble wrap or storing them in a basement as opposed to out in the elements. On the other hand, you could always plant them in wooden containers, baskets, or plastic instead of terra-cotta or thin ceramic pots.

To get the most bang for your bulb, layer them inside containers. Plant the first row deeper than the directions call for (it'll be fine in a pot), then add an inch or two of soil before placing more bulbs into the pot. Repeat.

For a brilliant, extended show, you can layer the same variety. Bulbs aren't the type to reflower (during the same season), so consider planting a bulb type that flowers a little later so the blooming period is staggered. Also, try planting a larger bulb variety with some smaller ones.

Stacking: Living Color Every Season

The most beautiful and interesting flower beds and borders are those where the view is ever-changing. This doesn't happen by accident—it's by design. To have a lush and blooming garden for the longest period of time is the Holy Grail for gardeners. Flower borders are prime real estate for planting, so that flowers are blooming for every season possible. There are several names for this planting style, but I refer to it as "stacking the garden."

It's all about creating layers of flowers using plants that bloom at different times. Each gardener may take a slightly different approach, but they're all seeking the same thing—an ever-changing landscape of color.

Since you read the beginning chapters of this book, let's say that you know which colors (or which plants) you'd like to plant. Make a list of the plants you want (be sure that they're available in your area or you'll be mail ordering). The next step is to group the plants into categories.

Group plants that bloom in the late winter or early spring in one section. Some of these plants will be bulbs like daffodils, crocus, or snowflakes. But there are also many annuals, including pansies, stock, and snapdragons, that wake up in the cooler weather. There are perennial spring bloomers like primroses and verbascum, too. Be on the lookout for a few that bloom in the late spring and early summer.

TIP THYME

Try this stacking trick: when you're digging a hole to plant a perennial, make it extra wide and plant another perennial in the same hole. The plants may bloom at the same time, but you plant one that blooms a little earlier than the other for a longer show.

Choose two plants that have roughly the same growing habit so that one doesn't overwhelm the other. Be sure that their requirements are the same, such as they both like hot, dry areas.

Consider some flowering shrubs, as they add strong backbone to the garden and live on for many years. Flowering shrubs such as ceanothus, azalea, hibiscus, camellia, and spiraea are all valuable additions to the ever-evolving garden.

The next thing you want to do is make a rough outline sketch of your planting area and make little figures (or use initials) that represent the plants. To create a nice balance in the bed during the seasons, place varieties from each flowering time at regular intervals throughout the garden. Be sure to plant several of each variety together so they make a clear statement during their bloom time. Start with placing the late winter/early spring bloomers around the bed, then late spring/early summer bloomers, then summer, and finally fall flowering plants.

TIP THYME

Need to fill in a little? Consider using grasses in your border to add some nonflower interest. Purple moor grass and prairie dropseed will offer texture and color all year.

Some gardeners stack their garden by using only long-blooming plants. Coreopsis, dianthus, balloon flower, penstemon, black-eyed Susan, and yarrow are all examples of long-blooming perennials. Annuals that offer nearly nonstop blossoms include petunia, zinnias, verbena, and cosmos. Of course, before you're done with your planning, give some thought to a few varieties that have interesting foliage.

Roses in Small Spaces

Roses have always been the queen of the garden. For many gardeners, roses are so special that if given the opportunity (and the land), they'll create a rose garden specifically. Even if you're not an avid rosarian, I'll bet you can think of a rose variety or two that you admire.

Currently, the trend is to plant roses in perennial beds among other herbaceous perennials, annuals, and shrubs. This plays right into the hands of the small-space gardener in that it takes advantage of every square inch of soil. If you can't resist the bigger rose types such as the hybrid teas, grandifloras, and some of the old-fashioned roses, the best way to use them in a small space is as specimen plants (focal points).

In other words, if you choose a larger rose, you may be able to fit only a few (or just one) into the landscape. Rest assured that you will find containers big enough to house them even when they're fully mature, but these guys can get *big!* Before you plant a behemoth of a bush, look into the other rose types. Whether you plant them in the landscape or containers, there are those that are especially suited for little landscapes.

Polyantha roses are short and compact with a shrubby habit and usually only grow 2' to 3' tall. They're excellent for the front of a perennial garden bed and make a stunning backdrop when you find them in their climbing forms. Polyanthas come in white, red, yellow, orange, and pink. When these showy gals decide to bloom, the 1" flowers just keep coming.

TIP THYME

To help ward off foliage diseases, do your best to water the soil and not the leaves of your rose bushes. If you want to squirt aphids or debris off of the bush, do so early on a sunny day so that the leaves dry quickly.

Another nice choice for small gardens are the floribunda roses. Floribundas were created by crossing polyanthas with hybrid teas. The cross turned out to be a good one, and what we ended up with was a full, attractive shrub with hybrid tea–like flowers—but in massive quantities.

Floribunda flowers may have the form of the elegant hybrid teas, but they bloom in sprays like the polyanthas. The 3' to 5' bush has no rival as a colorful shrub with a stunning impact. Floribunda roses make excellent cut flowers and are available in the same colors as the hybrid teas.

Miniature roses are exactly what they sound like—tiny versions of their larger shrub cousins. Everything on them is in perfect miniature scale, from their little leaves to their tiny buds and flowers. They're perfect for container gardening and offer blooms throughout the season.

PLANTING PITFALL

One of the biggest mistakes you can make is to not cut back your roses while they're dormant. Roses should be pruned every year, both for health and performance.

Last, but certainly not least, are the climbers and the ramblers. Like everything else grown vertically, these fit into small-space gardens admirably. They give you the roses you crave while taking up precious little ground space. Although it's true that many of them can end up climbing over a building, it's nothing that routine pruning can't solve. A climbing rose is truly at the mercy of the gardener.

If you want roses, you can have them, no matter how little room you have. The question will be, how many rose bushes can you have? And that will depend on the rose type(s) that you choose.

Plant a Potted Rose into a Garden Bed

Planting a container-grown rose bush is easy to do as long as you're capable of digging a hole. If you're not up to the task, have a helper do the digging for you. Thoroughly water the rose bush in its container the day before you plant it. This step will loosen the soil in the pot, moisten the roots, and hydrate the plant.

Do a little research on the rose that you purchased. Most roses need full sun to thrive, but some of them will do quite well in light shade. Some need protection from cold wind and can be planted near walls or other tall structures that act as wind barriers. Finding the right location in your yard or garden is the most important step, so know what your specific rose variety requires.

The best time to plant container-grown roses is in the spring, as long as the ground isn't frozen and you can dig. This gives the rose the longest possible time to become established before the next winter. That said, many gardeners plant potted roses whenever they're available.

A long stick can help you gauge how deep you're planting the rose before you've actually planted it. Right after you place the bush onto the mound in the hole, take a long, straight stick and place it across the top of the hole. Where the bud union is sitting will become instantly obvious and you can adjust accordingly.

What you'll need:

Potted rose bush

Shovel

Long, straight stick

What you'll do:

1. Dig a hole that's a little wider than the rose container. The sides of the hole should be as deep as the container, but you'll want to have a firm mound of soil in the center of the hole for the plant to sit on.

2. To remove the rose from its container, pick up the entire pot and press the sides together, moving your hands all the way around the sides and pressing as you go. You could also carefully lay the container on its side and roll it

while pressing gently on the sides. Holding on to the base of the plant (not the top branches), slide the bush out of the container.

3. Using your fingers, gently loosen the soil around the edges and bottom of the root ball. If you see roots that have coiled at the bottom of the container, gently straighten them as much as you can.

4. Place the rose on top of the mound in the center of the hole in the ground. The depth of the plant will be determined by your growing zone. For budded roses: generally speaking, the bud union (graft) will produce more canes if it's sitting above the soil line.

   This would be the perfect placement for a rose planted in an area that has mild winters. That said, a union that's exposed to extreme cold is more likely to freeze. In this case the bud union should be buried an inch or two below the soil line. If you're planting a rose that's growing on its own roots, this is less of an issue.

5. Once you have the depth right, fill the hole back in with the soil you dug out. Press on the soil to gently get rid of large air pockets and bring the soil around the roots.

6. Water your rose bush well. After the water has seeped into the ground, check and see if the bush has settled too far down. If it has, grasp the base at the union area and raise it up a little so that you can add more soil.

Growing Roses in Containers

As I mentioned earlier, the roses that have a smaller growing habit will be the happiest being grown permanently in containers. Roses like polyanthas, grandifloras, miniatures, small shrub roses, and patio types will have the best chance of success living in containers.

You can't make the mistake of choosing a container that's too large for a rose bush, because they like as much room as they can get. If you want the rose to have a couple of years in the same container, the smallest you'd want to use is a 5 gallon. Of course, if you have a baby miniature rose, you can plant it into something smaller temporarily, but it'll need to be transplanted as it grows.

If you choose a container such as a wine half-barrel or something similar, you'll have enough room to dress up the soil beneath the rose with a shallow-rooted annual. Of course, the decorative part of choosing a container is going to be all about personal taste and the garden style. But there are a couple of things to consider. If you use an unglazed terra-cotta pot, you'll be watering more often because it's so porous. You may want to stick with something that has a wide opening because you'll probably have to transplant your rose at some point and a tight neck is going to make that incredibly difficult.

> **TIP THYME**
>
> Is your container rose thirsty? Stick your finger into the soil and if you find that the soil is dry at 2" deep, it's time to water.

Roses won't respond well to soggy feet. So, other than plenty of room, the container should have enough holes to allow for good drainage. Small holes ($1/2$" or so) are fine, but in a small container there should be several. Large pots should have 4" to $5 3/4$" holes in the bottom. There are a lot of variations to this theme: if you make the holes larger, you'll need fewer of them; if they're smaller, you'll need more. It isn't rocket science.

Another thought on drainage is the use of container feet. These can be made of terra-cotta, cement, ceramic, or wood, and they're used as spacers between the pot and the ground. Not only are the feet a big help for keeping planted containers drained, but they help prevent water stains that show up when wet containers sit flat on cement or a deck. These spacers aren't mandatory, but they're really nice if you can get them. Pot dishes or saucers that sit underneath containers often come as a matching set with the pot. These also help prevent staining, but they should be emptied regularly.

Your container roses will need to be fertilized more often than their garden-grown friends because the nutrition leaches out quickly. Often gardeners will dilute the fertilizer solution (whether organic or synthetic) and feed them every other week.

If you're planting a potted rosebush into another container, the process is basically the same. You'll need enough potting soil to fill the container that you have for the rose bush. It's best to moisten the soil before you fill the container, because the soil won't settle much after you've planted and watered the rose, and there will be less adjusting.

Add enough potting mix to the container so that when the rose is set into the pot, the plant's graft sits a couple of inches below the rim of the container. The easiest way to get to this point is to simply add some soil and then place the rose bush into the container and see where it sits.

Now, set the plant into the center of the container and fill all the space around the root ball up with moist potting soil. Press down firmly on the soil to fill in any air pockets. Water the rose with a gentle spray until the soil is thoroughly wet and water drains out of the bottom.

Excellent Container Rose Varieties

Remember that some rose types are better suited for containers than others. Roses that stay on the smaller side when they're fully grown include shrub, polyantha, miniature, and floribunda roses.

Container roses:

- The Fairy: Polyantha, pink
- Baby Love: Miniature, yellow
- Flower Carpet: Shrub; pink, red, or white
- Cupcake: Miniature, pink
- Pillow Fight: Shrub, white
- Betty Boop: Floribunda, red and white
- Disneyland: Floribunda; blend of apricot, orange, pink
- Gourmet Popcorn: Miniature, white
- French Lace: Floribunda, creamy off-white
- Hot Cocoa: Floribunda, chocolate (almost dark purple)
- Sexy Rexy: Floribunda, pink
- Sunsprite: Floribunda, true yellow
- Knock Out: Shrub, ruby red
- Figurine: Miniature, porcelain pink
- Ballerina: Shrub; blend of pink, light pink, white
- China Doll: Polyantha, pink
- Rainbow's End: Miniature, blend of strawberry red and buttery yellow
- Sea Foam: Shrub, creamy white

- Sun Sprinkles: Miniature, yellow

- Crystal Fairy: Polyantha, white

The Least You Need to Know

- Small-space flower gardens allow you to get up close and personal with the plants and their scents.
- Bulbs can be layered in containers for a longer blooming period.
- Stacking the garden with layers of plant varieties ensures that you have something beautiful and interesting during every season.
- The best types of roses for container growing are miniatures, polyanthas, shrubs, and floribundas.

Other Small-Garden Themes

In This Chapter

- How herbs fit into small gardens
- What is a rock garden?
- A garden made for shade
- Easy wildlife gardening
- Plant a hummingbird garden

We've talked about some incredibly inventive ways to grow flowers, veggies, and fruit in small gardens—but I have news for you, we haven't come close to exhausting ideas. We're going to show you some other popular garden themes such as herb, rock, woodland, and wildlife gardens that fit just as easily into the small-space garden scene.

Herb Gardens

Most herbs are just a natural fit for small gardens. Most of them don't grow overly large and, if they threaten to, a snip here and a harvest there easily keeps them in check. Herbs don't mind sharing space with ornamentals in flower beds and make great bedfellows with vegetables. They can be squeezed into some of the most unlikely places, such as the holes in the cinderblocks of a raised bed.

The majority of kitchen herbs also take very well to containers, which is pretty convenient considering that one of the best places to have an herb garden is as close to the kitchen door as possible. This usually means on a porch, deck, or patio, which means pots or other containers. They have no problem growing in hanging baskets, tubs, and Woolly Pockets; if you're game, they're game.

Some of the easiest herbs to grow together in a large container are the following:

- Parsley
- Dwarf basil
- Lemon thyme
- Chives
- Oregano
- Savory
- Sage

Rosemary is a must-have, but it's a shrubby perennial plant that likes its space. My solution is to simply give the rosemary its own container. And the easiest way to get your herb garden up and growing is to purchase little starts from your local nursery.

TIP THYME

Mints can be incredibly invasive and are capable of taking over a garden in just a season or two. It's best to take a defensive approach from the get-go and grow them in containers exclusively.

If you're gardening on a balcony, try planting a short-but-wide container with a bouquet of varieties. You'll have a good selection of herbs while using less space. If you have only enough room to devote a very small space for a kitchen garden, plant those herbs that you use the most, such as parsley, chives, basil, oregano, thyme, and rosemary.

As if herbs' usefulness in the kitchen wasn't enough, another good reason to grow them is that they're some of the most laid-back characters you can grow. They have some basic needs, but they aren't picky, and most of them are very forgiving. As far as stylistic use in the yard or garden, herbs are as well suited to a formal layout as they are a casual one.

The old-fashioned knot gardens that consist of herbs clipped into formal, geometrical shapes and intertwined hedges may not be realistic in a small-space garden, but they could certainly be placed into geometrical sections and clipped accordingly to give the same impression. Or you could go with a more relaxed version that still offers some light structure, such as an herb wheel.

The Herb Wheel

If you only have a small space to devote to an herb garden, you might want to plant an herb wheel. You can literally use an old, discarded wagon wheel or construct one from scratch using bricks or wood scraps and making a wheel or pizza-shaped outline on the ground. Planting in-between the spokes is where your personality kicks in. If you're looking for culinary herbs, plant the spaces with your favorites.

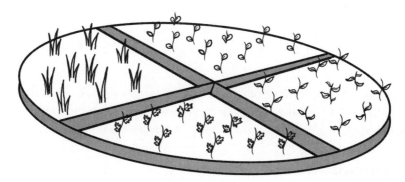

An herb wheel can offer a little structure to an herb garden.

If you're planting the wheel for added color or interest, try filling it with varieties that come in different colors, such as thyme, oregano, or basil. Don't forget to plant herbs with various textures, like sage or lavender. To immediately draw the eye to the wheel, add some annual flowers, such as marigolds or alyssums.

TIP THYME

Most herbs aren't big on fertilizers, so don't overdo it. Spreading a topdressing of compost every once in awhile is enough for them.

The Underappreciated Rock Garden

Find a sunny garden place anywhere in your yard. It might be a corner tucked away, a hot balcony, or the *hellstrip* in front of your house. This is the perfect spot to plant a rock garden.

You can create rock gardens with any number of sun-loving, heat-tolerant plants such as yarrow, stonecrop, and phlox, but rock gardens are best known for the little plants called alpines (rock plants) like alpine sedums, lewisias, and sempervivums. Because many alpines are tiny, slow-growing plants, they're perfect for small-garden enthusiasts who want to dabble in a lot of plant varieties. Colorful, sun-loving, rock-garden plants are plentiful, so this theme is easily tailored to the gardener's preferences.

Rock gardens are highly overlooked as a valued garden theme even when a gardener runs into the perfect setting. That's unfortunate, because they're not only drought tolerant (once established) and unique, they're beautiful and exciting in their own right.

If you happen to have a sloped area with a couple rock outcroppings, a pond, or a water garden, you're already halfway to a fabulous rock garden. If you're interested in planting a rock garden, but don't have any natural rocky areas, you can create the look yourself.

You've Got the Look

To begin with, find a space that sits in the sun for the majority of the day. Choosing rock that would naturally be found in your region is the ultimate in an authentic-looking outcropping, but it isn't a necessity. Limestone, sandstone, and granite will all work well here. To keep the yard garden unified (even outside of the rock garden area), try to use the same stone elsewhere in your yard.

You want to place the rocks just as you would plants—in odd-numbered groups. Just placing them on the ground isn't enough. Rocks should be sunk one third to one half into the earth to give the impression that they've been there forever.

Situate each rock so that the flattest side is down and the narrowest side up. Tilt the narrow end back toward the slope (if one exists) to help create a retainer for the plants, water, and soil. Tamp the soil down firmly to hold the rock in place.

When you plant the alpines, you'll dig little pockets at the back and sides of the rocks. You can add some good soil when you plant, as well. If you're making a gathering of rocks to imitate an outcropping, you can fill in the crevices with garden soil.

TIP THYME

Don't forget that drought-tolerant plants are only drought tolerant after they're established in the garden. Until then, water at weekly intervals, or more if temperatures in your area call for it.

If a rock garden sounds like the right garden for you, but you lack a slope or other characteristic place, make a level one in a flat area. You'll want to purchase ready-made cement edging. You can find them in different styles at home improvement and hardware stores.

Edging formed as rock shapes would be ideal for this project. Start with spreading a 2" layer of pea gravel over the area and then fill in the bed with a sandy-soil mixture for good drainage. Sink an odd number of rocks into the little bed and plant away!

Make a Hypertufa Sink

If you don't have any ground space, you can contain your rock garden in a hypertufa sink or trough by making faux rock. Hypertufa is meant to imitate real tufa, which is a naturally occurring porous rock that's not easy to find and is expensive when you do find it. Alpine-loving gardeners tend to make their own replicas with a hypertufa recipe. There are many recipes out there, but the one below is easy and straightforward.

What you'll need:

Thick disposable gloves

Dust mask

Goggles

Dishpan or another tub for mixing

Cardboard box for the primary mold

Smaller cardboard box for the center of the mold

Dowels

Hand trowel

Cotton fabric

Wire brush

Water

1 part Portland cement

1 part perlite

1 part dry peat (finely sieved)

Optional: 1 part fine builder's (concreting) sand (you can add the sand if you'd like to make the sink a little heavier and more durable)

Optional: Fiber mesh bonding agent (again, this will help prevent the sink from cracking or braking in areas that reach extremely low winter temperatures)

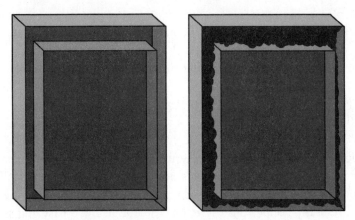

Try your hand at making a hypertufa sink (faux rock) to create an old-world-looking container garden.

What you'll do:

Be sure to put on the goggles, dust mask, and gloves so you won't irritate your skin, eyes, or lungs. Mix one part each of the Portland cement, perlite, and peat (and the sand if you're adding it). Also, if you're adding the fiber mesh, do that now.

1. First blend the dry ingredients well with your hands. Get all around the sides to be sure that everything is blended as evenly as possible.

2. Add enough water to the dry mix so that when it's squeezed, it holds its shape and yet doesn't drip water; it should look like cottage cheese. Your hand trowel can help mix at first, but most people end up using their hands.

3. Fill the bottom of the larger box with 1" to 2" of the mix. Spread it out evenly and then take the dowels and make a couple of drainage holes at the bottom.

4. Take the smaller box and center it inside the larger one. You can pour some sand in the smaller box for weight and stability if you'd like. Add the hypertufa mix into the crevices between the first box and the second to build the sides of the trough.

5. After the sides have been filled to the top, make the piece of fabric wet and cover the project.

6. After 36 hours, dig your fingernail into the trough. If you can make a dent, leave the trough alone for several more hours and try again. When it takes something as strong as a screwdriver to scrape it, then you can remove the sink from its cardboard mold.

7. At this point, you want to use the wire brush on the sides to give it texture.

8. Now place the trough in a shady area for two-and-a-half to three weeks.

9. After this final curing time, be sure that the lime from the Portland cement is leached fairly well from the sink. Fill it for the next week or so and let the water drain out, and it'll take the lime with it.

Some gardeners will make their troughs under a protected area during the winter. After they've cured completely, they'll place them out so that the rains can leach the lime out for them until spring. A stand-alone hypertufa garden is just fine by itself, but they're really special in a group setting, so plan to make a few. Better yet, invite gardening friends over and have a "garden sink" party.

Sink gardens are a natural place to plant alpine plants.
(Courtesy of Moss and Stone Garden)

A Woodland Garden

Many a homeowner has stood (hands on hips) at the head of a damp and shady area or side yard with a dismayed look and wondered, "What now?" Admittedly, shady and damp areas don't immediately scream, "Garden!" The trick with areas that don't seem like a traditional garden is to go with the environment, don't fight it.

You'll never grow watermelons on the shady side of the yard, but you can grow some herb varieties and, if you get morning sun, some lettuce as well. And here is where you can create a woodland setting that can hold its own against any garden theme. Woodland gardens are lovely things that have a romantic feel all their own—complete with woodland faeries. This is one garden that's at its best (and especially appreciated) on a hot summer day.

Other than shade, the key to a woodland garden is rich, loamy, humousy (organic-rich), damp soil. So bring in the organic matter and the compost and lay it on thick. Don't worry about tilling it in—just get the rich stuff on there. Damp soil is what will make this garden thrive. Not to worry, both the organic matter and the shade will help the moisture hang around longer.

Start with the trees or shrubs (canopy) first. We're talking about small garden areas here, so only consider trees that stay small or plant tall shrubs that you can prune into the shape of trees. Look for those that are "airy" as opposed to dense-leaved so the light can filter through and dapple the floor beneath—at least during the morning hours.

A small dogwood, redbud, or birch fills the bill nicely—and incidentally, one tree is all you need to create a small woodland area. If you plant evergreen trees, you may not have enough light to encourage the early spring woodland plants to rise and shine.

The next layer is the shade-loving shrubby plants and larger perennials. These can include azaleas, ferns, elderberry, viburnum, hostas, astilbe, foxgloves, primroses, columbine, and small rhododendrons. The woodland floor can house ageratum, wild ginger, shooting star, wood anemones, bleeding heart, heuchera, trillium, and so many more. No, a woodland garden won't suffer from lack of plant options.

If you're living in an apartment, you may not be working with a space as big or long as a side yard. But you may have a north-facing balcony or other buildings that block the sun, or maybe your balcony happens to be practically underneath large tree branches. You can use the same gardening principals by planting woodland plants in containers or portable raised beds on your balcony.

It's possible to plant a small tree in a large container or go for a shrub that will act as the canopy to your woodland container garden. Plant the smaller things in containers under the larger ones. Don't forget to plant bulbs or smaller shade lovers under some of the plants in the larger containers. You can achieve the same effect (even if it's to a lesser degree), but you will have a garden and there will be flowers. Check out Part 5 for plants that dig shady places.

Gardening for Wildlife

Gardening for wildlife is once again coming back into vogue. And why shouldn't it? After all, it involves utilizing the native plant species in your area; which only makes gardening easier. Wildlife gardening fosters good environmental stewardship, which is a powerful teaching tool for kids (and grown-ups).

It also brings us closer to the natural world around us, which can feel distant because residential and commercial development has eliminated much of the natural areas our wildlife needs to survive—let alone flourish. In fact, habitat restoration is actually at the critical point, so wildlife gardening just makes good ecological sense.

I may have lost you at this point, because you may be conjuring up images of large amounts of open space or wooded acreage. Let me assure you that this isn't the case. You do *not* need a lot of room to garden for wildlife and bring a little Eden to your yard.

There's an excellent program that's perfectly suited for any place where you can stick a few plants. For those living in the suburbs, consider doing some wildlife gardening on a side yard if you have plans for the main yards.

Backyard Wildlife Habitat Basics

The Backyard Wildlife Habitat program developed and promoted by the National Wildlife Federation (www.nwf.org) is the way to go for gardens of any size. Backyard wildlife habitats improve the quality of the environment by providing yards and gardens that nurture wildlife such as birds, bees, butterflies, and plants. By improving the air, water, and soil of our own backyards, we can once again help to nourish the wider natural world.

GARDEN GOSPEL

In a backyard wildlife habitat, there's no room for synthetic pesticides. Most are toxic to both insects and mammals, and using them in place of letting the natural balance of predatory and prey insects upsets the natural balance of the garden.

It's amazing that a project so simple and fun can have such a profound impact on the health of not only wildlife but our own yards and families. Building a habitat is one of the most educational and rewarding projects you can do with your kids. If this sounds like the garden you envisioned, read on.

> **TIP THYME**
>
> Don't forget to do some research on the native plants in your area. Native plant species will best provide for the needs of the wildlife in your area.

Wildlife habitats need four basic elements in order to support the natural world. Like all life, these include food, water, shelter, and a place to raise young. Although each species has some specific needs, by providing a wide range of these things, your habitat will support a variety of plants and creatures.

- **Food:** A little research needs to be done in order to find the plants and vegetation native to your area. Your goal is to plant a variety of vegetation for the year-round needs of wildlife. Local plant life will produce food such as acorns, berries, nuts, and seeds for animals. They will also provide pollen, nectar, and other things for insects and birds.

- **Water:** A constant source of reliable water is necessary in a wildlife habitat. Water needs to be available all year for inhabitants and passers-by. It can be supplied by setting up a birdbath, a waterfall, a small pond, or even a shallow dish.

- **Cover:** Cover is necessary for protection against the elements as well as predators. Sometimes native plants such as dense shrubs can provide shelter. Log or rock piles make good shelter, as do stone walls, evergreen trees, or brush. Ideally, shelters are places near the food and water since an animal has to come out of cover to get to them.

- **Places to raise young:** To complete the habitat, there have to be safe places to reproduce and raise young. This means different things to different species. Some good places are shrubbery, mature trees, brush, nesting boxes, ponds or water gardens, and "snags."

Snags as Homes

Speaking of wildlife homes, have you ever heard of a "snag"? I know that you've seen one. A snag is a dead or dying tree that's still standing. They're often removed from yards or land because a dead tree looks as if it no longer has value. Trust me, their woody lives are not over yet. A tree's full life cycle at this point is far from over.

When there's no sign of green left in a tree (and it's not dormant), it graduates to a snag, taking on a new ecological role. Snags are prime real estate for many mammals such as squirrels, deer mice, martens, raccoons, and bats, providing food, shelter, and nesting places. Butterflies, amphibians, and reptiles happen to be fond of dead trees, too.

GARDEN GOSPEL

Dead or dying tree snags end up with naturally occurring cavities in them, as well as some that birds and mammals excavate themselves in order to set up home. Snags provide habitats for over 85 species of birds, including wood ducks and owls. They provide homes for beneficial insectivores such as woodpeckers and nuthatches.

A standing snag provides a hunting lookout for birds of prey such as owls and hawks, and a place for songbirds to sit and sing. In fact, 85 species of birds call snags home. Even a fallen snag offers plenty of room for squirrels, raccoons, deer mice, bats, butterflies, and reptiles.

Woodpeckers find the soft, decaying wood of a snag easy to excavate while finding food and making a nest to raise little woodpeckers. As a fallen, decomposing log, a snag will entice foxes, skunks, bobcats, and opossums to set up home. Ask any third-grader about the wild creatures they find in tree snags.

You may not have some of the bigger wild critters meandering through your small yard or garden, but if you build a habitat, the wildlife will come. Having said this, if a dead or dying tree poses a threat to a home or is a potential danger for any other reason, it should be taken down. Of course, you could always consider moving the snag to another location and sinking it 2' into the ground, or placing it on its side in a more convenient location.

Hummingbird Gardens

These colorful flying jewels of the garden never fail to make us smile. You can find plenty of hummingbird feeders in stores, but why hang out a fake when you can offer them the real thing? Tiny hummingbirds need all the energy they can get and when you provide them with nectar flowers, a water source, and a place to perch, they'll be happy to hang around all summer long and then some!

Hummingbirds can use nearly anything to perch on, such as your trellis or hanging basket. But they'll be grateful for any small trees, shrubs, or climbing plants that you might have around the garden. These types of plants give them a place to stay hidden while they rest, as well as a potential nesting site.

Be sure to have a water source in your garden for the hummers such as a very shallow bird bath (1/2"). If it's any deeper, add some stones for easy entering and exiting. I've stood in my yard with the garden hose and placed my thumb partway over the end so that the water shoots up into the sky. The hummingbirds will boldly fly and dart through the water, paying no attention to me.

Last, but in no way least, are the nectar flowers that the teeny birds won't be able to resist. Just as you would do for any garden, try to stack the plants so that there's a nectar plant or two (or three) blooming all season long.

Butterfly bush: Takes full sun; 3'-10' tall (depending); 4'-8' wide; zones 5–10

Lupine: Takes full sun to part shade; 3'-5' tall; 1'-18" wide; zones 3–9

Columbine: Takes full sun to part shade; 18"-30" tall; 12"-18" wide; zones 3–9

Fuchsia: Takes part shade; 1'-2' tall; 1'-2' wide; zones 8–10

Starflower: Takes full sun to part shade; 24"-36" tall; 24"-36" wide; zones 9–11

Flowering tobacco: Takes sun to part shade; 36"-48" tall; 1'-1½' wide; annuals everywhere

Trumpet honeysuckle: Takes full sun to part shade; 12'-16' tall; 4'-6' wide; zones 5–10

Torch lily: Takes full sun; 30"-48" tall; 18"-24" wide; zones 5–9

Petunia: Takes full sun; 12" tall; 36"-48" wide; zones 7–10

Jupiter's beard: Takes full sun to part shade; 18"-36" tall; 12"-24" wide; zones 5–8

Lily of the Nile: Takes full sun to part shade; 12"-36" tall; 12"-16" wide; zones 6–10

Lobelia (ruby slippers): Takes full sun to part shade; 36"-tall; 12"-18" wide; zones 3–9

White mallow: Takes full sun; 24"-36' tall; 18"-24" wide; zones 3–8

Hyssop (apricot sprite): Takes full sun; 18" tall; 18" wide; zones 7–10

Stonecrop: Takes full sun; 4" tall; 12" wide; zones 3–8

Beardtongue: Takes full sun; 12"-18" tall; 12"-18" wide; zones 6–10

The Least You Need to Know

- Herbs are a natural fit for little gardens, as well as containers.
- Woodland gardens can be just as beautiful and interesting as a typical flower border.
- Rock gardens can be planted on slopes, constructed on flat land, or planted in hypertufa sinks.
- Creating a backyard wildlife habitat involves providing food, water, cover, and a place for wildlife to raise young.

In Lieu of Lawn

In This Chapter

- Should you keep your lawn?
- How to remove lawn the easy way
- Excellent grass replacements
- A fast and beautiful walkway built in a day

The term "grass" covers a lot of ground (pun intended) in terms of types and varieties. For most people, the word "grass" brings the image of lawn or turf grass that requires weekly mowing. You may have a lawn at your home, but there's plenty of information to be had on lawn maintenance. This chapter isn't going to focus on turf grass. Instead, we'll talk about grasses of the ornamental kind.

We'll get into the modern gardener's dilemma: lawn or no lawn? There are good reasons to get rid of it and good reasons to keep some, and we'll help you sort it out. We'll also talk about plants that can be grown in the direct line of traffic and live to see another day. Check out Chapter 19 for grass profiles.

Should You Swap Out Your Sod?

The short answer is, it depends. The important thing is that you ask the question. We're all used to having that green patch in front (and usually in back) of our homes. So used to it, in fact, that we take for granted that it "should" be there—but why? To begin with, lawns are attention hogs: they demand plenty of water, fertilizer, and mowing. Just this short list indicates how much time, money, and resources we expend to keep them happy.

But this might be an especially important question to answer when you have precious little space in which to garden in the first place! Ask yourself, "Do I use this lawn?" If you have three kids on soccer teams, it may get used often, and maybe it's right to keep it. On the other hand, if it isn't big enough to do much more than kick the ball a few feet, then you may be better off taking them to a real soccer field for practice.

Maybe you like the way a lawn looks. That makes sense. Lawns can make an area look and feel cooler than they are, which is a nice effect. Plus, after you pour all that money into them, they truly are green, and green is the right color for a garden, right? Green is lovely and there's nothing like the feel of cool grass on our bare feet … except that there *is* something like it. Have you ever walked on woolly thyme or bronze Dutch clover? Planting meadow grasses and flowers will also feel refreshing, and bring in the butterflies to boot.

Did you know that there's a wonderful new grass called Eco-Lawn? It's a blend of selected fescue grasses that are drought tolerant and lovely even when they're left unmowed. This special grass has the added benefit of growing well in the shade, too.

The truth is that there are many ornamental grasses and ground covers that can offer much of the same attributes that turf does—and more. If you really like (or use) your lawn, that's great. You can keep it and maybe just give up a little to your garden space. In any case, you should know that you have choices other than a lawn in your landscape.

How to Remove Lawn

There are a couple of ways to go about removing lawn. If you use an excavating approach, realize that this is a lot of physical labor, so you'll need to have a strong back and good stamina, or find someone (or two) with a strong back and good stamina.

If it's a tiny lawn, it may not be all that back-breaking, and it's certainly the fastest way to go about it. Many people thoroughly soak the lawn the day before removal. Then they take a sharp spade (a pointed shovel) and make slices into the sod that are as wide as the shovel. Once they have long strips, they slam the shovel into the root area of the lawn and push down on the shovel handle. Up comes a chunk of turf and they continue the process.

Some people will rent a rototiller and till up the entire area. This might look like it worked, but if you have grass that grows from stolons (like Bermuda grass), ripping it out doesn't work because it'll just grow back from the pieces left behind. For more on stolons see Chapter 17.

So while brute force may or may not be effective, it isn't always the easiest way. My favorite way to sacrifice some lawn for a garden bed or to put in another type of ground cover is to use the sheet mulching method. With this method we're gonna smother the grass to death—with no muscles involved.

What you'll need:

Water source

Cardboard boxes (without coloring)

Newspaper

Any combination of the following: wood chips (not bark), shavings, leaves, straw, compost

Topsoil or garden soil

What you'll do:

1. Start by mowing the lawn as close to the ground as possible. Don't clean anything up—just leave it all where it falls.

2. Cover the entire area that you want to reclaim with cardboard. Soak the cardboard until it's sopping wet. You can use just one layer of cardboard but it couldn't hurt to do more.

3. Now add the newspaper layer—lay it on there thick. Now wet the newspaper thoroughly. You can use a hose, but a sprinkler may soak it faster and take less time.

4. Spread out any type of mulch you have handy: leaves, wood chips, shavings, and so on. Wet down that stuff, too.

5. Last, add your topsoil or garden soil to the layers. You want to add as thick a layer as you can—a foot isn't too much. Water the whole area again.

The sheet mulching method is at its best when it's done toward the end of summer or the beginning of fall. This way it has the dormant season to smother the lawn and call in the decomposers, such as worms, to the revamped spot where they can work their magic and create some fabulous soil.

Ornamental Grasses

Grasses are a versatile option both as a lawn replacement and as an addition to the perennial bed. Ornamental grasses are related to the plain turf types that are part of traditional landscaping, only these grasses have personality. Their blades come up from clumps and arch outward. Ornamental grasses offer the garden color, texture, and even flowers … all of this and zero mowing.

TIP THYME

Ornamental grasses add a textural contrast to the garden that's pleasing to the eye.

Some ornamental grasses are tall, such as pampas and fountain grass. For most small gardens, the larger varieties won't have enough room to reach their potential. But there are the short, stocky grasses that fit beautifully into little landscapes, like Japanese blood grass and moor grass.

These petite grasses hold their own in container gardens, too. Many have striking and unique foliage that makes a bold statement on a patio or deck. Ornamental grasses also have a softening effect in the landscape.

Ground Cover in Place of Lawn

Okay, so you like the look of a green carpet of … something. You'd also like to skip mowing, use less water, and have something a little different in your landscape. Enter the lawn substitutes. Little landscapes are especially suited to lawn transformation because a) there's less work to do, and b) there's less money to invest.

TIP THYME

Before planting ground covers, be sure the area is free of weeds as they don't like competition. However, once established, you'll find that ground covers tend to crowd weeds out!

Be warned: none of these plants will hold up in a high-traffic area. Kids' soccer practice will have to be held elsewhere. But for light traffic, these living carpets offer less work, more interest, and fresh scent. Among the many attractive ground cover plants that make excellent lawn substitutions are …

- **Creeping thyme and red creeping thyme:** Don't confuse these with the common culinary thyme, which doesn't have the right prostrate habit as these thymes. Creeping thyme is very drought tolerant. In fact, it reacts poorly to overwatering, and excellent drainage is important. It has a wonderful scent. The red creeping thyme has dark-green leaves that turn to bronze as the temperatures dip. Flowers are a red-pink that fade to a lighter pink through the summer. Thymes should be replaced about every four or five years as they become woody and unkempt.

- **Woolly thyme:** Again, don't offer too much water once woolly thyme is established. I like the texture this thyme brings to the garden with its dusty-gray, furry foliage and pink blossoms. An added perk is that this soft herb feels fabulous on bare feet! Woolly thyme seems to make its home anyplace where the environment is dry.

- **Chocolate chip ajuga or dwarf bugleweed:** It's exactly what it sounds like: chocolate chip–colored foliage. Both in the spring and fall, it blooms in blue. Ajuga is one of the great ground covers that will grow well under trees, too.

- **Creeping mazus:** Both the lavender-blue and white flowering forms of mazus like their soil a little on the moist side. Its spring flowers resemble tiny snapdragons. Although mazus' stems form mats, it isn't aggressive enough to push out others and take over.

- **Sunny-side-up fleabane:** Fleabane is low growing and thick mat forming, with fernish foliage and a bazillion little white daisies with yellow centers. What's not to love?

- **Roman Chamomile:** This is an aromatic plant that has fernish foliage and daisy flowers. Chamomile has long been used as a lawn substitute because it deals with light foot traffic well.

- **John Creech Sedum:** This plant's bright-green stems grow close together and form an excellent mat as it spreads. John Creech has teeny, purple-pink flowers and the foliage turns burgundy come fall.

TIP THYME

Great ground cover varieties for sunny areas include blue fescue, lamb's ear, speedwell, bergenia, varigated sedge, varigated velvet grass, cranesbill, campanula, and candytuft.

- **Scotch moss:** This ground cover makes a lovely golden, mosslike carpet. In the spring, it blooms with little white, star-shaped flowers.

- **Bronze Dutch clover:** This clover's leaves are a garden standout with its red-bronze leaves edged in green, although the leaves will have more green in light shade and more bronze in the sun. In the summer, it blooms with pom-pom-type flowers.

> **TIP THYME**
>
> Some good ground cover varieties for shady areas are dwarf periwinkle, sweet woodruff, mondo grass, Solomon's seal, mock strawberry, and ajuga.

Make a Living Chessboard Walkway

A chessboard walkway utilizing concrete pavers and feet-friendly ground cover plants can be created in a day. The best part is that it's interesting, artistic, and inexpensive.

What you'll need:

Square concrete pavers—as many as you'll need for the length and width of the path

Walkable ground covers of your choice, such as creeping thyme, Scotch moss, bugle-weed, isotoma, or creeping mazus. Purchase the plants in 6-packs at your local nursery.

Square shovel

Garden soil (1 large bag)

What you'll do:

1. As long as you have a fairly level area to create, this walkway is very simple to install. With the square shovel, make the path ground as level as you can. If you'd like, you can dig out square, paver-shaped crevices to help secure the pavers and make them a bit more ground level, but it isn't necessary.

2. The goal here is to place the pavers so that they're spaced exactly one paver apart from each other. Only the corners of the pavers should meet. Once you lay the pavers out, fill the empty square spaces in with good garden soil.

3. Now dig shallow holes several inches apart from each other and plant your chosen ground cover until you have the "square" evenly filled in with plants. It's okay if you have some ground showing between the plants for now— they'll fill the square in during the season. For more texture, you could plant several ground cover plant varieties.

This walkway is completely adjustable according to how much space you have available. It could be made as narrow as one paver by making a single path that alternates between single squares of paver and the plant square. You could also lay it out so that the path is two pavers wide—remember to have the pavers on each side touching only at each corner so that there's space to grow the plants.

A variation on this theme is to make the chessboard a full patio square and add chessboard "pieces" on some of the pavers. Glazed pots, topiary trees, and cement animals and characters all make good ornamental playing pieces. By the way, some companies have oversized, wooden chess pieces available for outdoor use.

This easy chessboard walkway adds style and whimsy.

The Least You Need to Know

- If you don't actually use your lawn, could you do without some or all of it?
- The sheet-mulching method is physically the easiest way to remove lawn.

- For low-traffic areas, ornamental grasses and ground covers offer you everything that grass does, and more.
- A chessboard walkway is interesting, artistic, and inexpensive.

Small-Garden Water Features

In This Chapter

- The role water features play in the garden
- Construct an easy, in-ground pond
- Aquatic plants and their role in water gardens
- How to make a patio garden in a weekend

Water features have been a part of beautiful landscapes since humans have been creating gardens. They offer advantages that aren't just about visual beauty; if the water is moving, they can stimulate with sound, as well. A glimmer of water catches our eye and our imagination, and we usually can't resist. If the feature is just beyond our vision, the trickling water piques our curiosity and we're off in search of it. The sound of trickling water creates both a mentally and physically calming effect. Soothing background sounds are often referred to as "white noise," and moving water is one of the best of them.

Every type of water feature in the garden will attract wildlife, as it's necessary for their survival. And as far as garden style goes, they're simple to create and will become an instant focal point.

Water Gardens

There's no specific definition for a water feature other than the obvious fact that it features water. They run the gamut from exceedingly easy to quite involved:

- Bird baths
- Wall fountains
- Bubbling table bowls

- Self-contained tiered garden fountains
- Container or tub water gardens
- Small ponds

A wall fountain water feature fits into any garden, no matter how small.
(Photo courtesy of Jenny Peterson)

Water gardens bring beauty, interest, movement, and life to your garden or yard while adding a cooling effect to even the hottest places. Think of them as living art for the landscape. They can be created as in-ground structures or placed on top of the ground.

They come in so many shapes and sizes that it's hard to think of a place where they wouldn't be welcome. In fact, container water gardens are portable and can be temporary, which makes them quite practical for apartment and condominium balconies, and for those gardeners renting homes.

You can make water-garden containers with oversized glass bowls, ceramic planters, plastic planters, galvanized buckets or tubs, water troughs, and even bathtubs. Container water gardens can be moved to different locations and arranged in pleasing groups on a porch or patio. They also offer creative flexibility. There are no rules about the design—work with whatever excites you.

Important Note: Before adding any water feature to your yard or garden, please consider the age(s) of any children who could enter the garden. Kids should always be supervised around water. If that isn't possible, I urge you not to incorporate standing water into the yard.

A safer alternative would be installing a wall fountain in which the water spits into a "disappearing" reservoir beneath stones. Also, be on the lookout for designs in which the ceramic container is filled entirely with large river rock, which prevents standing pools of water.

In any case, water should always be considered a potential danger to children and pets.

Petite Ponds

If a pond is what your small-space garden is missing, your best bet is to go for the prefabricated, rigid liners that are found at garden centers everywhere. They're not only the easiest way to build an in-ground pond, but you're able to see exactly what the final product will look like and you're bound to find one in just the right petite size.

These prefab ponds typically have an irregular shape, which gives them a more natural feel once they're in place. Of course, you have the option of digging a small hole and lining it with a flexible black pond liner, which will remind you of heavy black garbage bag material (but much thicker). Creating a pond from scratch this way is completely doable—just a little more difficult.

The ideal place for a small pond is an area that receives some good hours of sunlight, but also isn't too close to tree understories. It might be obvious that you would keep it out from under deciduous trees, but even evergreens tend to drop their needles. This might not be the look you're going for. After your pond is in place, you'll want to "disguise" the top edge by placing plants, rocks, or some other attractive cover to create a natural-looking setting.

Whether you build an in-ground pond or a raised container water garden, it's bound to attract some wildlife visitors. Birds, frogs, toads, bats, dragonflies and damselflies, butterflies, bees, and other insects are going to be just as thrilled as you are with your new water feature.

Build a Small In-Ground Pond

As I mentioned earlier, using a rigid pond liner is the easiest way to install a pond unless you're creating a container water garden. The molded liners make the procedure so simple that it's a project for virtually any gardener. Thankfully, there are many sizes to choose from and they start as small as 40 gallons.

Before digging out even this small pond, you'll want to be certain that there are no water or utility lines of any kind in the vicinity of where you'll dig. In some places, the absence of any type of piping or lines may be obvious, but if you're unsure, then having the utility companies take a look first is your safest bet.

The only thing that could potentially stop you is if the ground is so hard that you can't dig into it with a shovel. So a great time for this project is in the late spring at the end of the rainy season. Otherwise you may need a little help.

What you'll need:

Prefabricated, molded pond liner

Spade shovel

Hand trowel

Level

Builder's sand

Access to water hose

Material for concealing the pond edge, such as plants, stones, pavers, etc.

Water plants (optional)

What you'll do:

1. First things first: locate your pond site. As I mentioned earlier, under trees isn't usually desirable. But look for an area that receives good sun.

2. Place the molded liner in its permanent spot and outline the pond. You can use a couple handfuls of the sand to sprinkle a line around the edge, or use a stick or hand trowel. Remove the pond from the outline and set it aside for now.

3. Dig out the soil inside the pond outline. At first, you can basically rely on your eyes to give you a general idea about the depth of the pond. But after you've dug quite a bit, place the pond back into the spot so you can see where you need to keep digging.

4. When you've gotten to the point where the pond nearly fits inside the hole, use the level to be certain that the pond is sitting correctly inside. Don't be in such a hurry that you don't check all sides of the pond.

5. Be sure there aren't any big or sharp rocks inside the hole and add 2" to 3" of builder's sand at the bottom. Place the pond back in the hole and check all the sides again with the level. If you need to add or remove more sand, do that now—just be sure that the pond is sitting firmly and evenly.

6. Fill in the gap between the pond liner and the ground with the soil you removed. Pack it down firmly.

7. Now fill your pond with water almost to the top. If you're adding water plants, leave some space for the water to rise as you add them.

8. Add the water plants to your new pond. Be sure to place the marginal plants onto the molded ledges on the side of the pond. Play around with the plant arrangement until you're happy with it.

9. Place pavers, stones, ground cover, or bog plants around the edge of the pond to disguise where the pond liner meets the earth.

Aquatic Plants

Aquatic plants are important to the water garden or pond in terms of both beauty and function. Many of these plants have attractive foliage, and nearly just as many have attractive flowers. But aquatic plants all perform a certain function in the life of a water garden or pond.

Those that live their lives on the outer edges of the pond, called marginals, prefer to grow in shallow water. The floaters that lie on the surface of the water help control the inevitable algae that grows in tubs or ponds. The submerged plants that grow in deeper water provide oxygen to the pond.

PLANTING PITFALL

Don't put aquatic plant species into any natural waterway, as they may be invasive and become uncontrollable in the wild. When choosing plants, the best thing you can do for the environment is to learn about the plant species that are invasive in your area, and avoid or confine them.

All of these plants work together to create a stable ecological system, and you should consider each type when you're purchasing aquatic plants for your water garden. Just like all plants, each species and variety will have its own personality and will have zones where it's at its best. A short list of aquatic plants follows for each category. If you see some that interest you, be sure to check with your local garden center and see if it's available in your area. If not, they'll be able to help you find something similar.

Floating Plants

Floating plants refer to those whose foliage rests on the water's surface. Like the much celebrated water lily, floating plants offer both visual interest as well as algae control. Algae only needs two things in the water to survive: a food source and sunlight. It can grow rapidly in ponds, especially if you have fish, due to the fact that algae finds fish waste especially delicious.

If you have moderate amounts of algae in your water garden or pond, there's no problem to speak of. In fact, algae is a sign of a healthy, thriving pond as well as a food source for fish. You just want to keep algae from taking over—and floating plants can help with this goal.

Generally easy to grow, floating plants help control the algae population in a couple of ways. First, they shade the water from the sun, eliminating one of the necessary components for algae to thrive. Like submerged plants, floating plants use nutrients in the water for themselves, thus robbing algae of their secondary life source.

Before purchasing floaters, talk to a knowledgeable employee at a local nursery and learn which aquatic plants do well in your growing zone. Of course, the easiest plants to maintain are those that winter over in your area. If you get tender plants, you can bring some of them indoors for the winter and then put them back in the water garden in the spring, or you can simply treat them as an annual plant.

Some floating plants actually do *too* well in a specific zone—that is, they may attempt to take over the entire pond. If you're attached and would still like to keep them as a water interest, there's an easy remedy for controlling invasive plants. Periodically, take a bucket or container and scoop about a third of the offending floaters out of the water garden.

TIP THYME

If you've scooped some floaters out of your water garden, don't let them go to waste! Instead, toss them onto the compost pile as a terrific food source for the microorganisms living there.

Here are some of the most popular floating plants:

- **Water lily:** Perhaps the most well known of the floating plants, the beautiful water lily flowers are usually the first thing that come to mind when you think of pond or water gardens. There's good reason for this. Not only are the blossoms so perfect that they seem unreal, some change color as they mature and some are even perfumed.

- **Fairy moss:** This is a delicate little fern type of floater. Fairy moss's green summer carpet is lovely in ponds. As the weather cools, the ferns become a pink-purple color. They're also an example of a floater that can become invasive, so keep them confined to your personal water garden.

- **Water lettuce:** Its fluted, rosette-shaped leaves make it attractive for ornamental purposes, yet it can be invasive in tropical and subtropical areas. Water lettuce can add texture and interest; just be sure to confine it to your water garden.

- **Floating heart:** Floating hearts are perfect for a water garden that has moving water. Water lilies prefer standing water, and these can be a nice substitute. Their flowers are fringed yellow or white and rise above the surface of the water.

- **Sensitive plant:** This floater has fern-type leaves that close up when they're touched (like their terrestrial cousin, mimosa). Neptunia is a member of the legume family and produces furry, 1" yellow blooms during summer.

- **Velvet leaf:** The velvet leaf or butterfly fern will grow in partial shade and can become invasive where the weather is warm. However, it's beautiful in home water gardens. Good to note: koi find them delicious.

- **Water hyacinth:** Water hyacinth is another lovely plant that should be confined. It's best when grown in a pond that sees a hard frost so the plants will die back. The base of the plant is bulbous and the thick leaves grow in a rosette pattern. Its summer flowers are quite showy with their lavender petals and touch of yellow.

Marginal Plants

Marginal plants are those that grow in varying amounts of water at the edge of a pond or slow stream. They bridge the gap between those plants that grow on shore and the true aquatic plants in the water. Most marginals are highly ornamental and perennial; both are virtues prized by water gardeners. They're perfect for growing in or near small water gardens or ponds.

Nearly all of these bog-loving plants usually need their roots surrounded by soil and can live in anywhere from 4" to 12" of water. Some of them will even thrive in simple murky mud. The water depth that make marginals the happiest will depend entirely upon the species. Be aware that you may have to acclimate your newly purchased plants to their permanent home.

Often water gardeners will create "shelves" in their water garden or pond for their marginal plants to rest on, because if you plant them too deep, you can, in effect, drown them. Late spring is the best time to choose and purchase marginal plants from your local nursery or pond store because the new growth has already begun to emerge, yet the plants haven't become root-bound waiting for a permanent home. Popular marginal plants include …

- **Sweet flag:** Sweet flag's leaves look very much like those of a typical garden iris. It's an easy plant to grow, and reaches 2' to 3' tall. It prefers to be planted in about 9" of water and situated in the full sun.

- **Lesser spearwort:** This hardy, low-growing perennial is perfectly happy in full sun or part shade. It has lance-shaped leaves and a reddish stem, and in early summer produces yellow buttercup-type flowers.

- **Umbrella palm:** This is an evergreen sedge that's leafless except for the umbrella-type spray of leaves at the top of the 3' stalks. Flower umbels (flower clusters that hang upside down) are produced during the summer. Plant umbrella palm in full sun to part shade.

- **Water snowflake:** Planted in at least 4" of water, these plants grow from rhizomes and form floating green mats. White, fragrant, and delicately fringed flowers bloom in the spring and may continue until late fall.

- **Variegated manna grass:** This fast-growing grass can end up nearly 3' tall. Its leaves are green-and-cream striped, with a pink tinge on the newest growth. Brown flower heads are produced during the summer.

Submerged Plants

The submerged aquatic plant group is often referred to as the "oxygenators," as these plants absorb carbon dioxide during the night and add oxygen to the water garden during the day. Nutrient-rich water in full sun is the perfect situation for algae growth. As a purifier, the submerged plants compete with algae by removing unwanted and excess nutrients from the water, which helps prevent algae buildup.

Oxygenating plants have unsupportive, weak stems, and therefore spend their lives completely under the water's surface. Instead of getting their nutrients through their roots in the soil, they get them directly through their leaves. Although most of these plants grow completely underwater, some of them produce flower stalks that will grow above the surface.

Usually, submerged plants are sold in bunches. A good way to decide how much to buy is to get about one bunch for every square foot of water. When you add them to the water garden, the stems can be pushed into gravel (or soil). The other option is to just let them free-float in the water.

All of these plants are easily propagated by taking 8" to 12" cuttings from the new growth during the summer. Every water garden has its own water habitat dictated by the garden area, plant life, sun situation, and water depth. So not all of the plants in the submerged group will survive in every pond. You may have to try a few varieties before you find the right one for that particular garden.

Some popular submerged plants are …

- **Parrot's feather:** The fernish foliage grows mostly submerged, but may also grow just above the water surface. Some species have flower spikes that poke an inch or so above the water in the summer.

- **Water violet:** This is actually a member of the primrose family. Its leaves are light green and it produces pale pink-lilac flowers on spikes in spring, which rise out of the water.

- **Starwort:** Fish enjoy nibbling on this tangled mass of leaves. The summer flowers are small and white, and the foliage underwater is sparse. The leaves on top of the water form thick mats.

- **Fanwort:** Fanwort is also a fish favorite and is often used as a food source in the cold months. Fish hide in the swirls of fanwort's leaves, too. It produces small white flowers in the spring.

- **Willow moss:** This plant is slow growing and prefers slow-moving water. It serves as a great place for fish to spawn, as the eggs easily stick to the willow moss's leaves.

- **Hornwort:** In the winter, hornwort will sink to the bottom of your pond. It's a good choice as an oxygenator because algae has a hard time competing with it.

- **Yellow water buttercup:** The water buttercup produces little yellow, buttercup-type flowers during the spring and summer. It's a noninvasive North American native that grows either submerged or floating.

- **Underwater arrowhead:** This plant offers excellent algae control. Arrowhead is one of the first submerged plants to grow in the spring.

- **Curled pondweed:** This plant may be invasive if allowed to wander. The seaweed-looking stems can grow to 6' long and have white summer flowers that poke just above the water surface.

Patio Water Garden in a Weekend

Container water gardens are easy to make and add instant beauty and life to your garden. After you create your first one, I promise it won't be the last!

When you're purchasing your container, remember that when it's full of water, it's going to be *heavy*. So the one you choose should be strong—a heavy ceramic planting pot is perfect. The best container choice would be one without predrilled drainage holes. Steer clear of the basic terra cotta pot; the water seeps out as it breaks down the pot's structure.

A few things to mention while you're choosing plants. You should only use aquatic plants in your container water garden. When you're out purchasing them, choose a small variety (three types always looks nice). Start by choosing one main plant as your focal point and then add a few more plants to accent the garden.

Look for different textures, such as one that grows upright and one that creeps along the water's surface. Don't bring home too many—a little goes a long way! Aquatic plants aren't shy about spreading and the idea isn't to completely cover the water's surface.

There are a lot of aquatic plant choices, but most people like to have a flowering water lily or lotus. They're free-floating plants and will help control algae. You could add a submerged plant as an oxygenator, and perhaps a decorative marginal plant.

What you'll need:

Suitable container for your water garden. A large ceramic pot or half-barrel works well.

Waterproof sealant for the inside of the ceramic container. This may not be necessary if the container is already sealed; however, many aren't.

Paintbrush for the sealant.

Several aquatic plants.

Pea gravel for weighing down the plant container and for building little mounds to raise plants up.

Water to fill the container.

*Clear caulking if you need to seal drainage holes in the bottom of the container.

*Plastic pond liner if you're using a half-barrel for your patio water garden.

*These items may or may not be needed to create your water garden.

What you'll do:

1. Prepare the inside of the container for holding water. If you're using a ceramic one, caulk drainage holes if there are any. You may also need to paint the inside with a waterproof sealer—do that step now (many people like to put a second coat over the first after it has dried). If you are working with a half-barrel, line the inside of the tub with a plastic pond liner.

2. Choose the location for your patio water garden. It's much easier to move around now than it will be when it's full of water. If you want to use aquatic plants that bloom, be sure to choose an area of the yard or garden that has plenty of sun. That said, modify that if your container is very small, as it may heat up too much in the summer heat. Try placing your container water garden in an area that has afternoon shade.

3. Fill the container with water. Rainwater would be ideal, but if it's tap water, typically you'll want to wait 24 hours before introducing plants into the pot.

4. Start arranging your water plants in the container. Sink your potted plants into the filled container and put some pea gravel into the pots to hold them at the bottom of the container. Gravel also holds the soil in place to avoid making the water muddy. By the way, the soil used in aquatic plants is designed especially for them—it's not traditional potting soil. So if you need more, be sure to look for the correct media.

While you're planting, be sure that the leaves are above the water line (with the exception of submerged plants like parrot's feather). If you need to, pile up some pea gravel or add fairly flat river rocks to make a little shelf for the pots if they're too short for the container.

Fountains

You can't go wrong with a sparkling fountain. An alternative to adding water movement to the garden without constructing a pond or a water garden is a fountain. Of course, there are the typical three-tiered fountains that have remained popular through the ages—large and small. But you can get smaller.

Urn bubbler fountain.
(Photo courtesy of Jenny Peterson)

Fountains can be constructed as a simple feature all by themselves. Such is the case with self-contained wall fountains and bubbling dish or urn fountains. No matter how many times we come across them, wall fountains always retain their mystery. Other than the wall of your home, they can be hung on a boundary fence or a faux doorway, too. They can spit water into a birdbath, tub, or pool, or all but disappear into a collection of rocks. There's a wide variety of this type of simple fountain that doesn't require a pool to fall into—in fact, many of them have a disappearing-water design.

TIP THYME

If your wall fountain tends to splash back against the wall of your home, you can protect the wall either by having a waterproof backsplash mounted behind the fountain or, at the very least, paint the wall with a sealant meant for that specific surface (for instance, a brick sealant).

Fountains can also be used in conjunction with a pool of water. They're often placed at the edge or in the center of a pond, or even in a container garden for added sound and decoration.

Disappearing pond.
(Photo courtesy of Jenny Peterson)

The way the water is dispensed from the fountain varies as well. Some are meant to trickle slowly, others have a steady stream, and still others actually have a deliberate spray or bubble. From an artistic point of view, the fountain styles are endless.

Fountains can range from traditional water-spitting animals such as frogs, fish, birds, and swans, to frolicking children, bubbling gazing balls, overturned urns, pouring watering cans, and any number of modern art structures. There are jets that spray straight up and create patterns in bell shapes and tulip shapes.

You'll find those that produce double domes or graceful, arching patterns. There are also those that allow you to change the pattern of the water when you get bored. Choose whichever fountain strikes your fancy and goes well with your garden theme or design.

The Least You Need to Know

- Water features in the garden act as focal points, adding beauty, movement, and sound.
- Don't release any aquatic plant species into any natural waterway, as they may be invasive and become uncontrollable in the wild.
- Aquatic water garden plants fall into the marginal, floater, or submerged categories.
- Before adding any water feature, always consider the ages of the children who will be in the garden. If kids will not be supervised, then a water feature shouldn't be part of your garden plan. If they are supervised, create a child-friendly design for safety.

Good Gardening Practices

All gardens—large, small, or in between—can thrive when you apply the same basic good gardening practices. We felt it would only be fair to let you in on what those are so your little space flourishes with healthy and gorgeous foliage, flowers, or food. This is the section where we let you in on the secret of great gardens—great soil and how to get it. We have a chapter that describes organic practices to defend your garden against pests (the bad guys) and introduce you to the beneficial insects (the good guys). Chapter 17 is devoted to helping you outsmart enemy number one: weeds. This is the part that will give you the tools to keep your well-planned garden thriving.

It's Always Been About the Soil

In This Chapter

- Determining your soil's personality type
- What is NPK?
- Why compost is king
- Organic fertilizer sources

It doesn't matter how big your garden is or what you're growing—if you want a fabulous garden, you need to concentrate on the soil. In this chapter, we'll talk about what "great" garden soil is and how you can get it. We'll also explain why compost is truly "garden gold."

Living, Breathing Garden Soil

Do you have dirt or soil? "Dirt" is a loose term that, from a gardener's point of view, has little in common with what's in their garden beds. Soil that doesn't have much nutritional value to offer plants is often referred to as dirt. Most gardeners prefer to use the term "soil" when they're talking about nutritionally rich garden earth.

The first thing you should know about soil is that it's anything but dead. Soil is full of billions and billions of living and breathing organisms that are invisible to the human eye. In the simplest of terms, soil is made up of organic matter, minerals, water, and air. All of these ingredients not only make up a stable medium for roots to hang on to, but also provide for plants' nutritional needs.

Soil Has Personality

Soil testing is about obtaining the specifics on the minerals and nutrients found in individual soils. Soil type or personality refers to the physical structure and texture of soil. This information provides clues to how porous a soil is and how well it will hold water, as well as giving you some hints to whether it's holding much nutrition at all. Knowing your soil's natural type tells you which plants will thrive in the soil that you already have. This will let you know how much amending to do to your soil before planting.

Texture is the relative proportions of sand, silt, and clay mineral particles in your soil. A soil that is sandy and coarse is referred to as a light soil, while a clay or fine-textured soil is referred to as heavy soil; there are many variations between the two. Still, just hearing those labels gives you an idea of how easy it would be to work these soils. But soil quality isn't all about physical work.

Lighter soils may be sparse in nutrients, whereas heavy soils may contain valuable nutrients that just can't be tapped easily due to its thickness. Although both soils will support certain plants, they both could be greatly enhanced with amendments.

The USDA classification system recognizes 12 basic soil textural classes. They can prove this with a diagrammed triangle that they ingeniously made look incredibly complicated. If you want to get that deeply into it, feel free to look that diagram up, but you may want to ask yourself if it's worth losing a growing season just to say you understand it (www3.hcs.ohio-state.edu/wiki/index.php/Soil_textural_triangle). In other words, it's interesting information, but you don't have to go that far.

Hands-On Method to Determine Soil Texture

Here's a method that allows you to get a general feel for your soil structure type. It isn't specific, but it's usually all you need to know.

- Take a palm-sized chunk of your soil in your hand (this is done one-handed, so you can go right on flipping through your seed catalogs with the other hand). Squeeze the soil together to form a slightly oblong ball.

- With your thumb, gently push the soil forward to make a "ribbon." If you can't make anything but crumbs, don't blame yourself. You have a coarse-textured soil—a loamy sand.

- If you can make a short ribbon to about a half-inch long, you have a medium-textured soil—loam. Smile … it's a nice one to have!

- If you can form a ribbon easily and it doesn't break off until about three-quarters of an inch long, you have clay loam—another medium-textured soil.

- If you can form a strong ribbon that seems to go on and on, you have a very fine-textured soil called clay. You might have to work a little harder on your soil by adding more organic matter (compost).

In any of those cases, the best thing for improving your soil is compost or composted manures. Adding a couple of inches of your homemade compost or bagged compost from a local nursery to your garden bed every year will soon have your soil teeming with good organisms and leave you with loamy and nutritional soil. In fact, it's hard to go overboard with compost, and I add it all year long.

What Is pH?

The pH scale is the way that chemists measure the acidity or alkalinity of the soil. The scale is drawn on a number line that ranges from 1 to 14. The lower the number is on the scale, the higher the acidity, and the higher the number is, the higher the alkalinity. The middle ground or neutral point of the scale is at 7. Numbers that fall to either side are either "sweet" (alkaline) or "sour" (acidic).

GARDEN GOSPEL

Acidity and alkalinity are important because they influence the nutrition that each plant receives. The acid or alkaline levels affect this by making them either more or less available to plant roots—depending on the plant species.

Most plants do very well with a neutral or slightly acidic soil. This is great news for the home gardener, who we hope is adding a lot of organic matter (compost) to the soil—which brings it closer to neutral. A few plants thrive in soils that are more on the acidic or sour side, such as rhododendrons, holly, azaleas, camellias, foxglove, and blueberries. The pH in soil can be organically lowered by adding peat moss, oak leaves, coffee grounds, or iron sulfate.

Some plants such as ceanothus, lilac, daphne, clematis, pinks, spirea, and forsythia prefer soils on the sweeter side. While most of these plants will do well in a neutral soil, if you have extremely acidic soil, you may want to raise the pH. Lime, wood ash (use sparingly), and oyster shells are all organic ways to achieve this. Compost is an excellent pH buffer (bringing soils to a neutral pH) for soils, and some gardeners feel that it can raise the pH to some degree, as well.

No matter what type of plants you prefer, small-space gardeners have the advantage in this arena. If you're gardening in a raised bed, you can simply amend the soil every so often to accommodate the plants you'd like to grow. The same goes for small in-ground plantings. In containers this type of soil maintenance is even easier.

Soil Testing

Soil testing goes beyond basic texture and pH level information. It's a more complex view that lets you know the minerals and nutrients in your soil. Although I think there's some usefulness in knowing the deepest chemical composition of your soil, it isn't always necessary. It's a way to get to know your soil on a more intimate level—or, I should say, levels. If you'd like to dig deeper (pun intended), there are three ways to go about obtaining this information.

First, you can purchase an inexpensive do-it-yourself kit at a local nursery. You can go for a basic model, or splurge and buy one of the most expensive ones. The basic ones are great fun and give you a fairly good idea about what's going on generally in your neck of the woods. The expensive ones are all the more accurate.

Your local Cooperative Extension office may also offer inexpensive soil testing. Their tests are a little more complete than the home tests. You could also contact a private laboratory, which is typically more expensive that the first two, but not horribly so. A private lab can give you the most complete report.

So how do you know if you should perform a soil test in your garden? Well, if you're gardening in containers, skip it for sure, considering you control everything from the get-go. People usually opt for this if they're gardening in-ground and observe that all (or many) of the plants are doing poorly, either from disease or a nutrient deficiency. If a home test indicates that things are truly off balance, the labs can sometimes shed further light on the situation as well as help you adjust the soil properly.

What Does "NPK" Stand For?

If you hang around gardeners or fertilizer bags long enough, chances are that sooner or later you'll run into the initials NPK. These letters refer to three of the main nutrients that plants need to thrive, and thus are the primary ingredients found in plant fertilizers. Whether the fertilizer comes in the form of chemical (inorganic) or organic fertilizers, the NPK content is measured and placed in the same order.

The type of plant you're feeding and which part of the life cycle the plant is in (growing, fruiting, or blooming) determines which number you want to see higher on fertilizer. Here's what the letters stand for and their nutritional function:

- **N is nitrogen:** It's the leaf and stem developer, and adding a nitrogen boost gets thing growing fast. Nitrogen is always appropriate for leafy veggies such as lettuce, kale, and Swiss chard. This makes sense because it's the leafy part that we're after.

- **P is phosphorus:** It's a valuable nutrient for flower and fruit development. Phosphorus also helps roots take quickly to the soil. If you're getting a ton of leaves and not enough fruit on crops such as pumpkin or tomatoes, you may need a boost of phosphorus.

- **K is potassium:** Plants develop healthy root systems and are able to resist disease easier due to potassium. It works right in tandem with phosphorus for fruit development.

Take a look at an organic fertilizer bag, such as blood meal. The bag may say "11-3-0," which means there's 11 percent nitrogen, 3 percent phosphorus, and 0 percent potassium.

When determining the right fertilizer, keep some basics in mind. While a plant is actively growing, it's a good idea to have that first letter (N) a little larger than the other two numbers. When the plant begins to flower, you could side dress it with a fertilizer that has a larger middle number (P). The last letter (K) is good for the general health of the plant.

If you're going to add fertilizers to your gardening program, you'll want to have a general understanding of the concept. A good example is in the case of tomato plants. While they're young, high nitrogen is just fine; the tomato plant is developing leaves and actively trying to reach a mature stage so it can fruit. However, once you see flowers, if you keep plying the dear thing with nitrogen, you're going to have more green than fruit—which we'll assume isn't the goal.

Although there's a staggering selection of both chemical and organic fertilizers on the market, more than ever gardeners are leaning toward the organic products. That's because in recent years we've learned the "Big Lesson" in soil health: providing our plants with NPK strictly through synthetic fertilizers has left little room for natural biodiversity in the soil and does little (if anything) for long-term soil productivity.

Although they're clearly useful in many cases, for the home gardeners, it's always better to focus on building the soil and encouraging biodiversity by making good use of organic matter. In other words, make some of your own earth.

Organic Fertilizers

Even if you're using organic products, you have a choice on how to obtain extra nutrition for your plants. Organic fertilizers can come in a ready-made blend, and it's the most expensive way to acquire fertilizers. But you can source out your own organics if you know what to look for.

Organic nitrogen (N) sources:

- **Grass clippings:** This is one of my favorite nitrogen sources. Call me cheap (and many do), but green grass freshly mowed from the lawn is an excellent source of free nitrogen.

- **Animal manure:** Fabulous manures come from cows, rabbits, horses, sheep, alpacas, llamas, and chickens. Think herbivore. We're not talking about animals that are primarily carnivores (meat-eaters) such as dogs or cats. Manure from meat-eaters can contain harmful pathogens that you really don't want to come into contact with. Usually the herbivore manures are composted before they're used in gardens, and many of them, such as cow manure, will burn your plants if not composted first. By the way, if you can get your hands on some bat guano (bat poo), that stuff is nitrogen gold.

- **Worm castings:** They don't have to be pure castings, of course. Castings by way of vermicompost is ideal (castings plus the organic matter that the worms composted while making the castings). It's also a superduper soil conditioner.

- **Coffee grounds:** Stop by your local Starbucks and snag a bag, or three. Many coffeehouses have the used grounds already bagged up and free for the taking. Sprinkle it around your azaleas, rhododendrons, blueberries, and the like for the acidity, but it also brings terrific nitrogen, too.

- **Alfalfa meal:** Not only does alfalfa offer a big bang of nitrogen, it's also a terrific organism activator for soil. So I toss some into my compost, too. Use alfalfa meal on the plants that are gluttons for food such as corn.

- **Blood meal:** It's exactly what it sounds like. It's dried blood from animals … but it's loaded with nitrogen.

- **Fish meal or fish emulsion:** This is seriously going to stink for a bit, but the smell doesn't last and your plants will love you for it. I prefer fish meal to the emulsion only because the emulsion is said to wash away faster.

Organic phosphorus (P) sources:

- **Rock phosphate:** The good news about rock phosphate is that it lasts a long time because it breaks down very slowly. The bad news is that it breaks down very slowly and the phosphorus doesn't become fully available to plants for possibly a year. But then, you've got time, right? Just add it and forget about it.

- **Bone meal:** Again with the dead animals. Bone meal is animal bones that have been ground into powder. It's highly phosphorus as well as loaded with calcium, but this is also a slow-releasing source. It's great for promoting flower blossoms as well as encouraging good root growth.

- **Colloidal phosphate:** This soft-rock phosphate is also called colloidal calcium phosphate.

Organic potassium (K) sources:

- **Kelp meal or liquid seaweed:** Another garden gift from the ocean, kelp meal is derived from dried seaweed. It's an excellent fertilizer as it contains a lot of trace minerals and hormones that give plant roots what they need to create strong plants. A popular organic fertilizing combination is kelp meal and fish emulsion.

- **Greensand:** Greensand is mined from mineral deposits that come from the ocean floor. It's good for general soil amending, as well as being high in potassium.

- **Granite meal:** Granite meal is finely ground granite rock that slowly releases potassium. It also helps create soil structure and improves drainage.

Compost

The question remains: do you need to add supplemental fertilizers to your garden at all? The answer is a definite maybe. If you're strictly container gardening, you may find it necessary to add some extra food once in a while because anything of value is eventually eliminated once the plant has used it up or it is flushed out by basic watering.

But if your small-space garden happens to be in the landscape or garden bed, perhaps not. As an all-around general soil amendment, there's nothing better than compost for your soil. Composted *organic matter* adds all kinds of nutrients and makes them easily available to plant roots, and this is good news for both garden beds as well as container gardens.

 DEFINITION

Organic matter is any material that originates from living organisms, including all animal and plant life, whether still living or during any stage of decomposition.

It's entirely possible for compost to provide all the goods that your garden needs. But that's not the entire picture. Some plants, such as heavy-feeding vegetables, may need to be supplemented with more nutrition. In any case, adding compost periodically to the garden beds is a great place to start.

Keep in mind that synthetic fertilizers may temporarily mask poor soil, but they don't actually solve the problem. They simply mask it. Compost, on the other hand, changes the structure of the soil—making it nutritionally rich.

The key to healthy plants is soil that's rich in organic matter. So great garden soil is all about having as much organic matter involved as possible—this is where compost comes in. Compost is the finished product of broken-down organic plant and animal matter.

In its "finished" form, compost becomes *humus*. Humus makes complex nutrients in the soil easily available to plants. A soil that's full of life-sustaining humus is often called "friable," meaning that it has a full, loamy texture and crumbles easily in your hands.

 DEFINITION

Humus is the product of degraded plant and animal matter that's nearly completely broken down. It's compost at its richest in organic matter.

Compost can add any number of nutrients to the soil, depending on what materials are added to the compost pile. Other micronutrients that add value to the compost are copper, iron, iodine, zinc, manganese, cobalt, boron, and molybdenum. It adds value to soil by providing it with nitrogen, phosphorus, potassium, and other minerals. It can also eliminate the need for synthetic fertilizers and can ward off plant diseases.

More Reasons to Worship Compost

Compost immediately improves garden soil by introducing organic matter and microbes. Living, healthy soil is only the beginning. Compost has more in store for you:

Compost extends your growing season

Composted soils enable the gardener to plant earlier in the growing season and harvest later in the season. Compost improves average soil structure by bringing it to a loamy, friable state. Nutritionally rich soil with good structure is able to hold heat better than poor soil. For the gardener, this means the soil warms up faster and stays warm longer.

Compost acts as a pH buffer

For most plants, the most desirable pH is neutral—neither too acidic nor too alkaline. If a gardener is generous with applying compost to garden soil, the gardener doesn't have to worry about the pH levels as much—if at all.

When humus is plentiful in soil, vegetable crops and flower beds are simply less dependent on pH levels in the soil. Due to its biochemical structure, humus acts as a buffer for soils that fall slightly to one side of acidic or alkaline. This not only takes the guesswork out of an average pH level, but in many cases, it can take the pH factor out of the equation entirely.

Compost saves water

Compost increases soil's capacity to hold water by a wide margin. For instance, a dry soil low in nutrients may only hold 20 percent of its weight in water. Compare this to a dry soil that's high in organic content, which can hold up to 200 percent of its weight in water.

Also, due to the poor crumb structure of soil that's low in organic matter, it can be washed away easily by storms or even everyday watering. Lost topsoil results in even lower fertility, creating a vicious cycle. Compost preserves and enhances soil structure and helps fight erosion, keeping healthy soil under the plants where it belongs.

Compost protects against plant diseases

Researchers have discovered another virtue of compost that doesn't get as much publicity as it should: it's valuable for plant-disease resistance. The beneficial microorganisms produced by composting organic materials render plant pathogens inactive. So compost can help wage the battle against certain soil-borne diseases.

The Least You Need to Know

- It's easy to determine your soil's basic structure by using a simple hands-on method.
- NPK are letters that refer to the three main nutrients that plants need—nitrogen, phosphorous, and potassium, which are the primary ingredients found in plant fertilizers.
- Compost can extend the seasons; save time, money, and water; act as a pH buffer; and offer nutrition to plants.
- Synthetic fertilizers temporarily mask poor soil—they don't solve any problems.

The Best Defense Is a Good Offense

In This Chapter

- Attracting beneficial insects to your garden
- Beneficial insects and the plants that attract them
- Why you should consider organic garden practices
- Using Integrated Pest Management
- Choosing organic pest controls

Your garden is now growing, thriving, and off to a great start. So how do you protect it from the insects and critters that would like to make your Garden of Eden their dinner? Should you use the nearest pesticide and shoot up the place, or go organic? Do organic practices really work, and how do you use them? Are some of those creepy-crawlers actually good guys that we can put to work? Those are the questions we're going to answer in this chapter.

The Argument for Organic

So why practice organic gardening? Does it really work? Aren't the pesticides, herbicides, and other expensive chemical fertilizers on the store shelves simply more effective? In recent years the term "organic gardening" has gone from hip buzzword to nearly ignored in a sentence simply because the term feels overused.

That said, to this day I overhear people stating that organic gardening techniques don't work nearly as well as synthetic chemicals for controlling pests and disease in the yard and garden. I think that gardeners who adhere to this theory either aren't actually practicing organic methods or aren't doing so for long enough.

First of all, synthetic chemicals may seem to work faster initially, but in the long run they don't work any better. And more often than not, they end up doing more harm than good. Don't forget that the pollinators necessary to the garden are also in the path of chemical pesticides, as are our bodies and the environment. Herbicides eventually create superweeds and threaten soils, waterways, wildlife, and human life. Inorganic fertilizers can be safe, but they do little to actually amend the soil (which is the real goal, after all) and can damage lakes, streams, and ponds due to runoff.

Organic gardening practices still offer the best, most earth- and people-friendly practices for maintaining a healthy balance in the garden—and a greater balance in your wallet.

Ideally, wouldn't it be grand if no one ever used chemical pesticides or herbicides again? In reality, each gardener has their own tolerance level and you need to define that line for yourself. For instance, most organic gardeners know that they'll have to put up with a few leaves with holes in them or perhaps lose a few seedlings to snails. Of course, there will be situations where you may need to break out the bigger guns, but did you know that the heavier artillery can be nontoxic chemicals, or at least less toxic? Take a look at the Integrated Pest Management (IPM) section later in this chapter.

TIP THYME

As a small-space gardener, you probably have neighbors living next to you and possibly a family in your home. Utilizing as many organic practices as you can in your yard and garden is extremely healthy and responsible to the environment and people living around you.

Here, again, is the beauty of gardening in small spaces. Organic garden practices don't get any easier than when you're gardening on a small plot. Pest and weed control methods are not only easier physically, but the techniques work better because you're not waving a gardening flag the size of three football fields in the face of the would-be pests. Wide expanses of land covered in blossoms or vegetables call in the pests in a big way.

Beneficial Insects

Not all insects are created equal. Some bugs—such as aphids, snails, slugs, and the Colorado potato beetle—see your heirloom garden and immediately hear the dinner bell. These are the bad guys. The *other* guys are known as the "beneficial" insects, and they're like knights in shining armor for your plants.

The beneficials take care of just enough bad guys to maintain a harmonious balance between gorgeous, healthy plants and a few munched leaves. Organic gardeners find beneficial insects especially helpful since they don't use chemical pest controls in their garden or yard. With these natural soldiers on our side, we can eliminate—or at least reduce—the use of potentially harmful synthetic pesticides.

Beneficial insects fall into two beneficial categories. Predator insects carry the heavy artillery, diligently devouring the bugs that devour your garden. Predatory insects include ladybugs, ground beetles, soldier flies, and lacewings. The pollinators make it possible for the garden to produce vegetables and flowers. Remember that more creatures than just insects can act as a plant pollinator. Wind, birds, and mammals are all pollinators, as are humans. But insects such as butterflies, honey bees, and blue mason bees do the lion's share of spreading pollen throughout the garden. The idea is to invite as many beneficials from both classes into the yard and garden as possible.

Recognizing the Good Guys

It's important that gardeners learn to recognize the difference between friend and foe. It's always best to identify your local critters so that you don't accidentally wipe out your own troops. You'll want to know which plants are particularly attractive to your beneficial insect team. In fact, many beneficial insects don't look like the friendly type at all.

Take ladybug larvae, for example. On one hand we have the mature adults who are colored a cheerful red and resemble a very tiny, shiny Volkswagen. Ladybug children, however, are just about as off-putting as it gets. They're painted a rough red-orange and black with a prehistoric alligator form. If you didn't know what they are, no one in their right mind would let one live.

You can find beneficial insect images online and in organic gardening books. Field guides are another excellent insect photo source, offering information not only on the good and bad insects, but also where you'll find them and what plants whet their appetite. *Mac's Field Guide Bug Identification Page*, available at Amazon.com, is one of the handiest references I've had hanging around the garden shed. This laminated sheet has pictures of beneficial insects on one side and garden pests on the other.

If you're really not sure what bug you've found, feel free to catch one in a jar and bring it down to a local nursery for proper identification. I strongly recommend that you find a nursery instead of a retail garden center. People at garden centers may be able to identify your insect, but it's easier to trust the actual nurserymen who grow plants and have experience with insects. If the species can't be identified, then your local Cooperative Extension office can surely help.

Without bashing commercial retail garden centers, there are a few reasons to patronize your local nursery as opposed to a large retail garden center. The first one is that the small nurseries have a tendency to hire people who truly have plant and pest knowledge, while the big, retail centers don't seem as concerned about this aspect of plant sales. This isn't a hard-and-fast rule, and certainly there are some knowledgeable people at the big chain stores, too. But I've had better luck at nurseries. I think one of the reasons is that the independent nurseries very often grow the plants right there at the back of their retail store (or on their land elsewhere), which gives them hands-on experience with raising plants and battling the pests.

The other reason to support your independent nursery is that those big chains are driving the smaller nurseries (families) out of business. It makes good sense to help keep family-owned businesses alive in your community.

The Not-So-Subtle Art of Seduction

Plants want to stay in existence just as much as we do. In order for that to happen, the flowers need to be pollinated in order to set the fruit that carries future generations in its seeds. A plant's main goal is to spread its seeds as far as possible to ensure that the species continues. Like people, plants rely on seduction to get the job done.

Each plant species has evolved to be provocative to insects in its own way. Bees can be lured by a perennial's bright petals. Butterflies and birds can become dizzily drunk on oozing plant nectar. And others produce so much pollen that when the wind blows the neighbor next door becomes pollinated—literally. Your role in this romantic scenario is to play matchmaker between the insect suitors and the plants of their desire. The plants you choose should be rich in pollen, nectar, or color.

Seriously Seductive Plants

Plants produce flowers to reproduce themselves … end of story. Flowers may fascinate us, amaze us, and make our jaws drop at their beauty, but the fact that they're attractive to humans is just a happy coincidence. They've also had millions of years to perfect their own personal, provocative style. But there are plants that seem to be especially gifted in the art of seducing a wide variety of beneficial insects.

Once predatory insects are lured by the appetizers of color and pollen, they'll stay for the main course: the pests. Many beneficials are especially attracted to plants belonging to the umbel or aster families, such as zinnia or Queen Anne's lace. These plants produce composite (compound) which are flowers that grow in the center of large ray flowers. Fennel, tansy, dill, and cosmos also produce compound flowers.

The list below is in no way exhaustive. Don't forget to plant some local native plants, too. They're a natural food source for many insects and can go a long way in helping you achieve your goal. For more information on plants that attract specific beneficial insects to your small garden, you can contact your Cooperative Extension office.

TIP THYME

If you're having trouble finding seductive plants in the usual places, try your local native plant nursery. They're a valuable resource when you're looking for plants that attract beneficial insects.

Some beneficial insect-seducing plants are:

marigold   An annual flower that blooms from summer to fall. There are many varieties and cultivars of this perfect garden companion plant. The colors range from white, yellow, orange, to rust, with mixes of those colors. All zones.

tansy   This is a perennial herb whose yellow flower heads show up in mid- to late summer. It's known by many common names including mugwort and bitter buttons. Zones 4–10.

Queen Anne's lace   This annual blooms in frothy white flowers in the late summer. It's also known as bishop's flower and bishop's lace. Zones 3–9.

Sweet Cicely   This herbaceous perennial is also known as garden myrrh. It blooms in small white flowers May to June. The whole plant is very aromatic. Zones 3–10.

dill   This hardy annual blooms in yellow flower in midsummer. It's super for attracting beneficials. Zones 3–7.

stonecrop   Sedum is a perennial plant (and ground cover) with succulent leaves and, depending on the variety, can bloom from May to August or late in fall. The flowers can be red, purple, pink, yellow, or white. Zones 3–10.

lavender   This is an evergreen, shrubby perennial herb that blooms with little lavender, blue, white, or pink flowers. Zones 6–9 (depending on the species).

thyme   This perennial herb blossoms with white, pink, deep rose, or magenta flowers in late spring through summer. Zones 4–9 (depending on the species).

coreopsis   Also known as tickseed, most of the varieties of this sunflower family member are perennials, although some are annuals. They bloom profusely in the summer with yellow, orange reddish, and maroon flowers. Zones 3–9 (depending on the species).

catnip   This perennial herb is also known as catmint. It blooms in white, blue, purple, or yellow in the summer or fall. Zones 3–9 (depending on the species).

summer savory   This aromatic annual herb blooms in the summer with white or pink flowers. Zones 5–8.

floss flower   This annual blooms with fluffy blue or blue-and-white flower heads all summer. Zones 5–10 (but a frost will just nail them).

alyssum   Sweet alyssum blooms spring though fall with tiny white, pink, or purple flowers. It's usually a perennial but is grown as an annual. This compact low spreader has a sweet scent if you stoop to smell the blossoms. Zones 4–9.

Mexican sunflower   Tithonia varieties can be annuals or perennials. They have orange or orange-red flowers that bloom in late summer to fall. Zones 5–10.

red clover   Also called crimson clover, this annual has creamy yellow to deep-red flowers in the spring and summer. Zones 6–9.

lovage   This perennial herb blooms with small, yellow flowers in mid- to late summer. Zones 3–8.

black-eyed Susan   This perennial blooms with orange or yellow flowers in the late summer to midfall. Zones 4–9.

coneflower   These perennials bloom all summer long with white, pink, or purple-pink flowers. Zones 3–9 (depending on the species).

blazing star   Also known as gayfeather, this perennial blooms in the late summer and early fall in pinkish-purple or white. Zones 3–9 (depending on the species).

bee balm   This lovely plant comes in annual or perennial form. Its flowers are white, pink, red, or violet and bloom from midsummer to early fall.

fennel   This perennial is often treated as an annual since the bulbs are often harvested for culinary dishes. It blooms tiny clusters of yellow flowers in the summer. Zones 4–9.

cosmos   Cosmos varieties can be annual or perennial. It blooms all summer and into the fall. The flowers can be shades of pink, rose, crimson, lavender, and purple. They can also come in brownish-red (chocolate) and yellow. Zones 5–10.

yarrow   This deciduous perennial isn't limited to white or yellow blossoms any longer. Newer cultivars have given us orange, pink, and salmon in the summer and fall. Zones 2–9.

goldenrod   This is a woody-based perennial that blooms in the late summer to fall. The flowers are bright golden yellow to yellow-orange. Zones 2–8.

Meet the Predators

Although the insects below are useful pest predators, they can also double as effective pollinating insects. It bears repeating: these lists are not exhaustive. For the best information on the beneficial insects that will be hanging around in your garden, contact your local Cooperative Extension office.

spider   People are often repelled by these eight-legged creatures, but spiders are friends to the garden. They eat more insects in the garden than birds.

green lacewing   Also called the aphid lion, it's the green lacewing larva that eats 60 aphids per hour. They also eat other soft-bodied insects such as mites, mealybugs, spider mites, whiteflies, scale, and thrips. The adult lacewing is a pollinator.

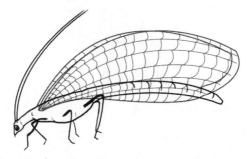

The lacewing is also called the "aphid lion" for his favorite snack.

ladybug   Adult ladybugs will eat 5,000 aphids by the time they die. Other ladybug prey includes bean thrips, mites, chinch bugs, Colorado potato beetles, and asparagus beetles.

ladybug larvae These little dudes are black and orange-red with a prehistoric alligator look. These spiny little creatures aren't much to look at, but they can eat 50 to 70 aphids in a day.

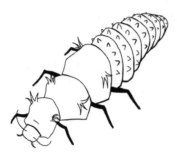

Ladybug larva looks nothing like their Volkswagen-bodied parents.

hoverfly Also called the syrphid fly, the larvae feed on soft-bodied pest insects.

praying mantid Although mantids certainly eat garden pests, they aren't big consumers and sometimes grab a good guy or two in the process.

minute pirate bug These tiny predators control small caterpillars, aphids, mites, and thrips. They are especially handy in the greenhouse as they like high humidity.

Minute pirate bugs happily offer their services of pest control.

spined soldier bug Potato beetles, tomato hornworms, and cabbage worms end up getting "harpooned" by this predator.

trichogramma wasp This wasp is one in a group of parasitic wasps that lay their eggs inside the larvae of garden pests such as cabbage worms, cutworms, and borers.

ground beetles   You may not see them much in the daylight hours, as they tend to hide among the plant debris on the ground. But at night they come out hungry!

assassin bug   These predators don't have much in the looks department but do have a voracious appetite for plant pests.

Meet the Pollinators

You'll be familiar with some of these pollinating insects, but there may be a couple that you haven't met yet.

honey bees   There are many different type of bees that can pollinate plants and some are around during different phases of the growing season, so it makes good sense to have a nice variety of plants to keep them coming around.

butterflies   Butterflies are a rather obvious pollinating insect. Although they may not be as effective as some other pollinators (they don't get a lot of pollen on their bodies), I'd invite them in no matter what.

lacewings   This is truly one of the most effective beneficials that you can have loitering about your garden. They're lovely as adults, dressed in light, bright greens and wearing fairy wings. Adults will pollinate and their children will eat the things that go crunch (on your plants) in the night.

moths   Moths are terrific pollinators but usually do so at night, so they end up pollinating plant flowers that are open during that time. One of the daytime pollinating moths is the hawk moth or hummingbird moth, which is out in the day pollinating like crazy. Hawk moths are usually mistaken for hummingbirds.

flies   Usually one of the biggest pests we can think of, right? Well, we aren't talking about houseflies here, but rather black soldier flies, tachinid flies, syrphid flies, and bee flies. In fact, flies are second only to bees for pollinating plants.

wasps   I know—I have you cringing now. But wasps are very effective pollinators. What can I say?

blue mason bees (and other native bees)   These little blue bees are also called orchard bees and are often mistaken for flies. Many a gardener has wondered why flies are enjoying their roses, never suspecting that they're actually this gentle pollinator. This big, blue, fly-looking bee isn't into stinging. In fact, only the females have stingers and they aren't inclined to use them. This might be partly due to the fact that they don't make honey and aren't busy protecting it.

Integrated Pest Management (IPM)

In plain garden-speak, Integrated Pest Management's (IPM) motto goes something like, "Don't use a bulldozer when a hand trowel will do." The idea behind IPM is to start with the least toxic remedy to a potentially bad situation and move up the ladder from there.

For the most part, IPM relies on the gardeners (and farmers) to monitor and gather information in order to ascertain which management technique (if any) is necessary. Here's how the Integrated Pest Management system is generally practiced.

Assess the Damage

Has all your baby spinach become a snail family's dinner? Or are there a couple of cosmetic blemishes on a few pieces of fruit? Has this pest moved all of his family and friends into your place? Or is it just he and his mate on a day trip? There's a big difference. It might sound odd, but sometimes you really don't need to do anything.

In the case of slightly blemished fruit, you have to admit that probably means that the natural balance of things is pretty stable. If that's the worry you have, then the natural enemies of the pest that are leaving a blemish or two must be plentiful in your garden. In fact, if this is the only worry you have, this is what we call "successful gardening."

Know Your Enemies—and Your Allies

The first thing to realize is that the mere presence of an insect does not a problem make. In other words, what kind of bug is it? How do you know it's eating your plants? Where there are bad guys, there are bound to be good guys. Learn to identify them and look for them.

Everyone has their personal tolerance level. One gardener may find some damage isn't a big deal, while another may find the same damage unacceptable. And yet another may decide that the plant with the problem isn't worth the hassle, and may choose to replace it with a more pest-resistant species altogether.

The Four IPM Control Categories

Gardeners who use IPM in their gardens combine the following controls to maintain a healthy and thriving garden:

These are the methods practiced using Integrated Pest Management:

- **Physical controls:** *Copper strips*, diatomaceous earth, and picking and tossing by hand work well for snail control. Sticky traps can be put out in a place where an undesirable amount of pests are setting up camp. These are good examples of getting physical.

> **DEFINITION**
>
> **Copper strips** are used to encircle a plant or placed on a tree trunk to keep slugs and snails away. Copper gives them a slight electrical shock when their bodies touch it. It doesn't kill them, but does act as a barrier.

- **Horticultural controls:** This includes choosing plant varieties that are labeled as disease or pest resistant. Companion planting can be used to either mask the scent of a desirable crop or to distract or confuse pests. Also, keep your plants healthy; healthy plants are the least susceptible to the bad dudes. Part of keeping plants healthy is to remove any foliage that could be diseased and discard it permanently in the garbage. Don't toss plant remains that you suspect to be diseased into your compost pile.

- **Biological controls:** Invite (or go out and purchase) other living creatures that eat insects and their larva. For the most part, if you don't use a lot of pesticides in your garden, you'll have a healthy supply of beneficial insects in your garden by default.

- **Least-toxic chemical controls:** There may come a time when bigger is better and a larger gun is necessary, but this is the last resort in the IPM lineup. The same general IPM principals are still applicable here. Start with organic pesticides such as insecticidal soaps, horticultural oils, and other controls derived from plants. If you feel that you need to use synthetic chemical controls, please read the labels carefully and follow the instructions. (See "If You Have to Use Chemical Pesticides or Herbicides" in Chapter 17.)

Other Outstanding Organic Operatives

It's true that there are hundreds (probably closer to thousands) of tried-and-true gardening hints designed to keep plants relatively free of pests and disease. These tips were handed down as garden gospel because someone experimented with some way of controlling aphids on their roses or keeping slugs off of new seedlings—and it actually worked! For them, anyway.

I think the biggest lesson that I've learned through the years is that you have to be willing to experiment with a few techniques to see which ones work for you. Successful gardeners will be more than willing to share their bag of tricks with you. Try their ideas and then pass these tips along to other gardeners. Among the many things to try are some seriously outstanding organic practices that work well for nearly every gardening situation. They'll truly give you a leg up on keeping diseases at bay and pests under control.

Critters for Pest Control

Insect-eating birds such as chickadees, bluebirds, purple martins, swallows, nuthatches, and wrens can be wonderful adversaries for the gardener. They have a grand time feasting on annoying pests such as stinkbugs, cucumber beetles, caterpillars, grasshoppers, and aphids. Lure them to your yards with bird baths, nesting boxes, and suet feeders.

If you like the rhythmic sound of frogs in the evening, you're in luck. Toads and frogs are tops for natural pest control. They enjoy shady garden areas with perpetual damp spots. Toads are easier to keep around because they're happy with shallow water like sealed plant saucers half-buried into the soil. They're also masters at reducing unwanted garden pests. Don't overlook frogs as a good insect predator, but to keep them in your yard you'll need a substantially deeper water source such as a true pond.

Old-Fashioned Elbow Grease

Then there is some hand-to-hand, down-on-your-knees battling that you can do yourself. Never underestimate a blast of water from the hose. Have you seen what a fire hose can do to someone? A garden hose is just as effective against the agitators you're facing. Don't just aim the nozzle randomly at your plant like Rambo; focus on the underside of the leaves. Adjust the water pressure according to strength of the plant, too.

> **TIP THYME**
>
> Water blasts are especially effective for controlling aphids, and if the sheer force doesn't kill these soft-bodied beasts, it breaks their jaws or some other such horrible thing. Which, of course, pleases us to no end.

Pick pests off with your fingers and squish them. Or brush them off the plant with your hands and step on them. Drown them in a bucket of soapy water or give them to your urban chickens. Round up some skilled insect hunters such as your kids—or borrow someone else's kids. Be sure they're doing a search and destroy on the *bad guys.* Pay them and you may never have to worry about pest control again.

Natural-Born Killers

Backyard gardeners everywhere are doing their part to push pesticides out of the gardening picture for good and insecticidal soaps are helping them do just that. If you're battling soft-bodied pests such as aphids, whiteflies, mealybugs, soft scale, or spittlebugs, try showering them with insecticidal soap.

There are insecticidal soaps that have already been mixed and measured for you such as one made by Safer brand. You'll find them at nurseries, online, or through garden catalogs. Commercial insecticidal soaps are considered eco-friendly, low- or nontoxic, and typically state that they can be used on both ornamental plants as well as edible ones (always double-check the label for guidance).

Some gardeners have their own favorite soap recipes, but whichever type of insect brew you use, it's important to understand that using soap mixtures controls pests *after* they've already arrived on the plant. Insecticidal soaps aren't preventative measures—they're meant to kill the bugs that are already bugging you. Of course, there are homemade spray recipes that are made with ingredients such as hot pepper and garlic that are used on plants as a repellant as opposed to a killing agent. But that's a horse of a different color.

Homemade Insecticidal Soap. A simple mixture of 3 to 5 tablespoons of liquid dish soap (not detergent) and a bit of vegetable oil to a gallon of water works just as well. The trick here is that you want to use a dishwashing soap that doesn't contain a degreaser or you may kill more plants by burning their leaves than you do pests. This concoction is then poured into a hand-held spray bottle or garden sprayer and then used on plants when the sun is low and temperatures are cool (usually the morning hours).

Depending on the soap recipe and the pest, gardeners either coat the critter causing the insect's cells to collapse, affect their nervous system, or simply become immobilized (therefore easy to spray off with the hose). Once the soap has dried, it's no longer effective.

Don't forget that it's best to try a small test spot on plant leaves before spraying an entire plant with any soaps. Most do just fine, but a few may be adversely affected. Signs that plants aren't reacting well are spots on the leaves or brown edges or tips.

Nontoxic, Low-Toxic, or What? Insecticidal soaps are placed in the very low-toxic category. In fact, many people claim that Safer brand is nontoxic to people and pets, as well as safe for beneficial insects. I think that for the most part that's true—it's virtuously harmless to mammals, although soaps can be slightly irritating to the eyes or skin. But the other school of thought is that anything that kills anything can't be considered *entirely* nontoxic.

While insecticidal soap may be considered safe for families and pets, there's a good chance it may take some of the beneficial insects down, too. So a good rule of thumb is to use the soap only on the plants that have been invaded with pests and to read commercial labels carefully while applying. As an organic gardener, I think this is a terrific alternative to many other pest control methods.

Horticultural oils work a lot like the insecticidal soaps in that they are meant to coat the insects in order to kill them. These oils kill eggs as well as mature insects. Oils fall into two general categories: dormant oils used in the late winter on trees and plants before they leaf out, and summer oils used when temperatures outside are over 40° but under 85°. Before you apply oil (petroleum) products, be sure that you know which type of horticultural oil you should use in order to avoid damaging or killing your plants.

It's also wise to do a little research on the tree or plant you're using the oil on. Japanese maples are known to be extremely sensitive to dormant oils, and a blue spruce may be stripped of its blue color by them. The summer oil sprays are much lighter, so plants have fewer reactions to them.

Pyrethrins are natural insecticides derived from pyrethrum daisies. They basically attack the central nervous system of insects. Pyrethrins are acceptable for organic gardening practices; technically, they aren't 100 percent nontoxic, but they're pretty darn close. They're also biodegradable and take just a few days to break down in the sunlight.

It's worth mentioning, however, that pyrethrins don't discriminate between the bad insects and the good ones, so they are a good choice if you need to use a low-impact insecticide, but don't use them to saturate the garden, either. Don't confuse pyrethrins (or pyrthrum) with the synthetic counterpart, permethrin.

Diatomaceous Earth (DE)

Diatomaceous earth (DE) isn't only inexpensive and effective, it's also nontoxic to kids, birds, and pets. And yet it destroys ants, earwigs, slugs, beetles, ticks, fleas, cockroaches, and bedbugs. As these pests move across the powder, it sticks to their feet and legs, only to get into their joints and exoskeleton.

DE is made up of crushed fossilized skeletons of diatoms and algae. Some people claim that the DE is jagged and sharp, so it works like little pieces of broken glass and scratches up the insects' bodies, then dries up their fluids. I've heard a slight variation of that theme that says, instead of scratching up their bodies, the DE is absorbed into the bug's breathing tubes as well as their joints, eyes, and so on. It doesn't really matter exactly *how* it works—just that the pests quit eating and death isn't far behind.

To humans and pets, DE feels like powder and is completely harmless. That said, you don't necessarily want diatomaceous earth in your lungs, so wear a dust mask when you're applying it. One thing you need to know is that there are different grades of diatomaceous earth. You don't want the stuff used for keeping swimming pools clean; you're going to purchase horticultural grade DE.

DE isn't an instant kill; it could take days or weeks to be rid of pests completely. But you will be rid of them without sacrificing anything else.

The Least You Need to Know

- Use beneficial insect-attracting plants to lure predatory and pollinating insects to the garden.
- Organic garden practices are superior to chemical warfare and keep a healthy balance between pests and predators in the garden.
- There are many excellent organic choices for controlling pests, such as wildlife, water, hand picking, soap sprays, oils, diatomaceous earth, and pyrethrins.
- Integrated Pest Management offers progressive stages of pest control.

Outsmarting Weeds

In This Chapter

- Presprouting technique
- How to use solarization
- Mulch and ground cover
- Using chemical pesticides and herbicides safely

In order to outsmart weeds, we first need to assume that they may be smarter than us. Let me make this clear for you: they *are* smarter than us. That may sting a little, but the fact is that weeds have had thousands and thousands of years to adjust to just about everything nature—never mind us gardeners—throws at them. They've become masters at stealing water, robbing nutrients, and generally taking over gardens since time began. They show up both as aggressive annuals and persistent perennials. The good news is that weeds *can* be outsmarted. *Ve have our vays.*

Even better news is that, as far as weeds go, those of us with small-space gardens have a big advantage over gardeners with big acreage. The techniques that follow are used by seasoned gardeners everywhere. But when they're put to use by small space gardeners, I promise you that that you'll probably never have to reach for the herbicide.

Come into My Parlor

Weeds can reproduce by seed, *stolon*, and root pieces. One technique for getting many springtime weeds out of the way from the start is to let them sprout (often called presprouting). That's right—encourage them to show themselves early on in the season, then, "Whack! Off with their heads!" This weed-control style works best in a vegetable garden bed. Presprouting can be used for beds in the ground or with raised beds.

> **DEFINITION**
>
> **Stolon** is an above-ground plant shoot that presses horizontally against the ground and produces roots at the node (where the leaf attaches to the stem).

Simply plan your attack by acting as if you're getting the garden bed ready to plant. Get this garden together well before you actually plan on planting vegetables for the season—say, about four weeks before your true planting schedule. Add whatever amendments you'd normally put into the garden bed—compost, garden soil, whatever. Rake the bed so it's smooth and really inviting. Then water it regularly. It'll only take a couple of weeks for tiny weed heads to sprout.

These first weeds are typically annuals, but anything can show up at this point. When they've grown around 2" tall, take a flat or stirrup hoe and knock them all down by scraping the soil at their feet. The first presprouting will give you an advantage, but you might as well water the bed again and let more rise—just so you can take them down again. Whacking presprouted weeds won't rid you of trouble entirely, but it's a terrific head start.

Let Them Fry

While we're in a killing frame of mind, let's talk a little bit about solarization. This is another weed control that works best in actual garden beds (raised or not), such as those used for vegetables. It's for killing weeds in areas that you won't mind covering up for a while; this would *not* be the right weed control for a perennial garden.

This technique works best in a sunny area. It's as easy as removing all the plants from the bed during a hot month like July. Cover the entire bed with clear plastic sheeting. Make it as smooth as you can and then reinforce the edges so the plastic stays in place over the garden.

The idea is to let the sun do the killing by heating the soil up to temperatures high enough to fry the weeds' seeds. This technique also destroys pathogens in the soil that attack plants, so that's a plus. This can take five to eight weeks, so, although solarization does work, you lose that garden space for a couple of months and you may notice the biggest difference after a season or two. If you're using solarization in an area where you're planning a new garden bed, then you're not losing a season at all.

> **TIP THYME**
>
> Don't forget that when you use solarization to kill off weeds and bad bacteria, you've also killed off some of the good bacteria and fungi in the garden soil. The best idea is to reintroduce the good bacteria by adding fresh compost to the soil before you replant the garden.

Covering Ground

The praises of covering bare soil in landscaping, flower borders, or vegetable beds is sung by gardeners everywhere. It's one of the single best gardening techniques that you can practice. Covering naked soil …

- Drastically reduces weeds by blocking the weed seeds from the sun and smothering them. If you plant a ground cover as living mulch, the weeds also have a hard time competing for water and nutrients.

- Retains moisture by slowing down evaporation and allowing water to remain available to plant roots. This can be especially important if you live in an often drought-stricken area like California.

- Insulates plant roots and flower bulbs against temperature fluctuations.

- Prevents soil erosion from wind and heavy rain. If you plant a living mulch or ground cover, between their fibrous roots and their leaves, they'll actually bind the soil.

All of these benefits will save you time, money, and effort. There are a number of ways to blanket the soil. One of them is to use the traditional mulches you see in neighborhoods everywhere. These mulches may be organic or inorganic in nature. Both work well, but the organic mulches will need to be replenished, since they eventually break down into the soil.

Organic Mulches

Organic mulches are products of former living things. That is, they were once alive and now they're dead—but they're just as useful. The extra perk that comes with using organic mulch is that it eventually breaks down and builds the soil, both in volume and nutrition.

Examples of organic mulches include the following:

- Shredded bark
- Wood chips
- Compost
- Grass clippings
- Dry leaves
- Pine needles (for areas that house acid-loving plants such as azaleas)
- Sawdust
- Straw
- Newspaper
- Cardboard

Inorganic Mulches

You may be wondering why rocks, pebbles, and sand are on the inorganic list; after all, they're not necessarily man-made. They're all natural products, but they aren't organic in that they didn't originate from something that was once alive, and they won't break down into the soil.

Here's a partial list of inorganic mulch material:

- Landscape fabric or cloth
- Black plastic
- Glass
- Rocks and pebbles
- Sand

Living Mulches

Ground covers are often called "living mulches." These soil-huggers of the plant world offer the same wonderful attributes as the other mulches, but with a few extra perks. I use ground cover as living mulch every chance I get; it adds beauty, texture, and scent to the yard. I especially love the herbs like woolly thyme; the bonus is the lovely feeling on bare feet!

Common ground covers include the following:

- Low-growing herbs
- Low-growing geraniums (true geraniums, not pelargoniums)
- Mosses
- Vining plants (and vegetables)

The Right Mulch in the Right Place

Before you decide which mulch is for you, consider the area that you need to cover. Foundation landscapes and perennial flower borders are basically considered "permanent" beds in that you're not going to be switching out plants each season. The better choices for these gardens are the inorganic mulches, ground cover (living mulch), and shredded bark or wood chips.

TIP THYME

Flower beds located in the front yard may not look their best with straw placed at their feet. On the other hand, don't overlook using several layers of newspaper as an organic backup underneath the top layer of shredded bark, either.

Vegetable gardens are the best place for mulches such as newspaper, straw, and grass clippings. These organic mulches break down in a reasonable amount of time. So by the time a new season rolls around (and new crops), you won't be disturbing the mulch materials. As far as newspaper, I could sing its praises every day (and I do). Newspaper is a fabulous organic mulch. Most people have it readily available to them, and if they don't, their neighbor does. It's 100 percent biodegradable and the critters in the soil love it.

TIP THYME

Other handy mulch ideas are the vining crops such as pumpkins, squash, melons, cucumbers, and zucchini. These vegetables can act as ground cover for taller crops like pepper plants, sunflowers, and corn.

I usually make it about five layers thick or more, as newspaper decomposes pretty quickly. If the wind is blowing it around while you're trying to spread it out, just dampen the newspapers with some water. Cardboard works exactly the same way, but it'll last longer. Cardboard makes terrific paths between vegetable rows.

Compost is the ultimate mulch in any garden situation. It has the added benefit of being loaded with turbo-nutrients that leach into the soil immediately. Compost also builds soil texture and tilth.

Herb gardens receive the biggest benefits from using sand as mulch. Containers planted with succulents like it, too. Those herbs that hail from the Mediterranean thrive in brilliant sunlight and detest soggy feet.

Sand reflects and intensifies the sunlight on the plant … exactly what herbs crave. Placing a layer onto the herb bed will not only make the sun stronger, but it has the perfect drainage property for herbs, which don't tolerate wet feet for very long. The type of sand you want to purchase is mason's sand—not children's sandbox sand, nor beach sand. Those grains are too fine. Use 1" of sand in an outdoor herb bed and about $\frac{1}{2}$" for your potted herbs.

Glass mulch is the creative gardener's dream. There's no limit to how you can use and design with it. Little garden areas, paths, walkways, container gardens, and fish ponds can be beautifully accented with this unique mulch material. It's predominately recycled glass, so that's a win-win for the environment and your yard.

Work on Your Timing

No matter how great the gardening advances, sometimes nothing compares with good old-fashioned manual labor. I don't make these garden rules; I'm just the messenger. Hand pulling weeds whenever you can is often the very best way to stay one step ahead. The key with pulling weeds, of course, is the timing.

Annual weeds start and finish their entire life cycle within one year. Weeds such as lamb's quarters, carpetweed, annual sedge, chickweed, crabgrass, knotweed, and Japanese clover should be pulled up *before* seed heads are formed. This is key to weed eradication, because if you let those little seed heads mature, they're going to scatter themselves silly all over your yard and garden—leading to a bigger battle.

Try ridding the yard of annual weeds right after a rain. In fact, annual weeds tend to miraculously pop up right after a spring rain. This is the perfect time for the presprouting technique we talked about earlier. The annual weeds you've pulled can be added to your compost pile because the seed heads haven't formed, so there's no way for them to reproduce. Some vegetable gardeners will pull them up and then bury them right in the veggie bed for added nitrogen. The key here is the lack of seed heads.

Perennial weeds are horses of a different color. They include bindweed, dandelion, purslane, Queen Anne's lace, burdock, nut grass, Bermuda grass, and curly dock, to name a few. It's still best to rid your garden of them before seed heads form. But this group also reproduces by stolon, runners, and tubers underground. Perennial weeds should be completely dug out of the soil to be sure that the entire structure has been removed. As far as the compost pile goes, I don't let perennial weeds near mine. It may be okay for some perennial weeds, but one or two bad experiences will make you swear off this practice.

If You Have to Use Chemical Pesticides or Herbicides

We all have our limits, and there may come a time when you draw the line and say, "Enough is enough." But before you grab the nearest heavy artillery and start shooting up the place, let me just leave you with a few general guidelines:

- Keep children and pets out of the garden area where pesticides or herbicides are being applied until the product is completely settled or dry. Don't eat or drink during the application.

- Store chemical pesticides and herbicides in their original packaging in a dark, cool place.

- Read all product labels very carefully and follow the directions on how to safely handle, apply, and store.

- Chemical products should be applied to plants on a dry day that's free of wind, with moderate temperatures.

- Always wear a face mask, long-sleeved shirt, gloves, and goggles while applying chemical pesticides. Avoid inhaling the products or touching your skin or face with your hands after the application.

- Wash the clothing used for the application separately from other laundry and wash your hands and face immediately afterward. Thoroughly clean the application equipment, too.

- Be certain that the product you're using is safe for food crops before applying it to the vegetable garden.

- Keep pesticides from reaching swimming pools or other bodies of water such as streams or ponds.

Pesticide Labels

Chemical pesticides and herbicides have their ingredients listed, as well as how to specifically use the product on their label. They also have one of four words to describe how harmful they are to humans or the degree of toxicity:

- **Caution:** This is the lowest toxicity. A product labeled this way can range from relatively nontoxic to slightly toxic. The approximate human lethal dosage is an ounce (in the case of a slightly hazardous product) or more (say, over a pint for a fairly nontoxic product).

- **Warning:** A product with a warning label is moderately toxic or hazardous. The human lethal dose is approximately 1 teaspoon to 1 ounce.

- **Danger:** This would be a highly hazardous product and is best kept out of the house entirely. The lethal human dose is pesticide specific, so read the label very carefully.

- **Danger Poison:** Usually accompanied by a skull-and-crossbones image, this means that the product is highly toxic. The lethal human dose is anywhere from a small taste to 1 teaspoon. This would be another example of a product that home gardeners are better off not using.

The Least You Need to Know

- Presprouting is most effective when it's done a couple of times in the early spring.
- Solarization is primarily for gardens such as vegetable beds, where plants are replanted each season.
- Mulch comes in several forms: organic, inorganic, and ground cover (living mulch).
- When using chemical pesticides or herbicides, apply them as the label states and keep away from people and animals.

Plants for Small Spaces

This handy plant index will give you a place to start by introducing the smaller plant varieties or those that have the type of growing habits we like for small spaces. Here, you'll find more than just plant names on a list. This part is all about showing off the personalities of the various plant varieties. There's a chapter on annuals and perennials, which are broken down into sunny and shady categories.

Chapter 19 profiles climbeing plants, ground covers, and grasses. The last chapter has tree and shrub profiles with some introductions to evergreens and flowering shrubs to make the most of a little land (or containers). After meeting the plants that thrive in small gardens, you'll realize that you're anything but limited.

Annual and Perennial Plant Profiles

This chapter lists some annuals and perennials that are perfect for small-space gardens, and most of them take to container life well. Annual plants are perfect for bringing in instant color or for filling in spaces between perennial plantings.

Perennials are the "secondary" bones in the garden—second only to trees and shrubs. They anchor and give permanence to garden structure, and best of all they come back year after year, usually bigger and better, without you having to do anything!

Shade-loving annuals and perennials may have lovely flowers, but many of them are loved for their fabulous foliage. What follows are merely some examples of what will grow well in shady places of your yard or garden. So don't stop with just this list in hand.

Figure out just how much shade you have and peruse a local nursery. Remember to plant bulbs that pop up as a pleasant surprise in the garden year after year without any help from you.

Annuals for Sunny Places

Common Name: Bacopa
Botanical Name: *Sutera cordata*
Height: 1"–2"
Width: 2'
Zone: Anywhere as an annual
Personality: Bacopa is truly a perennial plant for zones 9 through 11, but it's often used as an annual, so I placed it here. This is one of my hands-down favorite versatile, fill-in, trailing plants ever. It's easy to care for and is a fast grower. The flowers come in snowy white, pink, or lavender.

Common Name: Clove pinks, cheddar pinks
Botanical Name: *Dianthus gratianopolitanus*, feuehexe, or firewitch
Height: 10"–12"
Width: 12"
Zone: 3–8
Personality: Clove pinks are a perennial dianthus, but there are biennial varieties such as Sweet William, too. Many are grown as an annual, so don't get confused.

Common Name: Floss flower
Botanical Name: *Ageratum houstonianum*
Height: 6"–24"
Width: Up to 12'
Zone: 5–10
Personality: This sweet and unique-looking flower is a fast grower that blooms in the spring with colors of blue, pink, or white.

Common Name: Heliotrope, cherry pie
Botanical Name: *Heliotropium arborescens*
Height: 18"–36"
Width: 12"
Zone: 10–11; anywhere as an annual
Personality: Heliotrope is a tender perennial that's most often planted as an annual. It blooms in purple, blue, or white fragrant flowers in the summer. It has a fruity cinnamon and vanilla scent—hence its other moniker, cherry pie plant.

Common Name: Love-in-a-mist, devil-in-a-bush
Botanical Name: *Nigella damascena*
Height: 14"–20"
Width: 6"–12"
Zone: All zones
Personality: Love-in-a-mist is so named for its delicate blooms that are surrounded by fennel-like leaves. Then there's devil-in-a-bush, love's alter ego. The name refers to the balloon-shaped seed pods that have little horns on their heads that seem to be hiding behind the spidery foliage. It flowers all summer in blue, white, purple, sky blue, rose, or yellow.

Common Name: Moss rose
Botanical Name: *Portulaca grandiflora*
Height: 8"
Width: 8"–12"
Zone: Anywhere as an annual
Personality: Moss rose has fleshy, succulent-type leaves and is quite drought tolerant once it's established. Blooms summer to early fall in colors including yellow, white, rose, lavender, pink, and orange.

Common Name: Nasturtium
Botanical Name: *Tropaeolum majus*
Height: 6"–13"
Width: 1'–2'
Zone: Everywhere as an annual
Personality: Nasurtium varieties come in dwarf and trailing types, so know which ones you're looking for when you're selecting a variety. Don't forget nasturtiums add peppery flavor to salads (just be sure no chemicals were used on the plants if you're going to harvest them for food).

Common Name: Petunia
Botanical Name: *Petunia x hybrida*
Height: 6"–18"
Width: 6"–14"
Zone: Anywhere as an annual
Personality: Showy petunia flowers come in almost any color you can think of and bloom in the spring and though the summer.

Common Name: Zinnia
Botanical Name: *Zinnia elegans*
Height: 8"–4' depending on variety
Width: 12"
Zone: 3–11
Personality: Zinnias flower in summer through early fall in brilliant and bold colors of red, purple, yellow, apricot, pink, white, green, and orange. They adore hot weather and abhor their leaves splashed with water—so water at the soil line.

Annuals for Shady Spaces

Common Name: Amethyst Flower
Botanical Name: *Browallia*
Height: 1'–2'
Width: 6"–12"
Zone: 2–11
Personality: Amethyst blooms profusely in early spring and into winter (depending on the variety and the zone) with deep-blue flowers. It likes damp soil that's rich in organic matter, and is excellent in containers such as hanging baskets.

Common Name: Coleus, flame nettle
Botanical Name: *Coleus blumei*
Height: 12"–18"
Width: 18"–24"
Zone: 9–11; anywhere as an annual
Personality: To be fair, coleus is actually a perennial plant, but it's so cold sensitive that it's used in most areas as an annual so we'll place it in this section. Coleus is loved for its textured leaves that come in a host of colors, including lime, burgundy, pink, and variegated.

Common Name: Fuchsia
Botanical Name: *Fuchsia*
Height: 1'–6'
Width: 1'–5' wide
Zone: 8–10, but mostly anywhere as an annual
Personality: In small gardens, fuchsias are truly at their best in containers that let their decorative blossoms hang down. Modern varieties come in many shade of pink, lavender, and maroon. Hummingbirds adore them.

Common Name: Garden balsam
Botanical Name: *Impatiens balsamina*
Height: 1'–3'
Width: 1'–2'
Zone: Anywhere as an annual
Personality: Balsam is an old-fashioned, Victorian favorite that belongs to the impatiens family. Its tiny flowers bloom in late spring to early fall in shades of pink, apricot, orange, purple, and white.

Common Name: Impatiens, Busy Lizzie
Botanical Name: *Impatiens walleriana*
Height: 6"–12"
Width: 6"–9"
Zone: Anywhere as an annual
Personality: Impatiens enjoy morning sun, but would rather be shaded from the harsh afternoon sun. They come in a wide array of colors, including red, apricot, pink, white, purple, orange, rose—and every shade in between. They bloom in late spring all the way to the middle of fall.

Common Name: Lobelia
Botanical Name: *Lobelia*
Height: 1'
Width: 1'–2'
Zone: Anywhere as an annual
Personality: Lobelia is a plant-it-and-forget-about-it annual that blooms in blue flowers with white throats in late spring to late fall. It grows excellently in containers, on slopes, and in borders.

Common Name: Pansy
Botanical Name: *Viola x wittrockiana*
Height: 4"–8"
Width: 8"–12"
Zone: Anywhere as an annual
Personality: Yes, violas can be perennials, but because most people use them as annual bedding plants, we're putting them in with the annuals. Pansies bring a ton of color and can flower during the winter, spring, or summer.

Common Name: Polka dot plant, freckle face
Botanical Name: *Hypoestes*
Height: 12"–18"
Width: 9"–12"
Zone: 10–11; anywhere as an annual
Personality: This is a tender perennial that comes back the following year only in the warmest climates; therefore, it's most often used as an annual. The pink foliage with splashes of green is eye-catching and adds a little fun.

Common Name: Sweet potato vine
Botanical Name: *Ipomoea batatas*
Height: 1'–2'
Width: 1'–5'
Zone: Anywhere as an annual
Personality: These are gorgeous, fast-growing, and easy plants to grow. Their various leaf shades of green to purple are the stars of the sweet potato show.

Perennials for Sunny Places

Common Name: Bee balm
Botanical Name: *Monarda spp.*
Height: 12"–18"
Width: 12"–24"
Zone: 4–9
Personality: Monarda blooms anywhere from midsummer to early fall in shades of purple, rose, and lavender. It likes its soil moist and, true to its name, bee balm attracts bees and butterflies.

Common Name: Dwarf balloon flower
Botanical Name: *Platycodon grandiflorus*
Height: 6"–8"
Width: 8"–12"
Zone: 3–9
Personality: This plan blooms all the way through the summer in deep blue, star-shaped flowers. Especially excellent for rock gardens.

Common Name: Garden phlox
Botanical Name: *Phlox spp.*
Height: 15"–36"
Width: 2'–3'
Zone: 3–9
Personality: There are any number of phlox types available (from ground cover to the tall garden variety), and all are suited to small gardens. This particular one makes a sweet statement in a garden as it sits up tall and attracts all kinds of nectar-loving wildlife.

Common Name: Lantana
Botanical Name: *Lantana*
Height: 2'–3'
Width: 4'
Zone: 8–11
Personality: Lantana is one of my favorite perennials. From summer to fall, it flowers in colors ranging from orange, red, yellow, white, rose, and pink, and in all color combinations thereof. Lantana is a butterfly magnet and drought tolerant.

Common Name: Penstemon, beardtongue
Botanical Name: *Penstemon*
Height: 12"–18"
Width: 9"–12"
Zone: 3–9
Personality: Once established a bit, penstemon is drought tolerant. It blooms like crazy through the summer with pink, rose, scarlet, and red-orange tubular flowers that hummingbirds find irresistible.

Common Name: Pentas
Botanical Name: *Pentas lanceolata*
Height: 18"
Width: 18"
Zone: 8–11
Personality: Pentas have a long blooming period, which prompted me to add them, but if you aren't in their favored zones of 8 through 11, you'll have to grow them as an annual. This is an all-time butterfly and hummingbird favorite plant.

Common Name: Pincushion flower
Botanical Name: *Scabiosa columbaria*
Height: 24"–36"
Width: 15"–18"
Zone: 3–9
Personality: Pincushion puts on its flower show in late spring through early fall in colors of white, pink, and blue-violet. Scabiosa prefers well-draining soil and doesn't like to be overwatered.

Common Name: Tickseed, bigflower coreopsis
Botanical Name: *Coreopsis grandiflora*
Height: 18"–24"
Width: 18"–24"
Zone: 4–9
Personality: Tickseed flowers from late spring to early fall in bright, sun-yellow, daisy-type flowers. It's drought tolerant and will self-seed for next year's blooms.

Perennials for Shady Spaces

Common Name: Astible, false spirea, goat's beard
Botanical Name: *Astible x arendsii* Amethyst
Height: 18"–24"
Width: 15"–18"
Zone: 3–9
Personality: This astible has pink or mauve flowers during the midsummer. It likes moist soils, but doesn't like to have its roots drenched, either.

Common Name: Bleeding heart
Botanical Name: *Dicentra spectabilis*
Height: 24"–36"
Width: 18"–24"
Zone: 2–9
Personality: This is a beautiful woodland plant that produces pink or white little hearts along a long wand in the late spring or early summer.

Common Name: Coral bells
Botanical Name: *Heuchera sanguinea*
Height: 12"–18"
Width: 9"–12"
Zone: 3–9
Personality: Heucheras are most often grown for their rich, green-to-bronze-colored evergreen leaves. But many types—such as coral bells—have lovely flowers of white, scarlet, or deep red, too. Flowers show up in the late spring through the summer.

Common Name: Foamflower
Botanical Name: *Tiarella*
Height: 6"–10"
Width: 1'–3'
Zone: 3–8
Personality: Foamflower's foliage is usually a medium green, but there are varieties with variegated leaves that have a mounding habit. This plant is happiest in part to deep shade and it produces bottle-brush flowers mostly in the late spring, but they'll continue to make an appearance throughout the summer. This is an excellent woodland ground cover.

Common Name: Hellebores, Lenten rose, Christmas rose
Botanical Name: *Helleborus orientalis*
Height: 12"–18"
Width: 15"–18"
Zone: 4–9
Personality: Hellebores are long-lived and easy-to-care-for perennials. Pink, purple, white, or rose flower clusters appear in late winter to the middle of spring. They hang as if nodding on the end of their stems.

Common Name: Hosta, plantain lily
Botanical Name: *Hosta spp.*
Height: 2"–3'
Width: 6"–6'
Zone: 3–9
Personality: Grown for their dramatic, showy foliage, hostas come in more sizes, shapes, and leaf colors than ever. Again, many shade-loving hostas produce dainty but lovely flowers.

Common Name: Lungwort
Botanical Name: *Pulmonaria*
Height: 6"–12"
Width: 6" up to 3'
Zone: 4–8
Personality: This early-blooming perennial shade-lover comes in an amazing number of varieties, from the leaf colors and patterns to the amazing flowers. There's a lungwort for everybody and every shade garden.

Common Name: Solomon's seal
Botanical Name: *Polygonatum spp.*
Height: 1'–4'
Width: Around 1'
Zone: 3–9
Personality: Solomon's seal has an elegant form and handsome leaves. It has light-green foliage and bears small, white, tubular flowers in late spring and early summer.

Common Name: Trillium, sweet bath, wood lily, sweet wakerobin
Botanical Name: *Trillium spp.*
Height: 1'–3'
Width: 6"–12"
Zone: 4–9
Personality: Trillium is a North American woodland native that blooms in late spring. The flowers can be red, white, or chocolate-brown, depending on the variety. Trillium goes dormant during the summer, so be sure to stack your garden with other shade-lovers to fill in where sweet bath disappears (it'll be back next year).

Flower Bulbs

Common Name: Cyclamen
Botanical Name: *Cyclamen spp.*
Height: 4"–12"
Width: 9"–12"
Zone: 5–9
Personality: Cyclamen is a great choice for growing under native oak trees. The cyclamen that florists carry will be more tender than those adapted to the outdoors. Also, the cyclamen you find at your local nursery will more than likely have fragrant flowers.

Common Name: Daffodil, jonquil
Botanical Name: *Narcissus*
Height: 4"–16"
Width: Varies as they multiply each year
Zone: 4–9
Personality: Daffodils are a welcome harbinger of spring. They bring sunshine to a world coming out of the cold months. They're also deer resistant, and we like that.

Common Name: Daylily
Botanical Name: *Hemerocallis*
Height: 2'–6'
Width: 1'–3'
Zone: 3–8
Personality: Fragrant, summer-blooming lilies are always a pleasure. Asiatic lilies are easy to grow, and make great cut flowers, too.

Common Name: Freesia
Botanical Name: *Freesia*
Height: 12"–18"
Width: 9"–12"
Zone: 8–11
Personality: Freesias have a rainbow of hues including yellows, pinks, reds, blues, purples, and white. Their late-winter to early summer flowers are elegantly poised at the end of their stalks and release a sweet, heady fragrance.

Common Name: Iris
Botanical Name: *Iris*
Height: 4"–48"
Width: 6"–24"
Zone: 3–10
Personality: There are a ton of iris cultivars, so you should look around your nursery (and neighbors' yards) and decide which cultivar and variety you like best. In any case, iris is a show-stopper (especially the fancy bearded types) and definitely worth having. Iris blooms in the spring or summer depending on the variety.

Common Name: Oriental lily, star gazer
Botanical Name: *Lilium*
Height: 2'–6'
Width: 1'–3'
Zone: 3–8
Personality: Perfume plus! Plant a lot of them because you're going to want to bring some of these fragrant beauties indoors to enjoy. Summer flower colors include shades of red, pink, orange, yellow, and white.

Common Name: Ranunculus
Botanical Name: *Ranunculus asiaticus*
Height: 10"–18"
Width: 9"–12"
Zone: 8–11
Personality: Ranunculus flowers in the late spring and summer, in colors including pink, white, red, yellow, orange, and salmon. The papery petals are arranged like petticoats under a party dress, giving it a so-perfect-it's-fake quality.

Climbers, Ground Covers, and Grasses

In this chapter, we have some specific plants that enjoy growing vertically. Remember it's only a sampling, so don't stop here when looking for ways to grow up. If you're looking to replace some turf, you'll find some good options here. If not, consider planting some ground cover anyway, to finish off the look of a yard, or act as a living mulch by retaining moisture in the soil and suppressing weeds.

Don't overlook the grasses, which may not wow you with flowers, but instead bring texture and interest with their foliage.

Vines and Climbers

Common name: Clematis
Botanical name: *Clematis*
Height: 5'–18'
Width: 3'
Zone: 4–9
Personality: Clematis is the darling of the climbing world. She's not only a fast climber, but her flowers are absolutely charming and come in colors of purple, blue, pink, yellow, and white. Expect them from spring through summer, and even the fall.

Common name: Climbing roses
Botanical name: *Rosa spp.*
Height: 6'–10'
Width: 2'–6'
Zone: 4–11
Personality: There are literally climbing roses by the dozens and in every color of the rainbow. Peruse your local nursery for the varieties that grow well in your area. Don't forget that you'll have to help them along by securing their canes to a structure every now and then. Situate them in full sun.

Common name: Hyacinth bean
Botanical name: *Lablab purpureus*
Height: 10'–12'
Width: 1'–2'
Zone: 10–11; elsewhere it's an annual
Personality: Hyacinth bean produces fragrant purple or white flowers midsummer through midfall. They're followed by purple seed pods during the summer and through the fall.

Common name: Mandevilla
Botanical name: *Mandevilla spp.*
Height: 10'
Width: Varies
Zone: 9–11
Personality: Mandevilla produces large, trumpet-y, pink, red, or white blossoms. They bloom heaviest during the summer, but will flower periodically through the rest of the season, too. This is an evergreen in the warm zones; otherwise it should be considered an annual.

Common name: Morning Glory
Botanical name: *Ipomoea tricolor*
Height: 6'–12'
Width: 1'–2'
Zone: 10–11; use as an annual everywhere else
Personality: Morning glory flowers are absolutely breathtaking. They come in all shades of blue, pink, purple, rose, and white. But do a little research before you plant them. They can be incredibly invasive in some zones and just fine in others.

Common name: Passion flower vine
Botanical name: *Passiflora*
Height: 5'–20'
Width: 1'–3'
Zone: 6–10
Personality: The passion flower is an extremely exotic-looking and amazing work of art. This plant likes its feet wet and its face in the sun. It blooms midsummer to the late fall with flowers in varying shades of pink, purple, and lavender. Bees and butterflies are as captivated as you will be with this climber. Be sure that this plant isn't invasive in your area.

Common name: Pink jasmine
Botanical name: *Jasminum polyanthum*
Height: 12'–15'
Width: 4' and up
Zone: 9–10; otherwise considered an annual
Personality: Pink jasmine's sweet-scented pink-white flowers blossom in the late winter through the midsummer. The leaves differ from the star jasmine in that they're light green and paper thin.

Common name: Star jasmine, confederate jasmine
Botanical name: *Trachelospermum jasminoides*
Height: 3'–20'
Width: 4'–10'
Zone: 6–10
Personality: Star jasmine grows well in full sun to part shade. The white, star-shaped flowers are extremely fragrant, so place it by a window or door where the scent can be fully appreciated. This drought-tolerant evergreen has thick, deep-green foliage.

Ground Covers

Common name: Bronze Dutch clover
Botanical name: *Trifolium repens Atropurpureum*
Height: 3"–6"
Width: 12"–18"
Zone: 4–9
Personality: This clover creates a blanket of bronze leaves that are edged in light green—an eye-catcher for sure. The summer clover flowers are white. Bronze Dutch clover can take a little light foot traffic.

Common name: Bugleweed
Botanical name: *Ajuga reptans* (chocolate chip), also called *A. reptans* (valfredda)
Height: 4"–6"
Width: 12"–18"
Zone: 3–9
Personality: Ajugas are valued for their ground-hugging, bronze-green foliage. Chocolate chip produces deep-blue flowers in midspring through the early summer. Ajugas can take light shade as well as sunny places.

Common name: Creeping mazus
Botanical name: *Mazus reptans*
Height: under 2"–4"
Width: 18"
Zone: 6–9
Personality: This ground cover does well in areas from full sun to shade. Creeping mazus likes to be watered regularly. It blossoms with lilac flowers in the spring and looks wonderful in a woodland setting.

Common name: Dead nettle
Botanical name: *Lamium maculatum*
Height: 8"–12"
Width: 3'–3'
Zone: 4–9
Personality: Dead nettle is a must-have in the shade garden. It has very defined, variegated leaves that bring the light into the darker places of the garden. Although primarily desired for its leaves, dead nettle does bloom in the spring and summer with little pink, purple, or white flowers.

Common name: Isotoma, or blue star creeper
Botanical name: *Isotoma fluviatilis* or laurentia
Height: Ground hugger
Width: 18"–24"
Zone: 5–9
Personality: Excellent for areas that see foot traffic. This lovely ground cover produces darling tiny, pale-blue flowers in the spring and summer.

Common name: Roman chamomile
Botanical name: *Chamaemelum nobile*
Height: 6"–12"
Width: 1'–3'
Zone: 4–11
Personality: Roman chamomile isn't the same plant as its German cousin *(Matricaria recutita)* that grows tall and lanky. This type stays low to the ground and forms an excellent ground cover mat. It blooms in little white flowers in spring through midsummer.

Common name: Scotch moss
Botanical name: *Sagina subulata* (aurea)
Height: Under 6"
Width: 9"–12"
Zone: 4–9
Personality: Scotch moss's foliage is a chartreuse, and it blooms in the spring to summer with little white flowers. It's a great ground cover and just as nice for rock gardens. Some people have had skin reactions when handling Scotch moss.

Common name: Stonecrop
Botanical name: *Sedum spurium* "John Creech"
Height: 3"–6"
Width: 12"–20"
Zone: 3–9
Personality: John Creech likes full sun to light shade and is perfect for rock gardens and beautiful between pavers. Its foliage is light green and dense.

Common name: Sunny-side-up fleabane
Botanical name: *Erigeron scopulinus*
Height: ½"
Width: Varies
Zone: 4–9
Personality: Fleabane has dark-green, thick foliage and blooms in tiny white daisies. Wonderful for walkways or paths that are in sun or part shade.

Common name: Woolly thyme
Botanical name: *Thymus serpyllum var. lanuginosus*
Height: Under 6"
Width: 9"–12"
Zone: 4–9
Personality: Woolly thyme is extremely drought tolerant once it's established. It's heavenly on the feet, but be careful when it's in bloom because the bees like it, too.

Ornamental Grasses

Common name: Blue fescue
Botanical name: *Festuca glauca*
Height: 6"–12"
Width: 6"–12"
Zone: 4–9
Personality: Blue fescue's color is at its silvery-blue best in full sun, but will tolerate light shade. It prefers cool and dry conditions—and won't last long in heavy clay areas. Blue fescue often goes dormant during the summer months.

Common name: Blue oat grass
Botanical name: *Helictotrichon sempervirens*
Height: 12"–18"
Width: 20"–24"
Zone: 4–11
Personality: Blue oat grass's foliage can only be described as metallic blue—just beautiful. Its wheat-colored flowers show up in the early summer and grow a couple of feet above the leaves.

Common name: Dwarf fountain grass
Botanical name: *Pennisetum alopecuroides* (hameln)
Height: 2'
Width: 2'
Zone: 5–9
Personality: The foliage on dwarf fountain grass grows upright and then arches. In the late summer the silver seed heads appear. In the fall, the foliage turns varying degrees of orange. It likes regular watering, but this grass doesn't like to be overwatered.

Common name: Dwarf ribbon plant
Botanical name: *Phalaris arundinacea* (dwarf garters)
Height: 12"–20"
Width: 20"–30"
Zone: 4–9
Personality: This compact grass has foliage of big interest. The variegated leaves are striped white. Its summer flowers show up as a soft white-tinted pink and turn brown in the late summer.

Common name: Golden variegated hakone
Botanical name: *Hakonechloa macra (aureola)*
Height: 12"
Width: 14"–18"
Zone: 4–8
Personality: Plant hakone in partial sun. The bamboo-type foliage on this hakone is bright yellow streaked with green lines. This grass is lovely in those shades, but, come fall, the leaves turn a passionate pink. Be careful not to plant hakone in too much sun or the yellow on the leaves will turn a red-brown. This is a seriously handsome plant.

Common name: Golden variegated sweet flag
Botanical name: *Acorus gramineus* (ogon)
Height: 10"
Width: 15"–18"
Zone: 5–11
Personality: Sweet flag (ogon) has strappy, buttery-yellow, swordlike leaves with green striping. It's a terrific plant for containers, too. It likes its feet wet—don't let it dry out much.

Common name: Maidenhair grass, miscanthus
Botanical name: *Miscanthus sinensis*
Height: 3'
Width: 12"–18"
Zone: 5–9
Personality: *M. sinensis* (little kitten) is a compact ornamental grass that behaves itself so well that it's perfect for containers, too. It's a fast grower but remains small even when it's mature. If you're interested in a miscanthus with a little pizzazz, check out the striped variety, *M. sinensis* (zebrinus).

Common name: Purple moor grass
Botanical name: *Molina caerulea*
Height: 1'–3'
Width: 6"–12"
Zone: 4–9
Personality: Purple moor grass has dense clumps of variegated leaves. In the summer, its light-yellow flower stalk shoots up to about 3' and then arches over. During the fall, the inflorescence becomes a tan color. Moor grass enjoys a moist soil, do it makes sense to plant it in a boggy area if possible.

Small-Space Trees and Shrubs

All gardens—no matter how small—have room for at least one little tree, considering that many grow well in containers. Here's where you'll find some of the best small garden trees for shade, fruit, and structure. By the way, the little dwarf conifer "trees" can be found in their own section at the end of this chapter.

I've grouped the shrubs into a few general categories. These groups are shrubs that are evergreen, shade tolerant, or those that show off. The show-offs are those that are interesting in more ways than one. After that, there's the dwarf conifers that are not only interesting, but stay fabulously small with little or no help from you.

Trees for Little Gardens

Common name: Chaste tree
Botanical name: *Vitex agnus-castus*
Height: 10'–20'
Width: 10'–20'
Zone: 6–9
Personality: The drought-tolerant chaste tree produces white, blue, or lavender flowers in early to midautumn. In the colder areas such as Zone 7, it'll stay on the shorter side. In the hotter areas such Zone 9, it can reach 20'.

Common name: Citrus trees (dwarf varieties)
Botanical name: *Citrus*
Height: 4'–6'
Width: 10'–16'
Zone: 9–10 (colder zones if in container)
Personality: This includes all the dwarf citrus such as Meyer lemon, Kaffir lime, and Owari Satsuma mandarin orange. Dwarf citrus trees make excellent container plants for balconies or patios. Unless you live in a warm winter climate, you'll probably have to bring your citrus indoors or at the very least, under shelter for the cold months. They're so worth it, not only for the fabulous fruit but for the heavenly scented spring flowers.

Common name: Cockspur hawthorn
Botanical name: *Crataegus crus-galli*
Height: 15'–25'
Width: 15'–25'
Zone: 4–7
Personality: This an all-around winner of a tree. We love it for its attractive autumn leaf color and early summer blooms. The bees and butterflies also love the flowers. Its little red fruit feeds the birds in late summer to fall.

Common name: Columnar apple trees
Botanical name: *Malus domestica*
Height: 7'–9'
Width: 1'–2'
Zone: 4–9
Personality: These are the apple trees that grow straight up. They're interesting trees and produce normal-sized apples.

Common name: Crape myrtle
Botanical name: *Lagerstroemia indica*
Height: 3'–20' depending on variety
Width: 10'
Zone: 7–9
Personality: Crepe myrtles can grow fairly tall. However, there are many varieties that stay on the short side, including the dwarf Moned, easily maintained at 3' to 4' tall. But there are varying heights in between the smallest and the tallest.

Common name: Dwarf flowering crabapples
Botanical name: *Malus spp.*
Height: 6'–12' depending on the variety
Width: 8' depending on the variety
Zone: 4–9
Personality: Crabapple trees are often grown for their beautiful flowers, but the little fruits are also edible. Look for the dwarf varieties of this species such as Camzam, Tina, and Molazam Molten Lava.

Common name: Dwarf red powderpuff
Botanical name: *Calliandra haematocephala* (Nana)
Height: 3'–5'
Width: 4'–7'
Zone: 9–11
Personality: This evergreen shrub is excellent for container gardening. The hummingbirds will hang around for these fluffy blossoms, too.

Common name: Flowering dogwood
Botanical name: *Cornus florida*
Height: 6'–25' or taller
Width: Depends on variety
Zone: 5–9
Personality: Some dogwoods grow to 20' or taller, but many hang around 10', and the dwarf Nana stays at a petite 6' tall.

Common name: Fringe tree, old man's beard
Botanical name: *Chionanthus virginicus*
Height: 12'–20'
Width: 12'–20'
Zone: 3–9
Personality: The fringe tree is considered either a large shrub or a small tree, depending on your definition. In May, fragrant, creamy-white blossoms are suspended from the branches. In the fall, the shrub produces deep-blue fruit.

Common name: Golden chain tree
Botanical name: *Laburnum* × *watereri*
Height: 12'–25'
Width: 9'–16'
Zone: 5–7
Personality: This tree produces gorgeous wisteria-looking flower clusters up to 2' long. Look for the 12" to 15" tall Aureum for smaller gardens.

Common name: Japanese maple
Botanical name: *Acer palmatum*
Height: 6'–25'
Width: Depends on variety
Zone: 6–8
Personality: Japanese maples are the darlings of the small garden. Varieties include breathtaking colors of red-auburn, as well as deeply lobed leaves to distinctly lacy ones.

Common name: Japanese tree lilac
Botanical name: *Syringa reticulata*
Height: 20'–30'
Width: 15"–2'
Zone: 3–7
Personality: A fabulous small and showy tree, it produces foamy sea or creamy-white flowers in the late spring or early summer. This tree shows off again in the winter with its shiny, copper-colored bark.

Common name: Kousa dogwood
Botanical name: *Cornus kousa*
Height: 20'–30'
Width: 15'–30'
Zone: 5–8
Personality: The Kousa dogwood is just a beautiful specimen of a tree. Early summer flowers are creamy white, which give way to a pinkish-red fruit during late summer. Its dark-green leaves turn red-purple to scarlet in the fall.

Common name: Magnolia
Botanical name: *Magnolia*
Height: 10'–15'
Width: 5'–10'
Zone: 3–9
Personality: Magnolias are perfect for small gardens and have lovely pink-purple spring blossoms that look like tulips.

Common name: Redbud
Botanical name: *Cercis canadensis*
Height: 20'
Width: 20'
Zone: 4–9
Personality: The easy-to-grow redbud has lovely pink or white flowers in the spring and heart-shaped leaves. Violet-blossomed Ace of Hearts grows only to 12' tall and 15' wide.

Evergreen Shrubs

Common name: Boxwood
Botanical name: *Buxus microphylla*
Height: 3'–5'
Width: 3'–5'
Zone: 4–9
Personality: Boxwood might be less than exciting, but it's also an incredibly versatile evergreen. It's the perfect shrub for edging and for clipping as a hedge or topiary. But don't overlook its usefulness as a specimen plant. Boxwood can be trained to a "natural" pyramid shape (not clipped looking).

Common name: Camellia
Botanical name: *Camellia*
Height: 6'–10'
Width: 4'–10'
Zone: 7–9
Personality: (See "Shrubs That Show Off.")

Common name: Cotoneaster
Botanical name: *Cotoneaster horizontalis*
Height: 1'–5'
Width: 3'–8'
Zone: 3–9
Personality: Cotoneaster may be known best for its low-growing habit and bright-red berries come summer. There's plenty of cotoneaster varieties to choose from, including evergreen, semievergreen, and deciduous types.

Common name: Euonymus
Botanical name: *Euonymus fortunei*
Height: 1'–3'
Width: $1\frac{1}{2}$"–3'
Zone: 3–8
Personality: These evergreens are cute little shrubs that often have variegated or golden leaves depending on the variety. They're easy to maintain and grow in an "orderly" fashion.

Common name: Glossy Abelia
Botanical name: *Abelia x grandiflora*
Height: 3'–4'
Width: 4'–5'
Zone: 5–9
Personality: Evergreen to semievergreen. (See "Shrubs That Show Off.")

Common name: Hebe
Botanical name: *Hebe x franciscana* (Variegata)
Height: 2'–4'
Width: 2'–4'
Zone: 9–10
Personality: This is another lovely little evergreen shrub that happens to have some cute, pink-purple blossoms in summer through fall. It's compact and handsome, with dark-green leaves. Variegata has leaves that are edged in a creamy yellow, which makes it a standout in the garden.

Common name: Rosemary
Botanical name: *Rosemarinus officinalis*
Height: 5'–6'
Width: 4'–5'
Zone: 7–10
Personality: Rosemary stays much smaller when grown in containers. Plus, it's easily pruned to restrict growth. If rosemary is winter hardy in your zone, you won't want to be without it. It demands very little attention and doesn't mind if you skip a watering or two. Great for rock gardens and other hot places, rosemary smells delicious as you brush past and it pulls double duty as a culinary herb. This reliable herb makes a great landscape plant and blooms little blue flowers randomly throughout the year.

Common name: Santolina, cotton lavender
Botanical name: *Santolina chamaecyparissus* or *C. incana*
Height: 1'–3'
Width: 1'–3'
Zone: 6–9
Personality: Santolina is a compact evergreen shrub with gray-white to silver-gray leaves. It bears bright to lemon-yellow scented flowers in mid- to late summer.

Common name: Yew
Botanical name: *Taxus*
Height: 3'–12'
Width: Varies
Zone: 4–8
Personality: Yews make terrific evergreen backbones for any garden. They're easy to grow, dependable, and there are many to choose from. Although some varieties can grow quite tall, there are plenty of them that are well suited for the small garden. Adpressa Fowle grows to a mature size of 6' × 16', and Nana is a dwarf variety that grows to 3' × 6'.

Shrubs That Show Off

Common name: Azalea
Botanical name: *Rhododendron*
Height: Depends on variety
Width: 3'–6'
Zone: 5–9
Personality: Azaleas are a smaller version of the rhododendron group and are admired for their spring flower display. There's a vast array of azaleas (both evergreen and deciduous) to choose from, so ask a local nursery which ones grow well in your area. Azaleas love their acidic soil and dappled shade. Plenty of azaleas get extremely tall, but there are some compact beauties, such as Dwarf Red, which stays a petite 2' to 3' tall and wide.

Common name: Beautyberry, French mulberry
Botanical name: *Callicarpa*
Height: 4'–6'
Width: 4'–6'
Zone: 5–10
Personality: Most beautyberries are deciduous, but before they lose their leaves you get to enjoy the fall clusters of berries. Some varieties have lovely pink-purple fall foliage, too.

Common name: Blueberry
Botanical name: *Vaccinium*
Height: 2'–12'
Width: 3'–8'
Zone: 3–9
Personality: Blueberry bushes are really coming back into vogue. Not only are they used as edible landscaping plants, but they have darling little white-to-pinkish bell-shaped flowers in the spring. Blueberry leaves turn orangeish and red in the fall. This is a super attractive shrub that comes in compact varieties that are perfect for containers as well as the highboy bush that is appropriate as hedges. Most blueberries are deciduous plants, but one or two new varieties keep their leaves year-round.

Common name: Bridal-wreath, spiraea
Botanical name: *Spiraea prunifolia*
Height: 4'–6'
Width: 4'– 6'
Zone: 4–9
Personality: This shrub produces breathtaking double white flowers in mid- to late spring. It has an arching branch habit whose foliage turns bronze to red in the fall.

Common name: Butterfly bush, summer lilac
Botanical name: *Buddleia davidii*
Height: 6'–12'
Width: 4'–15'
Zone: 5–10
Personality: I know that I've raised an eyebrow or two by adding the butterfly bush to a shrub section. Many claim that it's a perennial, but the American Horticultural Society lists it as a shrub. There's such a fine line with this one that many people refer to it as a perennial-shrub. Keep it pruned well for small areas or plant it in a large container to restrict the growth. Blossoming, fragrant flower clusters appear from mid-July to frost.

Common name: California lilac, ceanothus, wild lilac
Botanical name: *Ceanothus*
Height: 3'–9'

Width: 8'

Zone: 7–9

Personality: Ceanothus enjoys an area of full sun and is drought tolerant once established. The evergreen types will bloom in purple, blue, and pink during the spring. The deciduous varieties' flowers will show up in the summer. California lilac varieties have some seriously intense and dazzling blue flowers. They're perfect for a wildlife garden, as they support all kinds of wild critters.

Common name: Camellia

Botanical name: *Camellia*

Height: 6'–10'

Width: 4'–10'

Zone: 7–9

Personality: This evergreen shrub has the most luxurious flowers. Many gardeners consider the camellia a rival to the rose. Bloom time depends on the camellia variety. While most blossoms are quiet for the winter, *Camellia japonica* waits for late winter to show off her brilliant blossoms. The thick-petaled, elegant beauties hang around for weeks. She's a class act that does well in borders, as a specimen plant, or in containers. *C. sasanqua* blooms in the fall. Camellias like protection from afternoon sun, or the leaves scald and they sulk.

Common name: Daphne

Botanical name: *Daphne*

Height: 1'–4'

Width: 1'–4'

Zone: 4–9

Personality: Daphnes come in evergreen or semievergreen varieties and are true show-off shrubs. They bloom with light pink flowers in spring, and have a wonderful fragrance. For fall or winter interest, they offer red berries.

Common name: Dwarf fothergilla

Botanical name: *Fothergilla gardenii*

Height: 2'–4'

Width: 2'–4'

Zone: 4–9

Personality: In the spring fothergilla blossoms with fragrant, white, bottlebrush-type blooms. But it's the fall yellow, red, and orange leaf colors that are the showstoppers. It makes a great woodland shrub.

Common name: Glossy abelia
Botanical name: *Abelia X grandiflora*
Height: 3'–4'
Width: 4'–5'
Zone: 5–9
Personality: Abelia is a fabulous evergreen or semievergreen foundation shrub for small yards. It offers showy, funnel-shaped, purple-tinged white flowers all summer long. The foliage turns purplish-bronze in the fall. This is a dainty-leaved shrub that's an easy keeper. Plant her in full sun for the best color advantage, but light shade works, too.

Common name: Holly
Botanical name: *Ilex*
Height: Varies widely
Width: Varies widely
Zone: 3–10
Personality: What's not to love? This handsome shrub with year-round color makes an ideal living fence or screen. One of the English holly's best features is the striking contrast between the glossy leaves and the bright red berries that the female plants produce in winter. This is one shrub that has tons of varieties to choose from. Tall, small, variegated, evergreen, and deciduous all describe the Ilex genus. Pruning is always an option for the hollies that grow naturally large, but keep your eyes open for the Dwarf Yaupon (such as Nana or the weeping *I. vomitoria* Pendula) and Japanese hollies like *I. crenata* Compacta.

Common name: Pieris andromeda, lily of the valley shrub
Botanical name: *Pieris*
Height: $2\frac{1}{2}$'–10'
Width: $2\frac{1}{2}$'–10'
Zone: 5–8
Personality: Big show-off here. This is an evergreen shrub that becomes covered with little bell-shaped pink, white, or red flowers during spring. While pieris is a plant that'll survive just fine in the shade, if you plant it where it'll receive some good morning sun, you'll have more blossoms. Not to be outdone, the leaf growth of pieris shows up in bronze, scarlet, and wine red. This is another acidic soil–loving plant. Watch for the dwarf varieties such as Valley Rose or dwarf Prelude.

Common name: Rose-of-Sharon, shrub althea
Botanical name: *Hibiscus syriacus*
Height: 8'–12'
Width: 8'–10'
Zone: 5–8
Personality: Rose-of-Sharon blooms with 4" to 5", trumpet-shaped flowers midsummer till frost. This hibiscus blossoms in colors of pink, white, purple, and crimson. The notched leaves are delicate and very attractive.

Common name: Summersweet, sweet pepperbush, white alder
Botanical name: *Clethra alnifolia*
Height: 3'–8'
Width: 4'–6'
Zone: 3–9
Personality: Summersweet brings fragrant white flowers that hang around for weeks. This shrub offers some fall interest with its yellow to golden-brown leaves. Sweet pepperbush likes its soil on the acidic side and tolerates shade quite well.

Common name: Viburnum
Botanical name: *Viburnum*
Height: 2'–15'
Width: 2'–10'
Zone: 5–9
Personality: Viburnums are loved for their superfragrant flowers that show up in the spring or sometimes the beginning of June. They're borne on one of three different flower head types: the round-ball type, flat clusters of florets, or in flat clusters surrounded by large flowers. These shrubs put on a glorious show in the fall with their brilliant orange-red leaves in autumn. This shrub can be kept quite compact by pruning the branches right after the flowers fade. Look for the dwarf Densa or Reifler's Dwarf if you'd like a naturally small variety.

Shrubs for Shade

Common name: Azalea
Botanical name: *Rhododendron*
Height: Depends on variety
Width: 3'–6'
Zone: 5–9
Personality: (See "Shrubs That Show Off.")

Common name: Dwarf fothergilla
Botanical name: *Fothergilla gardenii*
Height: 2'–4'
Width: 2'–4'
Zone: 4–9
Personality: Lovely for shady or woodland gardens. (See "Shrubs That Show Off.")

Common name: Dwarf hemlock
Botanical name: *Tsuga canadensis,* Jeddeloh and Bennett
Height: 5'
Width: 6'
Zone: 4–7
Personality: Although these conifers are usually much, much larger, both Jeddeloh and Bennett stay quite compact for hemlocks. Both of them will tolerate part shade.

Common name: Glossy abelia
Botanical name: *Abelia X grandiflora*
Height: 3'–4'
Width: 4'–5'
Zone: 5–9
Personality: Tolerates light shade. (See "Shrubs That Show Off.")

Common name: Camellia
Botanical name: *Camellia*
Height: 6'–10'
Width: 4'–10'
Zone: 7–9
Personality: This evergreen shrub has the most luxurious flowers. Many gardeners consider the camellia a rival to the rose. Bloom time depends on the camellia variety. While most blossoms are quiet for the winter, *camellia japonica* waits for late winter to show off her brilliant blossoms. The thick-petaled, elegant beauties hang around for weeks. She's a class act that does well in borders, as a specimen plant, or in containers. *C. sasanqua* blooms in the fall. Camellias like protection from afternoon sun, or the leaves scald and they sulk.

Common name: Hydrangea
Botanical name: *Hydrangea*
Height: 3'–15'
Width: 3'–15'
Zone: 3–9
Personality: There are a lot of lovely hydrangeas: mopheads, lacecaps, short, and tall. They have white (cream), blue, pink, and somewhere-in-between-lavender blooms from May through July. Bigleaf hydrangea will give you blue or pink blooms according to the pH levels in the soil. If the pH is between 4.5-5.0 (slightly acidic), then you'll have some lovely blue blossoms and at 5.5, you'll have lavender-purple. If the pH is from 6.0-6.5, you'll have purple to pink. Although hydrangeas are often planted in full sun, that will certainly depend upon your growing zone. If you live where you get some scorching hot sun, you'll be better off planting your hydrangea in part shade and out of the afternoon sun.

Common name: Pieris, andromeda, lily of the valley shrub
Botanical name: *Pieris*
Height: $2\frac{1}{2}$'–10'
Width: $2\frac{1}{2}$'–10'
Zone: 5–8
Personality: Pieris is good in shade, but flowers are better with at least a little sun. (See "Shrubs That Show Off.")

Common name: Summersweet, sweet pepperbush, white alder
Botanical name: *Clethra alnifolia*
Height: 3'–8'
Width: 4'–6'
Zone: 3–9
Personality: (See "Shrubs that Show Off.")

Dwarf Conifers

Common name: Arborvitae
Botanical name: *Thuja occidentalis*
Height: 1'–3'
Width: $3\frac{1}{2}$'–6'
Zone: 3–7
Personality: *Thuja occidentalis* comes in many varieties including the really tall types, too. So look for a dwarf such as Rheingold, Tiny Tim, and Hetz Midget.

Common name: Bald cypress
Botanical name: *Taxodium distichum*
Height: 3'
Width: 10'
Zone: 4–10
Personality: It bears repeating to look for the dwarf varieties of *Taxidium distichum* such as deciduous Secrest, which produces branches in a lovely horizontal shape. It likes acidic, moist soil.

Common name: Creeping juniper
Botanical name: *Juniperus horizontalis*
Height: 3'–4'
Width: Spreading plant
Zone: 4–9
Personality: This North American native is a low-growing juniper that pulls double duty as a ground cover. Dwarf variety examples are evergreen Icee Blue and Mother Lode.

Common name: Dwarf Alberta spruce
Botanical name: *Picea glauca* var. *albertiana*, Conica
Height: 6'–8'
Width: Roughly 4'–7'
Zone: 3–7
Personality: Conica's conical shape makes it the perfect miniature Christmas tree. It's excellent for containers and right at home in rock gardens or xeriscaping. Don't overwater.

Common name: Dwarf Colorado blue spruce
Botanical name: *Picea pungens*, Montgomery
Height: 3'–4'
Width: 3'
Zone: 2–9
Personality: Montgomery is a deer-resistant evergreen shrub that has great color and form.

Common name: Hinoki false cypress
Botanical name: *Chamaecyparis obtusa*, Minima
Height: 9"-12"
Width: 1'-1½'
Zone: 5–8
Personality: This Japanese conifer is interesting for its form as well as its bark. If you like the dwarf conifers, try to get Minima in your garden because she's a fabulous shrub. Watch for other dwarf false cypresses, too, such as Nana Aurea.

Common name: Mugo pine
Botanical name: *Pinus mugo*
Height: 5'–7'
Width: 8'–12'
Zone: 2–7
Personality: Mugo pines are highly adaptable to their environment and one of the hardiest of the dwarf conifers.

Common name: Norway spruce
Botanical name: *Picea abies*
Height: Depends on variety
Width: Depends on variety
Zone: 3–7
Personality: There are many dwarf varieties of the Norway spruce available right now, such as Coolwyn Globe, Frohberg, Pygmaea, Formaneck, and Maxwellii, just to name a few. They come in all shapes, including round, weeping, and pyramidal forms.

Common name: Oriental spruce
Botanical name: *Picea orientalis*, Tom Thumb
Height: 1½'–2½'
Width: 1½'–2½'
Zone: 4–7
Personality: Tom Thumb is stunning in a rock garden and perfect for any small space. The green and gold foliage is set in fingerlike layers. Look for the dwarf variety Nana, too.

Common name: Sawara cypress or Japanese false cypress
Botanical name: *Chamaecyparis pisifera* var. filifera, Sungold
Height: 6'–10'
Width: 3'–10'
Zone: 4–8
Personality: Sungold is gold to lime-green and is a weeping dwarf conifer. It's a gorgeous specimen in the rock garden.

AHS heat map   The American Horticultural Society's (AHS) heat zone map that focuses on the average highs in your zone, rather than the lows. The heat map gives you the average number of days that temperatures in your zone are at 86°F and above.

alpine plant   Plants that grow in high elevations (above the tree line), referred to as an alpine climate.

amend   When you correct or improve soil. It can refer to the nutrition available, or the organic matter, or altering the pH balance.

annuals   Plants that complete their life cycle within a year (germinate, flower, produce seed, and die).

beneficial insects   Insects that either prey on garden pests, spread pollen to flowers in the garden, or in any other way help plants complete the pollination process.

biennial   Refers to a plant that completes its life cycle in two years. Leaves are grown the first year and fruit and seeds are produced in the second.

buffer   Any compound that makes the soil less sensitive to acid and alkaline fluctuations.

cold frame   Cold frames are bottomless, box-type structures that have a transparent lid or door on the top that protects plants from cold weather. It acts as a miniature greenhouse and can extend the gardening season.

community garden   A piece of land cultivated by members of a community, particularly in an urban or suburban setting. Community gardening encourages citizens to grow their own food and donate any extra produce to local food banks.

compost   Organic matter that's been biologically reduced to humus. The term is used for both the process and the end product. *See also* humus.

cool-season vegetables   Vegetables that grow all through the cool months. These crops can be grown during two seasons: spring and fall. They need temperatures to hang around 40° to 60°. Examples are broccoli and cabbage.

drought tolerant   The term refers to those plants that naturally adapt to dry soil conditions. It's important to note that these plants should be regularly watered until well established.

fertilize   To supply nutrients to plants.

focal points   Items that are placed in the garden to purposefully stop the eye. They can be hardscaping, ornaments, or plants.

foundation plantings   Plants found around the foundation of a home. Usually the original foundation plantings are supplied by the builder and then may be replaced or added to by the homeowner.

friable soil   Soil with an open structure that crumbles easily when handled.

garden bones   Refers to permanent plants or hardscaping in the garden that gives the garden its basic foundation.

greenhouse   Refers to a building especially made to house plants for protection from cold weather.

guerrilla gardening   In its simplest form, guerrilla gardening is planting on a piece of land that isn't your own. Very often guerrilla gardeners will choose a piece of land that's been neglected or abandoned and give it new life with a small garden or ornamental plants.

hardpan soil   Topsoil that's so compacted that plant roots can't penetrate the earth.

hardscape   Generally refers to any man-made accents added to the yard or garden. It may be paving, walls, or other stonework. It can also refer to decks, fountains, arbors, walkways, garden decor, light fixtures, and patios.

hellstrip   This is a slang gardening term used for that rectangular strip of soil (or neglected grass) between the sidewalk and the street.

hoop house   Usually made with flexible piping (PVC) secured over a garden bed so that plastic can be wrapped over the top to protect plants from cold weather.

humus   The material that's formed after the breakdown of organic matter. It makes complex nutrients in the soil easily accessible to plants.

hypertufa   A sink or trough used as a planter that's made from a man-made imitation of a naturally occurring porous rock called tufa.

invasive plant   A non-native plant species that tends to spread aggressively and has adverse effects environmentally, ecologically, or economically on the habitat that it invades.

IPM   Integrated Pest Management, a sustainable pest management system that uses biological, cultural, and physical controls.

microclimates   Specific local atmospheric zones where the climate differs from the larger surrounding area.

microorganisms   Organisms (plants or animals) that are too small to be seen with the naked eye.

mulch   A protective covering of organic or synthetic material that's placed over the bare soil around plants to prevent weeds and erosion, retain moisture, and enrich soil.

NPK   Stands for nitrogen, phosphorus, and potassium, the three main nutrients that plants need to thrive.

organic matter   Any material that originates from living organisms, including all animal and plant life, whether living or in any stage of decomposition.

perennial   A plant that continues its life cycle for three or more years. It may produce flowers and seeds from the same roots year after year.

pH (pH scale)   The acidity or alkalinity of soil; the pH scale runs from 1 through 14 and measures the acidity or alkalinity of a soil. Soil is in balance when it falls between 6.5 and 7 on the pH scale. The lower the number is on the scale, the higher the acidity, and the higher the number is, the higher the alkalinity.

photosynthesis   This is the process of how plants create their own food. Plants use energy from the sun to convert carbon dioxide and water into simple sugars (carbohydrates).

potager   A potager is the French version of a kitchen vegetable garden. It's usually a pleasing mix of herbs, vegetables, and flowers.

potting soil   A mixed medium used for planting indoor and outdoor plants in containers.

root pruning   This is the technique in which parts of a plant's roots are cut off, which restricts the size of the plant or tree.

scion   A plant cutting that's selected to be the "top" or desirable half of the grafting set. The other part of that unit is the rootstock, which is visually unimportant.

side dressing   When nutrients in the form of fertilizer or compost are applied to the soil near a plant, but not directly under it, it's called side-dressing.

softscape   The plant part of the landscaping, as opposed to the hardscaping such as the patio, statuary, and so on.

starts   Plants that are started from seed in a nursery, brought to a garden center, and then sold to the public as baby plants.

stolon   An above-ground plant shoot that presses horizontally against the ground and produces roots at the node.

subshrub   A low-growing perennial whose woody stems are near the base of the plant, with the tips being more herbaceous. Examples are lavender, rosemary, and thyme.

top dressing   A soil amendment such as compost or fertilizer applied evenly over the surface of a garden bed.

topography   With regards to planting, refers to local details including natural and man-made features of the land.

trompe l'oeil   A style of three-dimensional painting that looks extremely realistic. Trompe l'oeil means to "deceive the eye."

USDA hardiness zone map   The U.S. Department of Agriculture's map dividing the United States into 11 growing areas. It's based on a 10°F difference. Microclimates within a zone, as well as rainfall, day length, humidity, wind, and soil types, also play a role in planting specifics. Therefore, this map is meant to be used as a general guide.

variegated   In botanical terms, the leaves or stems of a plant having more than one color on them. Plants with variegated leaves are especially useful for bringing light to shady areas.

warm-season vegetable   Vegetables that grow through the warm months. Warm-season vegetables find their sweet spot when temperatures are above 60°. They're usually planted during the middle to late spring or the beginning of summer. Examples are peppers and tomatoes.

xeriscaping   This refers to using plants that are drought tolerant in order to garden or landscape in a way that reduces or eliminates the need for supplemental water.

Resources for Small-Space Gardeners

Websites and Blogs

Visit the following websites and blogs for additional resources and innovative ideas for your small-space garden.

A Suburban Farmer
www.asuburbanfarmer.com
I couldn't leave my own blog out of the small gardening website mix. Its main focus is on family gardening and small-scale gardens.

Aha! Home and Garden
www.ahahomeandgarden.com
Another informative blog with great reviews of products for small-space gardening.

Beautiful Wildlife Garden
www.beautifulwildlifegarden.com
This team of wildlife gardeners offers their personal experiences. This website offers fascinating tips and facts for wildlife gardens.

Ecosystem Gardening
www.ecosystemgardening.com
This website delves a little deeper into the conservation of natural resources and explaining how to welcome wildlife into the garden.

Gossip in the Garden
gossipinthegarden.com
Beautiful ideas and inspiration for the small garden and yard.

Greenhouse Garden
www.greenhousegarden.com
This is a website that's packed with greenhouse gardening tips and advice.

Growing a Greener World

www.growingagreenerworld.com

No matter the garden size, we all strive to grow it green. This is a great blog for ideas on sustainable garden projects.

Guerrilla Gardening

www.guerrillagardening.org

A little on the naughty side—a lot on the nice. Come see what guerrilla gardening is all about.

Invasive Plant Species

www.invasive.org

This website has current information on any type of invasive species plants, insects, animals, and pathogens.

J Peterson Garden Design

www.jpetersongardendesign.com

Some of the most creative garden ideas anywhere are on this blog. The author, Jenny Peterson, is a landscape designer by trade, and the fabulous ideas just keep coming!

Life on the Balcony

www.lifeonthebalcony.com

There's a ton of great ideas at this blog for those primarily growing in containers.

My Earth Garden

www.myearthgarden.com

Michael Nolan produces an honest blog about gardening that tells it like it is—no punches pulled here. Just the truth, excellent tips, and good writing.

National Gardening Association

www.garden.org

You'll find an amazing collection of gardening information at this site. You can jump from here to their sister site for kids, Kids Gardening.org.

National Wildlife Federation

www.nwf.org

There's a lot of wildlife gardening info here, including the specifics on creating a backyard wildlife habitat.

Pronunciation Guide for Plants

www.finegardening.com/pguide/pronunciation-guide-to-botanical-latin.aspx

Don't know how to say it? Fine Gardening.com has a handy online guide that allows you to hear the botanical (Latin) plant names.

Truck Farm

www.truck-farm.com

The adventures of a mobile community farm—grown in a truck bed. It's just about the smallest-space garden around.

Urban Organic Gardener.com

www.urbanorganicgardener.com

Mike Lieberman takes you along on his growing adventures from his fire escape garden in New York City to his balcony in Los Angeles.

USDA Plant Database

plants.usda.gov

This is the Department of Agriculture's database. it has all kinds of good information for you including current botanical plant name changes.

Vegetable Gardener

www.vegetablegardener.com

If you're looking for answers on growing vegetables and herbs, this is the place for you. Go ahead and post your questions—the experts here can answer them.

Product Resources

We've gathered some product websites that offer excellent products and great service.

Authentic Haven Brand Soil Conditioning Tea

www.ahavenbrand.com

Here's where you find manure tea bags, which are especially convenient for the small-space gardener to use for giving plants the nutrition they need.

Clean Air Gardening

www.cleanairgardening.com

This site specializes in eco-friendly gardening tools, but you'll find a ton of composting supplies here, too.

Corona Tools

www.coronatoolsusa.com

Here's where you'll find reliable, sturdy garden tools that last forever.

Cyndi's Catalog of Garden Catalogs

www.gardenlist.com

This is the mother lode of gardening catalogs. Enter at your own risk.

EarthBox

www.earthbox.com

A portable, contained gardening system that works like a dream, this product was discussed in Chapter 5.

Eleanor's Garden

www.eleanorsgarden.com

Eleanor's Garden is a complete, compact, portable garden in a kit. I discussed this raised garden in Chapter 5.

Gardener's Supply

www.gardeners.com

Gardener's Supply is an employee-owned company that has a dazzling array of gardening tools and supplies.

Good Compost

www.goodcompost.com

These guys have a nice selection of composters and worm bins to choose from (plus they're nice folks).

Greenhouse Catalog

www.greenhousecatalog.com

This online supply catalog has every piece of equipment you could need for your home greenhouse. I like it because it has tons of houses for you to peruse to get an idea of the varieties available.

Greenland Gardener

www.greenlandgardener.com

Here you'll find excellent raised-garden-bed kits—plus there are helpful gardening articles.

Planet Natural

www.planetnatural.com

Earth-friendly supplies for you to peruse, along with beneficial insects for the garden.

Topiary Art Works

www.topiaryartworks.com

From the beautiful to the downright fun, Topiary Art Works creates many of the world's largest topiary pieces and the most involved topiary projects.

Woolly Pockets

www.woollypocket.com

This is the home of the wall pockets and stand-alone island pocket that I talked about in Chapter 5.

Plant Resources

If you're looking for the perfect plants for small gardens and yards, we have some of the best right here.

Annie's Annuals and Perennials

www.anniesannuals.com

Annie's whimsical place is right here in the heart of the San Francisco Bay area. She offers some of the best and most interesting plants around. Plus, they offer stellar service.

Baker Creek Heirloom Seeds

www.rareseeds.com

Baker Creek offers 1,400 heirloom varieties. All of the seeds they carry are open-pollinated, and all of them are non-GMO (Genetically Modified Organisms). The photography in this catalog is ridiculously stunning—you'll want to get it for that reason alone.

BBB Seed Heirloom Vegetable and Wildflower Seeds

www.bbbseed.com

The little seed company with the big heart. Pure, open-pollinated seed, great service, and nice people. Couldn't ask for anything more.

Botanical Interests

www.botanicalinterests.com

Botanical Interests carries both heritage and hybrid veggie, flower, and herb seeds. This catalog is loaded with lovely artwork.

Conifer Connection

www.coniferconnection.com

This nursery specializes in rare and unusual miniature, dwarf, and intermediate-sized conifers.

Nature Hills

www.naturehills.com

This website is loaded with information about plants, tools, fertilizer, and oodles of other things.

Iseli Nursery

www.iselinursery.com

Here's the place to find some fabulous dwarf conifer and Japanese maple varieties and the information to grow them.

Plant Delights

www.plantdelights.com

This is a wonderful resource for those searching for shade plants (although they have sun lovers, too). Tony Avent does a killer job describing his plants and entertaining you at the same time. Order a catalog just so you can read this thing from front to back.

Proven Winners

www.provenwinners.com

This company offers excellent, reliable, and beautiful plants for every garden.

Renee's Garden

www.reneesgarden.com

This is a fun site to peruse and is owned by Renee Shepard, who is renowned in the plant world. When you order your seeds, they come in lovely little packages; Renee's Garden Seeds are famous for their little watercolor portraits of each plant.

Stargazer Perennials

www.stargazerperennials.com

Another nice site for perusing all kinds of plants, including walkable ground covers.

Stark Bros

www.starkbros.com

Ohhh … these guys have wonderful plants, berries, and fruit trees, including the multigrafted fruit trees I talked about in Chapter 10.

Stepables

www.stepables.com

Find some terrific ground covers at this site. Many can handle foot traffic—plus they have some fabulous ideas for you.

Wildflower Farm

www.wildflowerfarm.com

This is the place to find wildflower garden seeds and the wonderful, drought-tolerant Eco-Lawn.

Books

Bartholomew, Mel. *All New Square Foot Gardening.* Nashville, Tennessee: Cool Springs Press, 2006. Step-by-step directions on using the square-foot gardening method for growing vegetables.

McLaughlin, Chris. *The Complete Idiot's Guide to Composting.* Indianapolis: Alpha Books, 2010. Find out just how easy it is to create your own garden gold for your heirloom vegetable beds.

McLaughlin, Chris. *The Complete Idiot's Guide to Heirloom Vegetables.* Indianapolis: Alpha Books, 2010. Learn about the joys of growing flavorful heirloom vegetables in your own backyard.

Nolan, Michael, and Reggie Solomon. *I Garden: Urban Style.* Cincinnati, OH: Better Way Books, 2010. An excellent book for anybody within city limits who would like to grow more than a houseplant. Gorgeous photos and tons of hands-on projects.

Soler, Ivette. *The Edible Front Yard.* Portland, OR: Timber Press, 2011. All the cool kids are doing it—growing food right in with the landscaping, and out front. Learn more about utilizing the space you have available to grow your own food.

Taylor, Lisa, and Seattle Tilth. *Your Small Farm in the City.* New York: Black Dog & Leventhal Publishers, 2011. An excellent book for growing vegetables in urban and suburban areas. They even get into farm animals.

Yang, Linda. *The City Gardener's Handbook.* North Adams, MA: Storey Books, 2002. An excellent and detailed guide to small-space gardening.

Common and Botanical Plant Names

These are the plants that I refer to as examples throughout the text. Within the book, I typically use their most common names. But using common plant names is never good enough. A plant called "bleeding heart" in California can be a completely different species than the one that gardeners call "bleeding heart" in Georgia.

Throughout this book I used plant names that weren't necessarily the botanical names. To be clear on the species that I was referring to, the following list has the plant's common name first and it's botanical name second. It doesn't necessarily include those plants that are discussed in the profiles.

African lilies—*Agapanthus*

American holly—*Ilex opaca*

Baboon flower—*Babiana spp.*

Bacopa—*Sutera cordata*

Balloon flower—*Platycodon spp.*

Bamboo Muhly—*Muhlenbergia dumosa*

Basil—*Ocimum basilicum*

Bayberry—*Myrica pensylvanica*

Beard-tongue—*Penstemon spp.*

Bee balm—*Monarda spp.*

Birch—*Betula spp.*

Black-eyed Susan vine—*Thunbergia alata*

Blanket flower—*Gaillardia aristata*

Bleeding heart—*Dicentra spectabilis*

Blue fescue—*Festuca cineria*

Blue star creeper—*Isotoma spp.*

Bluebeard—*Caryopteris incana*

Boston ivy—*Parthenosissus tricuspidata*

Boxwood—*Buxus spp.*

Bronze Dutch clover—*Trifolium repens Atropurpureum*

Bugleweed—*Ajuga*

California lilac—*Ceanothus spp.*

Candytuft—*Iberis sempervirens*

Canterbury bells—*Campanula spp.*

Cape plumbago—*Plumbago spp.*

Chives—*Allium schoenoprasum*

Chocolate cosmos—*Cosmos atrosanguineus*

Climbing hydrangea—*Hydrangea petiolaris*

Climbing nasturtium—*Tropaeolum polyphyllum*

Coleus—*Coleus blumei*

Columbine—*Aquilegias spp.*

Coral bells—*Heuchera spp.*

Crabapple—*Malus spp.*

Cranesbill (true geranium)—*Geranium maculatum*

Creeping mazus—*Mazus reptans*

Creeping thyme—*Thymus praecox*

Cup-n-saucer vine—*Cobaea scandens*

Daylilies—*Hemerocallis spp.*

Deadnettle—*Lamium spp.*Dogwood—*Cornus spp.*

Dwarf bugleweed—*Ajuga* x, "Chocolate Chip"

Elephant ear—*Colocasia spp.*

Elderberry—*Sambucus nigra*

English ivy—*Hedera helix*

False spiraea—*Astible spp.*

Fig—*Ficus carica*

Firethorn—*Pyracantha spp.*

Floss flower—*Ageratum spp.*

Fountain grass—*Pennisetum*

Flowering tobacco—*Nicotiana alata*

Foxglove—*Digitalis purpurea*

Gayfeather—*Liatris spp.*

Geranium—*Pelargonium spp.*

Glossy ableia—*Abelia* x *grandiflora*

Golden chain tree—*Laburnum spp.*

Gulf muhly—*Muhlenbergia capillaris*

Hens and chicks—*Sempervivum spp.*

Holly—*Ilex spp.*

Hollyhock—*Alcea rosea*

Honesty—*Lunaria spp.*

Honey locust—*Gleditsia tricanthos*

Honeysuckle—*Lonicera japonica*

Honeysuckle—*Lonicera pileata*

Impatiens—*Impatiens walleriana*

Hawthorn—*Rhaphiolepis indica*

Italian cypress—*Cupressus sempervirens*

Japanese barberry—*Berberis thunbergii*

Japanese black pine—*Pinus thumbergiana*

Japanese iris—*Iris ensata*

Japanese meadowsweet—*Spiraea japonica*

Japanese maple—*Acer spp.*

Japanese Sky Pencil holly—*Ilex crenata* 'Sky Pencil'

Juniper—*Juniperus spp.*

Lamb's ear—*Stachys byzantina*

Lavender—*Lavendula spp.*

Lavender cotton—*Santolina spp.*

Lemon thyme—*Thymus x citriodorus*

Lemon verbena—*Aloysia triphylla*

Lilac—*Syringa spp.*

Lily of the valley—*Convallaria majalis*

Love-in-a-mist—*Nigella damascena*

Lungwort—*Pulmonaria spp.*

Maiden grass — *Miscanthus sinensis*

Maidenhair fern—*Adiantum spp.*

Marigold—*Calendula officinalis*

Marigold (French)—*Tagates patula*

Meadowsweet—*Filipendula spp.*

Mexican feather grass—*Nassella tenuissima*

Mexican sage—*Salvia leucantha*

Mock orange—*Philadelphus spp.*

Mountain ash—*Sorbus aucuparia*

Mullein—*Verbascum spp.*

Nectarine—*Prunus persica*

Oregon grape—*Mahonia aquifolium*

Pansy—*Viola spp.*

Paper flower—*Bougainvillea*

Paperwhites—*Narcissus tazetta*

Passionflower—*Passiflora racemosa*

Persimmon—*Diospyros spp.*

Pink jasmine—*Jasminum polyanthum*

Plantain lily—*Hosta spp.*

Primrose—*Primula spp.*

Privet—*Lingustrum spp.*

Red cedar—*Juniperus viginiana*

Red creeping thyme—*Thymus serpyllum Coccineus*

Redbud—*Cercis spp.*

Rosemary—*Rosemarinus officinalis*

Russian olive—*Elegans augustifolia*

Savory—*Satureja spp.*

Scotch moss—*Sagina spp.*

Shooting star—*Dodecatheon spp.*

Smoke bush—*Cotinus coggygria*

Snake's-head fritillaria—*Fritillaria meleagris*

Snowflakes—*Leucojum aestivum*

Southern magnolia—*Magnolia grandiflora*

Southernwood—*Artemisia abrotanum*

Stock—*Matthiola spp.*

Stonecrop—*Sedum spp.*

String of pearls—*Senecio rowleyanus*

Sunflowers—*Helianthus annuus*

Sunny-side-up fleabane—*Erigeron scopulinus*

Sweet alyssum—*Alyssum spp.*

Sweet potato vine—*Ipomoea batatas*

Sweet rocket—*Hesperis matronalis*

Sweet William—*Dianthus spp.*

Tamarisk—*Tamarix tetradra*

Tea tree—*Leptospermum spp.*

Thyme—*Thymus spp.*

Tickseed—*Coreopsis spp.*

Tree Mallow—*Lavatera olbia*

Virginia creeper—*Parthenocissus quinquefolia*

White spruce—*Picea glauca*

Wild ginger—*Asarum spp.*

Winter jasmine—*Jasminum nudiflorum*

Wood anemones or windflower—*Anemone nemerosa*

Yew—*Taxus spp.*

Index

C

G

H

I

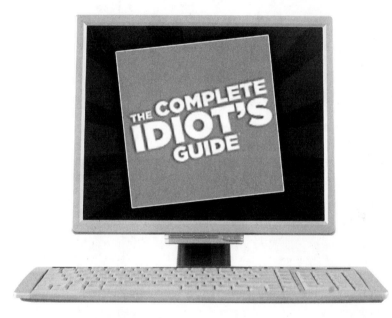

CHECK OUT THESE BEST-SELLERS

More than 450 titles available at booksellers and online retailers everywhere!

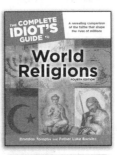

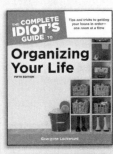

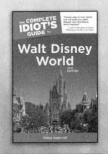
ALPHA

idiotsguides.com